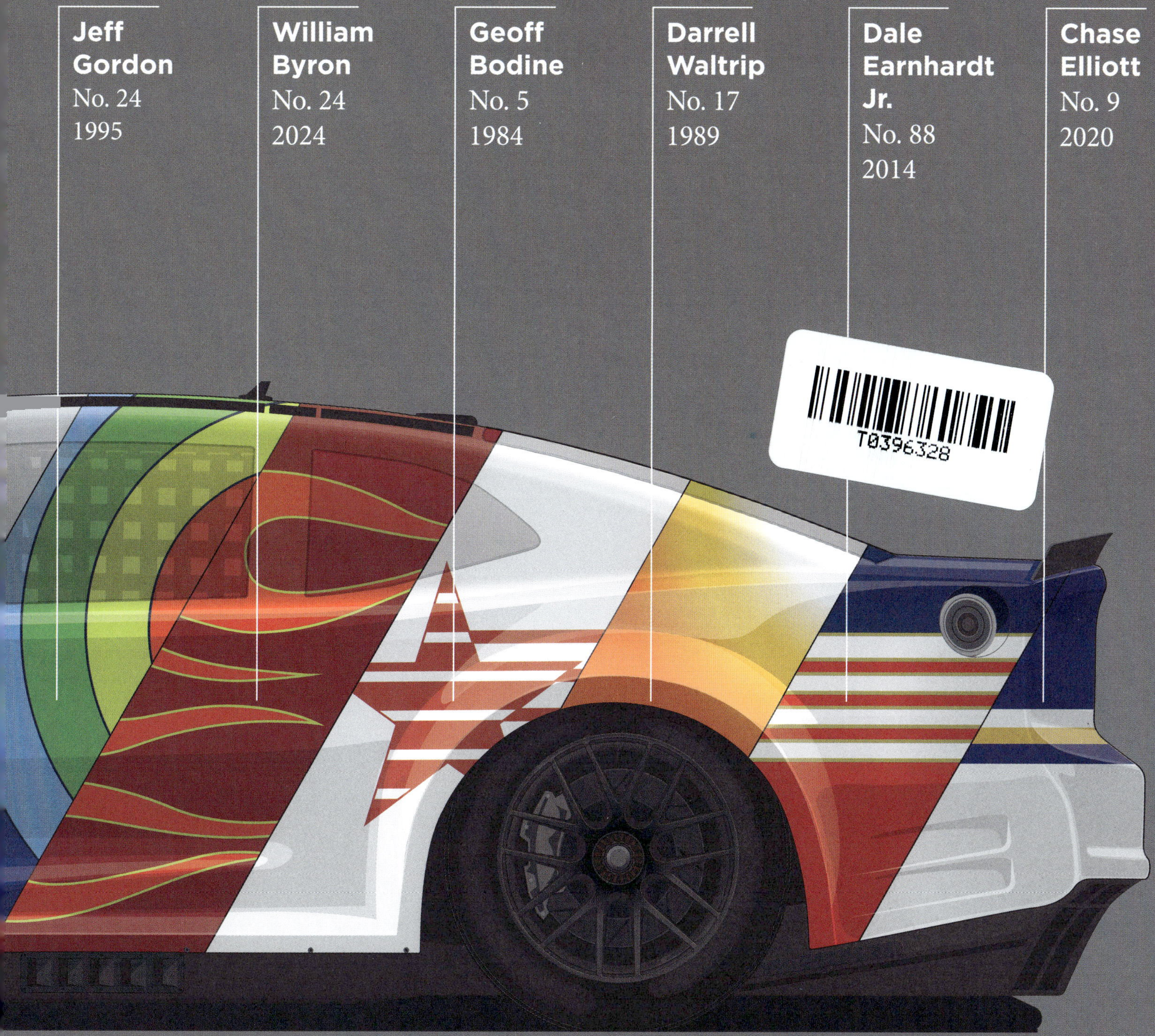

Jeff Gordon
No. 24
1995

William Byron
No. 24
2024

Geoff Bodine
No. 5
1984

Darrell Waltrip
No. 17
1989

Dale Earnhardt Jr.
No. 88
2014

Chase Elliott
No. 9
2020

T0396328

Quarto.com

© 2024 Quarto Publishing Group USA Inc.
Text © 2024 Ben White

First Published in 2024 by Motorbooks, an imprint of The Quarto Group,
100 Cummings Center, Suite 265-D, Beverly, MA 01915, USA.
T (978) 282-9590 F (978) 283-2742

All rights reserved. No part of this book may be reproduced in any form without written permission of the copyright owners. All images in this book have been reproduced with the knowledge and prior consent of the artists concerned, and no responsibility is accepted by producer, publisher, or printer for any infringement of copyright or otherwise, arising from the contents of this publication. Every effort has been made to ensure that credits accurately comply with information supplied. We apologize for any inaccuracies that may have occurred and will resolve inaccurate or missing information in a subsequent reprinting of the book.

Motorbooks titles are also available at discount for retail, wholesale, promotional, and bulk purchase. For details, contact the Special Sales Manager by email at specialsales@quarto.com or by mail at The Quarto Group, Attn: Special Sales Manager, 100 Cummings Center, Suite 265-D, Beverly, MA 01915, USA.

28 27 26 25 24   1 2 3 4 5

ISBN: 978-0-7603-9123-5

Digital edition published in 2024
eISBN: 978-0-7603-9124-2

Library of Congress Cataloging-in-Publication Data

Names: White, Ben, 1960- author. | Hendrick Motorsports (Firm)
Title: Hendrick Motorsports 40 years / Ben White.
Other titles: Hendrick Motorsports forty years
Description: Beverly, MA : Motorbooks, 2024. | Includes index. | Summary: "Hendrick Motorsports celebrates the NASCAR-champion team's 40th anniversary in competition. Forty stories from the 1980s to today relate the team's full history in this officially licensed book"— Provided by publisher.
Identifiers: LCCN 2024012591 | ISBN 9780760391235 | ISBN 9780760391242 (digital edition)
Subjects: LCSH: Automobile racing--United States. | Hendrick Motorsports (Firm)—History. | Hendrick, Rick, 1949- | NASCAR (Association)—History. | Motorsports—United States.
Classification: LCC GV1033 .W448 2024 | DDC 796.7206/073—dc23/eng/20240515
LC record available at https://lccn.loc.gov/2024012591

Design: Cindy Samargia Laun
Front cover, back cover, endpapers: Hendrick Motorsports

Printed in China

© 2024 HMS Holdings, LLC

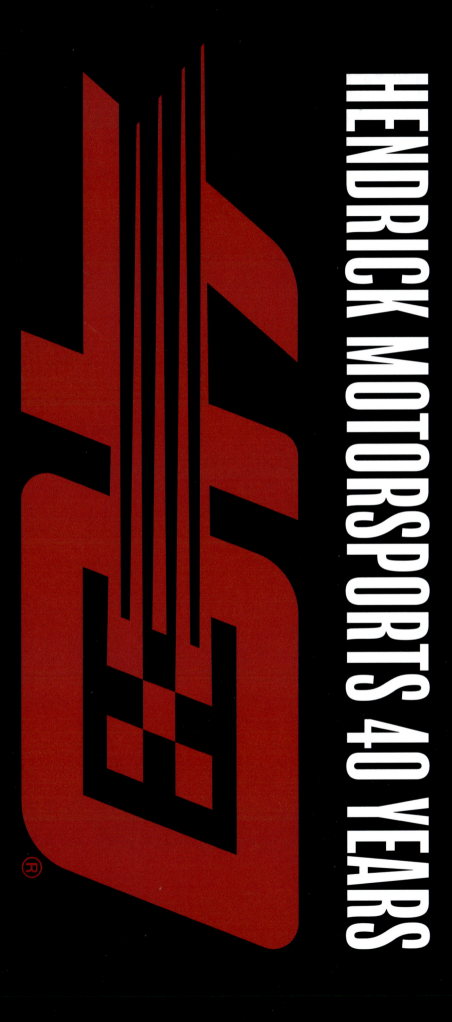

HENDRICK MOTORSPORTS 40 YEARS

NASCAR Racing's Greatest Team Celebrates Four Decades

BEN WHITE

FOREWORD BY
JEFF GORDON

AFTERWORD BY
RICK HENDRICK

FOREWORD BY JEFF GORDON 6   INTRODUCTION: TOBACCO FIELDS TO RACETRACKS 8

CONTENTS

SECTION 1 — 1980s — 13

#	Title	Page
1	An Unlikely Powerhouse	14
2	Keeping the Lights On: Martinsville Win Saves Hendrick Motorsports	18
3	The Road to Daytona	22
4	Hendrick Becomes a Modern Multi-Car Team	26
5	Shooting Star: The Brilliance of Tim Richmond	30
6	Like a Dream: Darrell Waltrip Arrives with Expectations	34
7	Ken Schrader Joins "Pop's Team"	38
8	Hitting the Road: The Corvette GTP Program	42
9	*Sidebar: Linda Hendrick's Steady Presence*	46

SECTION 2 — 1990s — 51

#	Title	Page
10	Going Hollywood: The Making of *Days of Thunder*	52
11	Ricky Rudd Brings Swagger and Strong Résumé	56
12	Changing the Sport: Jeff Gordon and the Rainbow Warriors	60
13	Home Game: Bragging Rights at Charlotte	64
14	T-Rex: Creating a Monster	68
15	Terry Labonte Ices Another Championship	72
16	Truckin': Jack Sprague Delivers Three Titles	76
17	This One's for You: Daytona Sweep Stirs Emotions	80
18	*Sidebar: It's All About People: Rick Hendrick's Winning Culture*	84

SECTION 3: 2000s — 89

#	Title	Page
19	Ricky Hendrick: An Emerging Leader	90
20	Stepping In: John Hendrick at the Helm	94
21	Live From New York! It's Jeff Gordon and *Saturday Night Live*	98
22	No. 24 Team's Fourth Championship Cements Place in History	102
23	Dale Earnhardt Jr.'s Move Rocks NASCAR	106
24	Seventh Heaven: The Jimmie Johnson and Chad Knaus Dynasty	110
25	The Triumph and Tragedy of Martinsville	114
26	*Sidebar: A Winning Combination: Hendrick Motorsports and Chevrolet*	118

SECTION 4: 2010s — 123

#	Title	Page
27	Talented Kasey Kahne Joins the Team	124
28	Chase Elliott: Second-Generation Champion	128
29	An Unconventional Path Brings William Byron on Board	132
30	Alan Gustafson's Winning Ways	136
31	Rick's Refuge: The Hendrick Heritage Center	140
32	*Sidebar: Hendrick Motorsports and the NASCAR Hall of Fame*	144

SECTION 5: 2020s — 149

#	Title	Page
33	The Enduring Legacy of Randy Dorton	150
34	1-2-3-4: Alex Bowman Leads Historic Dover Finish	154
35	269: A New Wins Record	158
36	Wasting No Time: Kyle Larson Dominates 2021 Season	162
37	Jeff Gordon: Takin' Care of Business	166
38	NASCAR to Le Mans: Garage 56 Goes Global	170
39	The Double: Larson Chases Crown Jewels	174
40	*Sidebar: 300 and Counting*	178

AFTERWORD BY RICK HENDRICK 182 · APPENDICES 184 · ABOUT THE AUTHOR 194 · ACKNOWLEDGMENTS 195 · PHOTO CREDITS 195 · INDEX 196

FOREWORD
PERSEVERANCE AND GRACE

I first met Rick Hendrick in the spring of 1992. I knew him only by reputation—that he had a successful NASCAR Cup Series team and also possessed a tremendous business background as one of the leading car dealers in the country. I was twenty years old and wanted to make a good impression. There was nothing more important to me at that time than for Rick to consider me as a possible driver for Hendrick Motorsports.

I was terrified, to be honest. It didn't take long for me to realize, though, what a genuinely nice person Rick was. I remember sitting in front of him at his desk and how he immediately made me feel at ease. In large part, that was because he was so humble and composed. He wasn't overpowering or intimidating, as I thought he might be. Instead, he was easygoing and extremely comfortable in his own skin.

Even though he has enjoyed incredible success as a NASCAR team owner and businessman over the past forty years, Rick remains exactly the person I met that day. He hasn't changed at all. You'll read more about that in the pages of this book.

We've worked together for just over thirty of those years. What I've learned is that Rick loves to play a role in seeing others succeed, and he takes joy in how all the little pieces combine to create something special. At the same time, when someone is struggling or in need, he is the first person to offer the shirt off his back. When you grow up in a small farming community, neighbors lift each other up during adversity and hardship. He's carried that approach throughout his life and in his businesses.

Although it was Rick's unparalleled vision that led Hendrick Motorsports to where it is, Linda Hendrick has been right by his side every step of the way. They've been a winning team since they married in January 1973, and they are closer than ever after more than fifty years together. They have always treated everyone at Hendrick Motorsports like family. Rooted in their faith, both continue to enjoy their own success in life, and as a result others have been able to share in that success. Rick and Linda have also experienced unimaginable challenges of their own, yet what they've been through has only strengthened their bond. Their perseverance and grace have inspired so many people.

It's been a long journey. Transforming Hendrick Motorsports from an upstart team to perennial champions has required inspired leadership and a lot of hard work from many talented people. Rick and Linda will be the first to tell you they didn't do it by themselves. Even more than all the wins and trophies, they've enjoyed building lasting relationships and creating life-changing opportunities for others in the process. They have always said people are the key to success. I'm fortunate to count myself among the ones they've touched along the way.

Spanning forty years and more than three hundred victories, the contributions of countless people have built Hendrick Motorsports into the greatest team in NASCAR history. This book is made up of their stories—just as Rick and Linda would want.

I hope you enjoy it.

INTRODUCTION
TOBACCO FIELDS TO RACETRACKS

The early morning summer humidity around Palmer Springs, Virginia, showed no mercy and crept higher by the hour. It was 1964, and somewhere on the spacious five-hundred-acre farm where tobacco, soybeans, cotton, and corn grew was fourteen-year-old Joseph Riddick "Rick" Hendrick III and his younger brother, twelve-year-old John Lewis Hendrick.

A young Rick Hendrick in a school photograph from the early 1960s. He began attending local short track races with his father, Papa Joe Hendrick, as a child.

As Rick stared out upon the sea of green tobacco leaves destined to be tied to brown five-foot tobacco sticks in the coming days, his mind was somewhere between the beautiful Corvettes he had studied in the latest magazines and his escape plan for getting out of the brutal sun, as far away from the long, lifeless rows of crop as he possibly could. To him, tobacco was a sticky, nasty substance that had no place in his everyday vocabulary.

The small crossroads settlement the Hendrick family called home also included some 1,500 other residents who shopped and worked eighteen miles away in South Hill, where grocery and retail stores were located. The town square was the center of city life, and young Rick loved to walk it and see the shiny cars and trucks in the public parking spots by storefronts.

The massive flat acreage owned by Joseph R. Hendrick Jr. spanned as far as the eye could see. It was left to him following his father's passing in July 1969 and the loss of his mother in May 1972. His two boys knew all too well the feel of tobacco juice, the climb to the top of barns to hang sticks for curing as well as every conceivable chore one could think of as the sons of a farmer. Early morning translated to cooler temperatures before a merciless sun began to rise over southern Virginia.

Rick and John were never afraid of hard work. With each wrap of string Rick flipped over each green stalk, or cucumber gathered to make a bushel, or load of hay tossed, his mental wheels turned about better ways to get away to make a living.

"Our dad gave us a quarter of an acre apiece, and that would make us about two hundred fifty dollars each summer," Rick remembers. "You're talking about in the early 1960s, and that was good money back then. I hated that work. I asked my dad if I paid a guy in my place, could I still get my crop, and he said yeah [*laughter*]. That guy was better at doing farm work than I was, so I hired him to do my part."

The elder Hendrick, known as Papa Joe, recalled the day Rick came to him with the "business proposition" to get out of the field, as told in *Twenty Years of Hendrick Motorsports* (2004): "Rick and John were real good boys at home and good mannered. Anything I asked them to do they would do. Let me tell you something. Rick never really was a farmer. He didn't like that too much. He was always in a business deal. If I told him I wanted him to do something that day on the farm, he would say something like, 'Well, Dad, Mr. Warren's boat is messed up and I can go over there and fix it and he'll pay me. Maybe you need to find someone to do my job.'"

Rick Hendrick alongside his first car, a 1931 Chevrolet. He was fourteen when he bought the five-window coupe, which he and Papa Joe built into this slick hot rod.

Papa Joe began work on the farm at 5:00 a.m. and then went to work at Burlington Mills as a supervisor from 4:00 p.m. until midnight. The next day, he would rise at 5:00 a.m. and do it all over again, six days a week. After church on Sundays, he would work on the farm and never seemed to take a day off.

"Dad was the hardest working guy I've ever met," Rick said. "And the thing that always impressed me with him was he could take up a hammer and an anvil and make anything. It wouldn't always be pretty, but it would work. He was super creative that he could figure out ways to do things. It was crude, but it worked.

"I think about his work ethic and his ability to figure out things. In general, the way he would get along with people and [how] everybody liked him, and he had tons of friends. He was a hardworking man. He worked in the tobacco fields and just never quit. He also taught me to work with my hands. On the farm, you often have to make things work and adapt the best way that you can. So many times, we had to make our own tools, pieces, and parts to get by."

John was also smart enough to realize that rising while it was still dark was the best way to beat the heat.

"During the summer, we worked from sunup until sundown in tobacco, cotton, cucumbers, and soybeans," John said in *Twenty Years of Hendrick Motorsports*. "When I was 12 years old, we might have 80 acres of tobacco and you'd do that by hand, pulling the leaves and tying them on tobacco sticks and were put in drying houses by the end of the day. We never had the machines of the bulk barns like they have today. We pulled it all and tied it by hand. I can tell you without a doubt I knew when I left there that I didn't want to do farming for a living."

Rick proved to be quite good at many sports, most notably baseball. Just after graduation from Park View High School in South Hill in June 1967, he was invited to a tryout with a Pittsburgh Pirates farm club but elected to follow his passion for cars, racing, and competition.

Rick and John's mother, Mary Hendrick, worked at the bank in Boydton, Virginia, as a teller and bookkeeper. She was all about numbers, and while Papa Joe and the boys raised the crops, Mary would make sure they received every dime due to them.

Rick's passion for cars, in particular Chevrolet Corvettes, became an obsession before he reached his twentieth birthday.

Introduction   **9**

When Rick began flipping Corvettes to make extra money in the summer of 1967 at the age of eighteen, the only way he could keep this fledgling enterprise going was with help from his mom and a promise to never falter on his word.

"He [Rick] would borrow money, buy the car, fix it up and sell it," Mary Hendrick said in *Twenty Years of Hendrick Motorsports*. "Then he would come into the bank and ask for another note and do the same thing. He wasn't old enough to sign the papers, so I had to do it for him. I'm proud to say I never had a problem with Rick on those notes. I never had a problem with Rick or John ever, I'm glad to say. I could not be more proud of them."

Rick always had a backup plan from the very beginning. When asked which parent he would go to for help first, he laughed and said, "I used to order stuff from Honest Charlie's cash on delivery and had it sent to my grandmother's house. That's how I got away with some things."

Rick wanted to drive oval track race cars, but Mary stopped that idea cold.

"Definitely not," Mary said. "Rick did do the drag racing, but when he built that car I thought he was building it to drive back and forth to school. Then I heard him crank it up one day. He said, 'Mom, come go for a ride with me.' He nearly scared me to death."

The compromise came through entering drag racing events with a maroon 1931 Chevrolet that he worked on day and night as a teenager. He built its V-8 engine himself and set numerous records at the local drag strip close to home. The Hendrick family made racing a family activity, putting the boys in the rumble seat and going to South Boston Speedway to watch late model races. Then they would go to the drag strip on Sunday afternoons and watch young Rick best his competition.

"I had that 1931 Chevrolet that my dad and I built," Rick said. "I would drag race at Person County Drag Strip in Roxboro, North Carolina. We built a 327 engine with used parts and won races with it."

"He talked about driving continuously," Mary said. "Wanting to race. I said, 'No way!' Then he finally persuaded us to let him drag race. He had been doing that, but we didn't know about it. At night, he would race different boys, you know, friends of his."

Rick remembers so much about his mom and dad and what a strong influence they had on his life. Papa Joe passed away on July 15, 2004, at age eighty-four. Mary Hendrick followed seven years later on August 8, 2011, at age eighty-eight.

"My mom was kind of the pillar of the family and the business head for the family," Rick said. "My dad was the creative one. She was a great mom to John and me. She ran the house and worked at the bank. She loved racing. She was always proud of us whatever we did, whether we were playing baseball or whatever. Like Dad, she was just hardworking.

"I think the main thing they taught us was that you need your neighbors because you never have everything you need. You have to depend on other people. You need your neighbors, and you need people. You have to depend on other people. Treat people with respect. Then they will want to do things with you and want to be friends with you and want to work with you.

"The need to have support from other folks is important because you might lose a barn or you might break a tractor, or you know, anything could happen. It was a real small community, and if somebody got sick, everybody jumped in. If somebody died, everybody supported. If somebody had any kind of issues or problems, they were always there for each other. And I think I've tried to keep that thought through my career. It's people first. I believe in servant leadership, but I believe in putting people first and putting people before profits. You'll make more, and you'll do more if you can keep everybody together."

He and Linda Myrick met one afternoon in Raleigh, North Carolina, at a gas station while Rick was working on a car. They were married in 1973 and rented a small home for one hundred dollars per month. Rick continued to buy and sell Corvettes, while Linda worked as an X-ray technician. Together, they cleaned cars and sold them for rent and grocery money. Rick also enrolled in a work-study program with Westinghouse Electric Corporation as a tool and die maker. His love for cars soon took center stage over any other career path.

By 1974, both Hendrick brothers were making huge professional strides. John attended school in Cincinnati, Ohio, followed by a year of business in Henderson, North Carolina. Rick was moving fast in automotive circles with a bright future. A sales opportunity at a car dealership in Raleigh served as the foundation for a successful future empire.

The hard work on the farm in Palmer Springs continued under the direction of Papa Joe. But soon, the Hendrick family would find themselves moving in an entirely unexpected direction.

OPPOSITE: Papa Joe Hendrick was a fan of stock car racing for most of his life. He and wife Mary's work ethic was a tremendous influence on Rick and John Hendrick.

1980s

SECTION 1

1 / AN UNLIKELY POWERHOUSE

Rick Hendrick sits in his office at City Chevrolet in Charlotte, North Carolina, in 1985. It remains his flagship dealership to this day.

By the spring of 1983, Rick Hendrick had scaled the corporate ladder as an automobile salesman, dealership general manager, and finally a successful car dealer. After five years, Hendrick owned four dealerships beginning in tiny Bennettsville, South Carolina. His business prospered under his leadership, and more opportunities were on the horizon in the years to come.

Stock car racing was a passion equaling his love for Corvettes and had been on his mind from a very early age. Local short-track racing was popular throughout the South. NASCAR's Cup Series races, known for decades as the Grand National Series, could be found through weekly radio broadcasts on the Universal Racing Network and Motor Racing Network, or on tape-delayed television broadcasts, most notably ABC's *Wide World of Sports* on Saturday afternoons.

Papa Joe also felt a passion for racing, having been involved with a local team since the late 1950s. Young Rick began going to races with his dad at around six years of age at Occoneechee Speedway in Hillsborough, North Carolina, as well as various short tracks around Richmond and South Boston.

"I remember I went with him to Martinsville Speedway when I was real young," Hendrick said. "I got an autograph from Richard Petty on a piece of paper, but I don't have any idea what happened to it. I also remember cheering for Rex White. He was the NASCAR champion in 1960, and he was driving the gold and white No. 4 Chevrolet then. That was in the early 1960s, so I would have been eleven or twelve years old. Many years later at the NASCAR Hall of Fame, Rex introduced himself to me, and I told him about pulling for him when I was a kid there in Martinsville. That was a special moment for me."

Papa Joe shared ownership in one of Clayton Mitchell's modifieds when the team ran the No. 97 and No. 98 Chevrolets wrenched by local car builder Frank Edwards. The Mitchell team eventually merged with Jack Tant's modified team and enjoyed five-time South Boston track champion Ray Hendrick (no relation) as their driver in the cherry-red No. 11 Chevrolet. Rick would ride his bicycle ten miles one way to Norlina, North Carolina, to Mitchell's shop just to help work on his cars. His pay? Free soft drinks from the small vending machine in the shop.

Twenty-five years later, Hendrick sponsored a Chevrolet dirt track car through his City Chevrolet dealership in Charlotte, North Carolina, owned by fellow South Hill resident Robert Gee, to be driven by rising star Dale Earnhardt.

Part of Hendrick's growing business enterprise included a high-performance parts distributorship, which helped create introductions to NASCAR drivers and mechanics who were customers.

Gee was known to be one of the best fabricators in the business. He already had the Budweiser Late Model Sportsman Series (now NASCAR Xfinity Series) entry built and ready for Charlotte Motor Speedway, and a driver who could put it up front and win. All he needed was Hendrick's financial support to build a fast engine to get it to victory lane.

"First off, I had been boat racing and drag racing, and I grew up in a town where Robert Gee was from," Rick said. "Jimmy Wright [piloting Hendrick's boat] was killed in a boat racing accident in Litchfield, Illinois, in 1982. After that, I didn't want to race boats anymore.

"So, when Robert called me, I got involved with his dirt car with the City Chevrolet dealership. Then he said, 'Would you like to be involved with me in the car that Earnhardt drives?' As it turned out, Dale won that three-hundred-mile race at Charlotte [in 1983]. I have a photo of myself and Dale in victory lane. A lot of people don't realize Dale Earnhardt won a race for me before Hendrick Motorsports was formed."

Behind the scenes, the wheels of business were moving fast. Sports marketing legend Max Muhleman had put together a potential deal that would garner news headlines around the world.

"Max called me and asked, 'How would you like to be partnered with the king of country music, Kenny Rogers, and have the king of NASCAR, Richard Petty, drive the car?' How could you not want to be a part of that?" Hendrick recalled. "C. K. Spurlock [Rogers' manager] was also part of the deal with his Gambler Chassis Company. The name of the team was to be All-Star Racing."

Harry Hyde, crew chief for driver Bobby Isaac when he won the 1970 NASCAR Grand National championship, had worked with several smaller Cup Series teams since his last Cup Series win with Neil Bonnett in 1977. Hyde was very eager to get with a top-flight team again and felt Hendrick was the man who could put him back on top.

"Harry Hyde was a hell of a salesman," Hendrick said. "He told me if he had a chance, he could build a car and go to Charlotte Motor Speedway and win. And I was dumb enough to believe him and that it would be that easy. That was like a road map to being part of something really special."

Driver Bobby Allison (left), team owner and engine builder Jack Tant (center), and driver Ray Hendrick (no relation to Rick) in the garage area at Martinsville Speedway in the early 1960s. Papa Joe Hendrick was a volunteer crew member with Tant's team.

Rick Hendrick sits behind the wheel of one of his race boats in the late 1970s. Hendrick was a regular drag boat competitor before starting his race teams in NASCAR.

Papa Joe Hendrick sits in the No. 5 Hendrick Motorsports Chevrolet parked in front of City Chevrolet in Charlotte, North Carolina, in late 1983. The car is painted with the first paint scheme before red and white colors were applied in January 1984.

Hendrick stored his boats in a building owned by Hyde, giving the former championship crew chief the opening he needed to sit Hendrick down and tell him his story.

"The very first time that Harry and I met was when Richard Broome [an employee who worked with the boats and a future Hendrick Motorsports crew chief] had the boats at Harry's shop," Hendrick said. "I would go over there on Saturdays, and Harry took me in his trailer, and he showed me pictures of Bobby Isaac and all these other drivers he had worked with. He showed me how he and Bobby had set all these records at the Salt Flats in Utah. He said that if he had a chance, he could come back to NASCAR and win. I believed him. So, when all that was going on with no intention of doing anything, I get the call from Max.

"At the time, Harry was as advanced as anybody in the sport. Harry was super creative. He had all these tricks and stuff that he did. Harry was equal to [team owner] Bud Moore. Harry was equal to the crew chiefs of that time. Crew chiefs back then were not engineers. Harry had an engineering mind without the credentials."

By late October 1983, Petty backed out of the deal. Not only was he committed to Pontiac and Hendrick to Chevrolet, the driver's primary sponsor, STP motor oil, balked at moving to an unproven team. With Petty's departure, Rogers and Spurlock's involvement lessened (ending after 1984) withdrew. That left Hendrick with Harry Hyde, two race cars, no sponsor, and no driver.

Geoff Bodine (left) talks with crew chief Harry Hyde during a race weekend at Daytona in 1984. In their first season together, they won Cup Series races at Martinsville, Virginia; Nashville, Tennessee; and Riverside, California.

2 KEEPING THE LIGHTS ON: MARTINSVILLE WIN SAVES HENDRICK MOTORSPORTS

Geoff Bodine (5) leads Bobby Allison (22) and Richard Petty (43) in the closing laps at Martinsville Speedway on April 29, 1984, before recording the first Cup Series victory for Hendrick Motorsports.

At 10:00 a.m. on Wednesday, October 2, 1983, Geoffrey Bodine walked into the lobby of City Chevrolet dressed in jeans, a dress shirt, and a blazer and took a seat. He wasn't there to buy a Chevrolet Monte Carlo off the showroom floor but rather to have his name painted on the roofline of the two red-and-white race cars on jack stands in the boat shed some twenty miles away.

Hendrick had already offered Tim Richmond a contract to drive the No. 5 Chevrolet and was waiting for an answer. With Petty out of the picture, the up-and-coming team owner needed someone proven to attract sponsorship for the upcoming season.

"I saw Tim and how much raw talent he had," Hendrick said. "I liked the flamboyant part of Tim. I liked the little bit of cockiness, but he could back it up, and I felt like I could harness it. So that was a sheer gut feeling like he had all this raw talent if we could put him in the right spot."

Hendrick had given Richmond until 3:00 p.m. that day to sign the contract and had called him to try to get an answer. Several messages had been left on his home answering machine to no avail. Seeing Bodine in the lobby, Hendrick told him it could be a long afternoon and that, to be fair, he was waiting to hear back from Richmond. Bodine replied that he would wait and that it was no problem.

"I admired that so much about Geoff," Hendrick said. "That showed me he was determined and how badly he wanted the ride, even though he knew we were a start-up team with very little to offer. He stayed and waited there for several hours. I finally called Tim and left another message and told him I was going in a different direction and had given the job to Geoff."

Bodine had one specific reason for wanting the ride with Hendrick, even though he wasn't completely unhappy with the ride he had.

"First off, I felt things were going well with Cliff Stewart's team, which was the team I was driving for in 1983," Bodine said. "Still, we were blowing engines and having mechanical issues. Plus, I felt Cliff needed to hire a couple more people, and he just didn't want to do that.

"Rick only offered me fifteen races and not the entire season. I didn't care about that. The main reason I wanted to go to Rick's team was Harry Hyde, and Rick knew that. Harry was a successful crew chief with Bobby Isaac, Neil Bonnett, and others. I felt I could learn so much from Harry. Hyde was smart and talented, and being with Harry would do so much for my career."

In mid-January 1984, All-Star Racing was unveiled at City Chevrolet. Hendrick, Bodine, and Hyde were introduced to the media, and they offered a glimpse of their red-and-white All-Star Racing Chevrolet. After interviews were completed, Hyde went back to work getting ready for NASCAR's season-opening Speedweeks and the Daytona 500, which were only a month away.

Hendrick had some firepower in his camp. Bodine, the young driver from Chemung, New York, was a great talent in the Northeast against fellow modified legends Richie Evans, Jerry Cook, Ray Hendrick, and Mike Stefanik.

Bodine at speed in the Cliff Stewart-owned No. 88 Pontiac at Daytona International Speedway in 1983. Bodine left Stewart's established team to join Hyde at Rick Hendrick's All-Star Racing because of the latter's experience as a championship-winning crew chief.

Bodine (5) passes Ron Bouchard (47) for the lead in the Sovran Bank 400 on April 29, 1984, at Martinsville Speedway just before winning his first Cup Series race and the first race for Hendrick Motorsports.

Hyde, a crusty, no-nonsense crew chief, had won NASCAR's Cup Series championship with Bobby Isaac fourteen years earlier while working for team owner Nord Krauskopf. Hyde helped Isaac secure thirty-six of his thirty-seven career victories in NASCAR. He also scored four wins with Dave Marcis and three with Buddy Baker in Krauskopf's Dodges and two more wins with Bonnett after J. D. Stacy bought the team from Krauskopf.

Hyde had worked with several independent teams but longed for the glory of the past. At fifty-nine years of age in 1984, some called him too old to make a difference in what was known as the modern era of NASCAR. Hyde saw it differently and felt he could bring a vast amount of knowledge and experience to a team. His method of doing things rubbed some people the wrong way, but he won races with an old-school, common-sense approach. Pairing the northern-born Bodine with the Kentucky-bred Hyde didn't make sense to most everyone in the garage area—except Hendrick.

With a fresh paint scheme, rented transporter, crew members, and a few volunteers, All-Star Racing set out to Daytona with hopes of a strong showing. Privately, Hendrick was feeling anything but optimistic.

"The deal with Petty, Kenny Rogers, and C. K. Spurlock had fallen through, and I was in too deep to turn back," Hendrick said. "I was walking down pit road there at Daytona, and I saw Bud Moore's team and Dale Earnhardt and [Richard] Childress and Cale Yarborough with Harry Ranier and the Wood Brothers, and I'm thinking, 'I just don't belong here.' We got into the practice and the one-hundred-twenty-five-mile qualifying race. Our car wasn't running great and falling back, and I'm so embarrassed. I just wanted to go back to the hotel."

On February 19, 1984, Bodine ended Speedweeks with a remarkable eighth-place finish in the Daytona 500 in their first outing in NASCAR's Cup Series. Over the next six races, Bodine logged a ninth at Richmond, Virginia, a sixth at Rockingham, North Carolina, and thirteenth at Atlanta. He finished twenty-fifth at Bristol, Tennessee, fourteenth at North Wilkesboro, North Carolina, and thirty-fifth at Darlington, South Carolina, after suffering a crash.

With seven races completed, Hendrick and Hyde had a difficult conversation. With little to no sponsorship to speak of, it was time to close the doors of All-Star Racing.

"I told Harry we couldn't go past Darlington, or I'd be putting my entire business at risk," Hendrick said. "We went to Darlington and finished thirty-fifth, and I thought that was it. Now, again, Harry was a great salesman. He kept saying, 'Just let us go to Martinsville. Bodine is good there. We can win.' He talked me into it."

Hyde was right. Bodine was very good at Martinsville Speedway, having won several major modified and late model races there. Bodine seemingly knew the feel of the track and knew how to nurse a car to the end better than anyone at the 0.526-mile short track.

"I had driven many five-hundred-lap races there before that race," Bodine said. "I knew how to stay off the brakes when a lot of drivers didn't. I went into that race in 1984 feeling I could win it. I wasn't nervous about it at all and wasn't thinking about having to close the doors. That wasn't in my mind at all when I crawled into the car that day. I honestly felt I had a solid chance to win that race.

"Part of the reason for that was I had a lot of confidence in Harry's setups back then. We had some good finishes in those first few races. I had confidence in the crew. I said to myself, 'Just do your job.'"

The entire landscape of the Cup Series was different in those days. Sponsorships were lighter, the car bodies were boxier, and the crews were much smaller in number. There was much more beating and grinding on the track. Simply surviving five hundred laps at Martinsville was a legitimate concern.

"Back then, it was harder to race there than it is today," Bodine said. "We didn't have big brakes. So, you really had to save your brakes. I knew that, and I understood that. And of course, Harry kept telling me on the radio to save my brakes."

Bodine passed Bobby Allison on the outside of turn four to take the lead with forty-nine laps to go. The laps clicked off, and as cars were being put in his rearview mirror, the emotion of a possible win began to set in. In the closing laps, the tears began to flow.

"I kept thinking something could still happen, but it was all starting to set in," Bodine said. "With five to go, tears were flowing down my cheeks. That's when I started thinking about all the sacrifices I put my family through. It was finally paying off. It was finally going to work."

While Bodine and Hyde enjoyed champagne in victory lane, Rick and Linda Hendrick were in a much more solemn setting in a late-afternoon church service in Greensboro, North Carolina. On the way home, they pulled over to a pay phone on the side of the road to call Rick's mother, Mary, to check on the results of the race.

"Mom said, dead seriously, 'You haven't heard? He blew up,'" Hendrick said. "I thought it was all over. Then she said, 'No, he won!' I about dropped the phone. I went back to Linda and said, 'You're just not going to believe what has happened. We won.' We couldn't believe it. Then we went straight to Bodine's house [in Pleasant Garden, North Carolina] and covered his entire yard in toilet paper. I don't remember how we found his house because we didn't have [GPS] or cell phones back then.

"It was such a relief to win. If we hadn't, there's no way we'd be here today."

Bodine went on to win two more races that year, at Nashville, Tennessee, on July 14 and at Riverside, California, on November 18 to close out the season.

"That first win at Martinsville was an incredible story that I'll always remember," Bodine said. "I'll forever be grateful to Rick for giving me the opportunity to drive for Hendrick Motorsports because of the great lifelong friendships I've made there, including my friendship that remains with him. Without that win, Hendrick Motorsports wouldn't be here today. I'm grateful to have been a part of it."

The leaderboard in turns three and four at Martinsville posts the results of the Sovran Bank 400. Bodine's car number is shown in the lead, followed by the car numbers of Ron Bouchard, Darrell Waltrip, Bobby Allison, and Neil Bonnett.

Geoff Bodine in victory lane, trophies in hand, after winning at Martinsville Speedway. The Chemung, New York, native led 55 of the final laps to secure the win.

3 / THE ROAD TO DAYTONA

Crew members from the No. 5 All-Star Racing team at Daytona International Speedway for Speedweeks in February 1984. Daytona marked the beginning for Hendrick Motorsports' full entry to NASCAR competition.

On Wednesday morning, February 8, 1984, Harry Hyde walked around the No. 5 Chevrolet that was set to load into the top of the All-Star Racing transporter. The paint was barely dry on the body, as well as on that of the backup car that had already been loaded ahead of it.

The fledgling team of a half dozen or so handpicked crewmen would soon head down Interstate 85, then Interstate 77, and finally onto Interstate 95 for the nine-hour ride to Daytona International Speedway. The twin 125-mile qualifying races prior to the Daytona 500 were set for February 16, and there was much to accomplish before those two events.

Hyde had been there before, literally, and figuratively. The excitement he was feeling was almost impossible to contain. The Brownsville, Kentucky, native had traveled to Daytona since becoming a crew chief in NASCAR's elite Grand National Series in 1965.

Hyde was a stickler for detail and organization and ran his teams with an iron fist, often drawing comparison to World War II general George S. Patton. Hyde was famous for keeping an index card in his shirt pocket with notes from each race recording what went right and, especially, what went wrong.

"Harry Hyde was meticulous about everything he did," said Buddy Parrott, a crewmember under Hyde who became a legendary

The No. 5 All-Star Racing Chevrolet sits on the grid at the 1984 Daytona 500. Geoff Bodine started the Rick Hendrick-owned Chevrolet in ninth alongside Tim Richmond (27) in 10th. Bodine finished an impressive eighth in his first race with the team.

Bodine pits for tires and fuel during the 1984 Daytona 500. Crew chief Harry Hyde had assembled a very capable crew for the race, though most were volunteers at that time.

Geoff Bodine, driver of the No. 5 Hendrick Motorsports Chevrolet, in victory lane after winning the 1986 Daytona 500 at Daytona International Speedway. This was Hendrick Motorsports' first Daytona win.

Darrell Waltrip and his No. 17 Hendrick Motorsports Chevrolet at Daytona International Speedway in February 1989.

crew chief in his own right. "We worked together when Bobby Isaac drove for him in 1969–1970. Harry knew what he was wanted right down to the last nut and bolt. You didn't understand him but what he was doing usually worked. Patton? Oh yeah. That's a great comparison. [*Laughter*] He should have driven a tank to work every day."

Hyde was traveling with Rick Hendrick's No. 5 Chevrolets, but by that February day in 1984, he had worked with a variety of great race drivers, including Bobby Allison, Neil Bonnett, Ray Hendrick (no relation to Rick Hendrick), and Buddy Baker to name but a few. Through 1977, Hyde had forty-five wins to his credit. He had worked with several teams for a few races here and there, but he longed to get back with a top team for a full schedule of Grand National races, to make that long awaited comeback at age fifty-nine. The smile on his face was difficult to contain.

Once in the garage area at the 2.5-mile track, Hyde and Bodine began working toward mission one: winning the Busch Clash of 1984 scheduled for Sunday, February 12. The Clash was a twenty-lap race for pole position winners from the previous season, and Bodine had made himself eligible by earning pole at Atlanta International Raceway (now Atlanta Motor Speedway) on March 27, 1983, while driving for team owner Cliff Stewart.

Prior to the start of the Clash, Bodine was having ongoing engine issues. The Chemung, New York, native started the twenty-lap event fourth, but by lap ten had dropped to tenth in the eleven-car field.

Bodine salvaged a fifth-place finish in the Clash, pulling toward the front in the final lap. In the 500 a week later, he excelled once again with an impressive eighth-place finish. Not every driver and team can claim a top-ten finish in their debut running of NASCAR's most prestigious race.

Two years later on February 16, 1986, Bodine won Hendrick Motorsports' first Daytona 500 with Gary Nelson making the strategic calls as his crew chief on pit road. It was only Bodine's fourth career Cup Series victory and the biggest win in the brief history of Hendrick Motorsports.

"I felt so good about that day at Daytona in 1986," Bodine said. "I knew we had a great chance to win that race. The car was good from the start. It came down to me and Earnhardt and those final pit stops. Dale overshot his pits and broke a transmission with just a few laps to go and we had enough fuel to make it all the way. Gary [Nelson] had the fuel figured perfectly and we weren't going to stop. It was the perfect day. Everything went our way and it was the biggest win of my career."

Over the next 38 years, Hendrick Motorsports would enjoy eight additional Daytona 500 victories coming with Darrell Waltrip in 1989, Jeff Gordon in 1997, 1999, and 2005, Jimmie Johnson in 2006 and 2013, Dale Earnhardt Jr. in 2014, and William Byron in 2024.

Waltrip went on to win the only Daytona 500 of his career in 1989. It was the second Daytona win for team owner Rick Hendrick (left).

SECTION 1: 1980s

4 / HENDRICK BECOMES A MODERN MULTI-CAR TEAM

Crew members from the No. 5 Hendrick Motorsports team unload tires in the garage area at Daytona International Speedway in 1986. This marked the first year the organization would run as a multi-car team.

Beginning with the 1986 season, Hendrick Motorsports was set to become one of the earliest full-time multi-car Cup Series teams in NASCAR's modern era. Petty Enterprises ran both Richard and Kyle full-time in 1981 and 1983, and Junior Johnson began running two full-time cars in 1984 with Darrell Waltrip and Neil Bonnett behind the wheels (Waltrip, in fact, won a championship in 1985). Now Hendrick Motorsports was poised to be the first team to make it truly work long-term.

What started in a boat shed two years earlier was now more than a race team—it was an organization that garnered a great deal of respect from long-established racing operations because of its ability to win, its fairness on the track, and its promising future. Many NASCAR team owners had come and gone, but Rick Hendrick seemed here to stay.

As the 1985 season came to a close, Geoff Bodine had logged ten top-fives, fourteen top-tens, and three pole positions for Hendrick Motorsports with no victories in twenty-eight starts. The chemistry between Bodine and Hyde had faded, prompting Hendrick to make personnel changes. In the fall of 1985, a second team was quietly being added to the fold.

"Bodine and Hyde were not getting along like before, and we had a new team coming on board," Hendrick said. "Geoff and Harry just weren't seeing eye to eye on anything, so I called them into a meeting. After my long talk about working together and the need to get along, Geoff agreed he would do all he could to make it work. Harry stood up and said, 'Geoff, you're a prick and a prima donna, but I love Rick more than I hate you.' [*Laughter*] I'm like, 'Wait, that's not what we're trying to do here.' I felt like what I was trying to say wasn't working at all and didn't go very far."

Hendrick Motorsports was building a reputation as a solid racing entity. Corporations were proud to be associated with them and looked for ways to have their product names on Hendrick's Chevrolets.

"We pursued the Levi Garrett sponsorship that we put with Bodine and crew chief Gary Nelson [in 1985]," Hendrick said. "Another company, Folgers Coffee, came to us and wanted to sponsor a team. So, I hired Tim Richmond to drive for us and put Harry Hyde with Tim and formed the number 25 team. I finally got the driver I wanted with Tim and felt Tim and Harry would work well together."

Bodine also thought the move was a boost, and it gave him the biggest victory of his career.

"I enjoyed working with Gary," Bodine said. "We had some great success together, which included winning the 1986 Daytona 500. I enjoyed working with Harry also. Harry taught me a lot about racing and a lot about winning. I loved Harry. But Gary did as well, and so did everyone I worked with at Hendrick Motorsports. I was a better driver for the time I spent there for sure. My last win for Rick was at North Wilkesboro Speedway in October of 1989. Rick and I knew we were parting ways, but it was still a great win for us."

In 1986, just two years after its inaugural Daytona 500, Hendrick Motorsports and Geoff Bodine stood in victory lane at Daytona International Speedway. It was the first of nine victories (through 2024) for Hendrick Motorsports in NASCAR's most prestigious race, and a tie for the all-time record.

Team owner Rick Hendrick posed for this driver photo before his start in the Busch Grand National Series race on August 2, 1987, at Road Atlanta. Hendrick started sixth and finished twenty-fourth after suffering clutch issues.

Hyde's reaction to the new plan with Richmond wasn't as smooth as Hendrick had hoped. The crew chief wasn't one to mince words and let his feelings be known rather quickly.

"I had built this reputation of raising up young 'uns, and I hated that damn thing," Hyde explained in *Twenty Years of Hendrick Motorsports*. "I hated it because it seemed like everybody wanted me to raise their young 'uns, and I wanted an experienced driver. I wanted a David Pearson or a Richard Petty. I wanted someone who already knew how to drive.

"I really didn't warm up to it [having Richmond as his driver]. In fact, in April [1986] I hated every minute of it because Tim was so defiant. He wouldn't stop long enough to listen to anybody. He was his own man and he was going to do it his way and the car had to do it his way.

"I was trying to drill into him that we were no good unless we thought 'five hundred miles.' You think five hundred miles on tires, pit stops, brakes, gas mileage, gearboxes, saving equipment, engine. He wanted to run any way he wanted to just about as long as the car lasted."

The turning point in the two men's relationship came when Hyde took Richmond to North Wilkesboro Speedway and, to prove his point, let Richmond run fifty laps the way he wanted and then fifty laps the way Hyde wanted. Hyde's tires were smooth. Richmond's tires were badly blistered. Richmond began to come around.

Their first victory came in the thirteenth race at Pocono Raceway in Pennsylvania on June 8, followed by six more wins coming at Daytona in July, Pocono in July, Watkins Glen and Darlington in August, Richmond in September, and Riverside to close out the season in November.

Richmond affectionately referred to Hyde as "Pop," as he had grown close to the old ironclad crew chief, almost like father and son. By year's end, they looked forward to the 1987 season. The potential for winning races and a championship reminded Hyde of the years he enjoyed with Bobby Isaac.

Ken Martin, director of historical content for NASCAR Studios, has seen Hendrick Motorsports grow from a single-car team in 1984 to a championship powerhouse. The key to decades of success as a multi-car organization, according to Martin, comes down to close interaction among its people.

"Many other team owners throughout NASCAR's history have fielded multi-car teams," Martin said. "In the modern era of NASCAR, beginning in 1972, most drivers would talk with team owners about driving for them but absolutely would reject any multi-car team scenarios. If that ever came up, their first reaction would be, 'I'm gone.'

"Rick has been able to make multi-car teams work for forty years because he has had this incredible ability to put the right people together in the right positions. The chemistry among them has been strong long-term. The result has been the remarkable success Hendrick Motorsports continues to enjoy."

Hendrick's tremendous faith in his vision and those around him was another key to taking the venture to the next level. A three-time champion was about to join Hendrick Motorsports in 1987, along with some very talented people. Storm clouds were also about to roll in.

Tim Richmond won his seventh Cup Series race of the season for Hendrick Motorsports on November 16, 1986. Richmond's victory count and his third-place finish in points saw the National Motorsports Press Association honor him as Co-Driver of the Year, alongside 1986 NASCAR Cup Series champion Dale Earnhardt.

5 / SHOOTING STAR: THE BRILLIANCE OF TIM RICHMOND

Tim Richmond poses with the winner's trophy at Watkins Glen International in Watkins Glen, New York, on August 10, 1986. Richmond led twenty-nine of the race's ninety-lap distance on the 2.4-mile road course.

Richmond, driver of the No. 25 Hendrick Motorsports Chevrolet, at the start of the 1986 Cup Series season. Richmond was fun loving and a fan favorite.

Richmond started the 1980 Indianapolis 500 in 19th position and eventually worked his way into the top ten. He led one lap and finished ninth after running out of fuel. Richmond was named Rookie of the Year for the race.

In 1980, a young, charismatic rising star named Tim Richmond was shaking up the open-wheel IndyCar world. He was handsome, smart, and a rebel of sorts who wore jeans, cowboy boots and hat, long hair, and sunglasses. The Ashland, Ohio, native was a fun-loving, easygoing guy who attracted the Hollywood starlets of his time and had a reputation as a partier. He didn't fit in, and Richmond loved it. He seemed to be living on the edge every minute, and that's what set him apart. It's also what made him a great race car driver.

In his first Indianapolis 500 start, Richmond won Rookie of the Year honors by finishing ninth and was famously driven down pit lane toward victory circle on the side of Johnny Rutherford's winning car after running out of fuel and being picked up by Rutherford on his victory lap.

In July 1980, Richmond came to NASCAR after crashing out of several IndyCar events in a row. D. K. Ulrich gave him five starts in 1980 and a full-time ride in 1981. He proved he could drive, catching the eye of wealthy team owner J. D. Stacy for the 1982 season after entering some one-off events with various owners. Later that year, he swept both races on the road course at Riverside, California, in Stacy's Buicks.

Team owner Raymond Beadle hired Richmond for a three-year deal from 1983 through 1985, during which he scored victories at Pocono Raceway and North Wilkesboro Speedway. The pairing lacked consistency, so when Hendrick asked for his services a second time, Richmond felt the time was right to move.

"Tim was clearly a sponsor's dream," Hendrick said. "He had it all with his great looks and ability to carry himself. Even his name was the perfect name from a marketing standpoint. He would come to meetings and charm everyone in the room. The downside to that was that you weren't always sure he would show for some of those very important high-level meetings. Tim had his own agenda and knew how to party. Sometimes a little too much. I was always worried if he would show up when I needed him to be there."

Richmond won his seventh Cup Series race of the 1986 season (thus the sign) on November 16 at Riverside International Raceway in Riverside, California.

The 1986 Cup Series season was nothing short of magical, as Richmond and Harry Hyde eventually jelled like no other driver and crew chief. The operative word was *eventually*, as they battled through incredible challenges throughout the first third of the season. At first they struggled to see eye to eye on chassis setups, tires, and even the weather, but despite all that they did manage three top-fives. There were also four finishes of twentieth or worse. Consistency didn't come until both decided to give in to the other and really listen to what was being said.

Richmond and Hyde then scored seven victories, their biggest being the Southern 500 at Darlington Raceway on August 31. Richmond finished third in Winston Cup points with thirteen top-five finishes, seventeen top-tens and was named Co-Driver of the Year alongside season champion Dale Earnhardt, driver of the No. 3 Richard Childress Racing Chevrolet.

As the 1987 season began, there were high hopes for a Winston Cup championship for the No. 25 Folgers Coffee team. Unknown to many, Richmond suffered a terrible offseason physically. After the NASCAR Awards Banquet in December 1986, he was hospitalized in Cleveland, Ohio. Still recovering in February 1987, he missed the season-opening Daytona 500, reportedly due to pneumonia. Though not widely known at the time, a weakened immune system due to AIDS was likely the reason behind his infection.

Richmond's Hendrick Motorsports Chevrolet was turned over to 1973 Cup Champion Benny Parsons, with the number changed to 35. Parsons finished second in the 500, and went on to record six top-five finishes and nine top-tens after twenty-nine starts.

Richmond returned at Pocono on June 14 for the Miller High Life 500 driving the famed No. 25 Hendrick Motorsports Chevrolet. Despite gearbox problems midway through the race, Richmond led

Richmond enjoys a champagne and beer shower after winning at Pennsylvania's Pocono Raceway on June 14, 1987, in his first start in the eight races that he entered that season.

82 laps and won by eight car lengths over Bill Elliott. Richmond competed in eight races in 1987, also winning at Riverside International Raceway, logging one pole position before his final race at Michigan in August of that year.

"I had tears in my eyes when I took the checkered flag. Then, every time anyone congratulated me, I started bawling again," Richmond said during postrace interviews at Pocono. Richmond made his final start at Michigan International Speedway's Champion Spark Plug 400 that August, finishing twenty-ninth with a blown engine.

As further health issues surfaced in Fall 1987, Richmond withdrew from the public to his home in Florida. Rumors of HIV and AIDS persisted, but he denied them. He was eventually hospitalized in West Palm Beach. Richmond died on August 13, 1989, and was laid to rest in Ashland, Ohio.

"Tim was a very flamboyant person with unbelievable talent as a race car driver," Hendrick said. "He was hard to harness at times but not afraid of anything."

Richmond logged thirteen Cup Series wins during his career, and many in the industry believe that had he continued competing, he would likely have become a Cup Series champion.

6 / LIKE A DREAM: DARRELL WALTRIP ARRIVES WITH EXPECTATIONS

Barney Hall (left), a Motor Racing Network announcer, interviews Darrell Waltrip prior to the 1989 Daytona 500. Waltrip drove for Hendrick Motorsports from 1987 through 1990.

During the winter months between the 1986 and 1987 seasons, there was little to keep motorsports writers busy at their respective news outlets. The countdown to Speedweeks at Daytona in early February was all that seemed relevant, other than the occasional test session at the 2.5-mile track.

In early January, a rumor-turned-fact kept typewriter keys clicking. One headline began to spread: "Waltrip to Drive for Hendrick Motorsports as Part of New Dream Team."

It was a huge surprise to everyone in the sport. Waltrip had indeed left Junior Johnson and Associates, considered one of the premier Cup Series teams. He would drive a third Chevrolet for Hendrick Motorsports with engine builder and crew chief Waddell Wilson. Wilson was coming over from Harry Ranier's Charlotte-based Ranier-Lundy Racing, leaving rising star Davey Allison to look for a crew chief.

From 1981 through 1986, Waltrip and Johnson enjoyed a very successful relationship that garnered three Cup Series championships and forty-three victories. The driver and team owner were considered the best of the best, and the powerful team based in Wilkes County, North Carolina, were thought to be virtually unstoppable.

Hendrick Motorsports had become a viable racing operation in a rather short three-year timespan. Hendrick and crew chief Harry Hyde had progressed mightily on a shoestring budget in 1984 and flourished quickly. Now they carried sponsorships from Fortune 500 companies and attracted a championship driver and top mechanics who could make them winners everywhere they raced.

The media dubbed the union of Waltrip, Wilson, and ace mechanics Gary DeHart and Eddie Dickerson "The Dream Team." They were known as some of the best mechanical minds in the business and the best money could buy.

34 HENDRICK MOTORSPORTS 40 YEARS

Waltrip drove for team owner Junior Johnson (left) before his departure to Hendrick Motorsports in 1987. Waltrip and Johnson won Cup Series championships in 1981, 1982, and 1985.

Waltrip thought he would be with Johnson for years to come until a quick comment from the moonshine legend changed their working relationship one October afternoon in 1986. Ironically, Waltrip wasn't looking to make a move. It was Johnson that prompted a call to Hendrick to put the deal together.

"I had just gotten a letter of intent from Honda to have a dealership, and I was so excited. I was beside myself," Waltrip said. "Rick and I were talking, and Rick said, 'Why don't you come and drive for me? I said, 'I'm just not sure I can. I'm still with Junior [Johnson] and happy up there. I'll probably just stay there.' And we sort of left it there and went on our way.

"I thought, well, I should run this by Junior and just let him know. I felt I should tell him about that conversation. So, I'm at Junior's office, and he's sitting at his desk. Junior was wearing one of those half-pairs of glasses on his nose, and he is staring down at some papers on his desk, and he never looked up.

"I said, 'Hey, Junior. Rick Hendrick sort of offered me a ride with Hendrick Motorsports for next year. I just thought you should know about it.' Again, he never looked up and still had those glasses on. He said to me, 'I'll tell you what, boy. Maybe you need to go on and take that job.' That kind of shocked me because I wasn't expecting that answer at all. Not at all! And so, I left the office and I thought, well, so much for that."

A conversation with his crew at Johnson's shop days later also prompted another unexpected response, as Johnson had already told them Waltrip was on his way out the door.

"I left the shop and ran to the phone as quickly as I could find one," Waltrip said. "We didn't have cell phones then. I called Rick and said, 'Hey, I've been thinking about your offer. Let's put that deal together.' And the rest is history."

Hendrick summed up Waltrip's personality by saying, "Darrell was a character and a super salesman, sort of like the way Harry

SECTION I: 1980s   **35**

Race winner Waltrip in victory lane at Charlotte Motor Speedway after winning the Coca-Cola 600 for Hendrick Motorsports on May 29, 1988. The Owensboro, Kentucky, native led 73 of the race's 400 laps.

Hyde was a super salesman. He would make you believe he could walk on water. I think Darrell was kind of a first-round draft choice at the time. If you could get Darrell Waltrip, you got a winner and you got a champion."

Hendrick had lined up Wilson, Dickerson, DeHart, Wesley Mills, and Pete Bingle to build and tune Waltrip's No. 17 Chevrolet. They were the best of the best and collectively contributed to nine victories from 1987 through 1990, including the 1989 Daytona 500. Though Waltrip and Wilson were considered a top-flight driver and crew chief, winners of NASCAR's biggest races, they ended up going different directions. Jeff Hammond, Waltrip's crew chief for most of his tenure with Johnson from 1982 through 1986, joined Hendrick Motorsports at Riverside, California, on June 21, 1987.

"We had some great talent assembled for The Dream Team," Waltrip said. "Waddell wanted to bring on some of his own people. He wanted to be in charge and make all decisions on the car, but I've always been able to make decisions on the car myself. So, we finally parted ways, and I got Hammond to be my crew chief. We had some wins, but the overall hope of multiple championships and large amounts of wins just didn't materialize. We did win races with Rick, including the Daytona 500, and that's what we need to take from that experience. We were successful."

Waltrip parted ways with the team at the end of the 1990 season to pursue a new venture of his own. He was partial to having a single-car team, while Hendrick Motorsports planned to always have multiple cars in their stable, even while "The Dream Team" was being built.

Team owner Rick Hendrick (center) with driver Darrell Waltrip (right) after he won the Daytona 500 on February 19, 1989. To Hendrick's right is Waltrip's crew chief Jeff Hammond. Waltrip had to nurse his No. 17 Hendrick Motorsports Chevrolet to victory at race's end with a near-empty gas tank.

"Rick called me into his office one day and said, 'We have a problem,'" Waltrip said. "'We're always going to have more than one car. Maybe three or four cars. Maybe five cars. Do you want to be in or out?' That was probably the only disagreement we ever had about that situation, until I decided in 1991 to go on my own and have my own team. Even then, he said he thought my leaving was a mistake but said he would help me any way he could, and he did. Rick is probably one of the very best friends I've ever had."

Hendrick felt "The Dream Team" was a great idea that simply didn't meet expectations.

"The good of The Dream Team was that you had a championship driver and a championship engine builder and crew chief with Waddell Wilson," Hendrick said. "You had it all with these talented guys. The problem is that when you put it together, if there's no immediate success, everyone wants to revert back to what they did somewhere else. Whereas if you build a team from the ground up and they've worked together from that point, they don't have that mentality of, 'We did this over here' or 'We did this over there.' It's too many personalities that sometimes just don't mesh for success."

7 KEN SCHRADER JOINS "POP'S TEAM"

Ken Schrader (center) stands between team owner Rick Hendrick (left) and Papa Joe Hendrick (right) in victory lane at Talladega Superspeedway on July 31, 1988, after winning the Talladega 500. It was Schrader's first victory for Hendrick Motorsports.

Schrader racing the No. 29 Louis Seymour USAC Silver Crown sprint car at Indianapolis Raceway Park in 1988.

Ken Schrader had already found success in the ranks of open-wheel United States Auto Club (USAC) Sprint Car competition—winning four USAC sprint car races, six Silver Crown races, twenty-one in USAC midgets, and twenty-four other midget races—before moving to NASCAR in 1984.

The Fenton, Missouri, native made headlines in newspapers through the Midwest on a weekly basis. His name was widely circulated as an up-and-coming star with huge potential for a possible ride in NASCAR's Cup Series.

Schrader also felt it was time to consider NASCAR as a possible next step. He made his debut at Nashville Speedway in the No. 64 Ford Thunderbird leased from Elmo Langley and finished nineteenth out of thirty cars. He ran four more races that season, his best finish being seventeenth at North Wilkesboro Speedway on October 14.

Then in 1985, he signed for team owner Junie Donlavey, winning Rookie of the Year honors. In 1986, Schrader twice finished in seventh place and logged two other top-ten finishes, ending up sixteenth in points standings for the second year running. Schrader won his first career pole in the spring of 1987 at Darlington Raceway. He led nineteen laps, finishing in fifth place for his first career top-five result. With nine other top-ten finishes, Schrader ended the season tenth in the standings.

"Things were working pretty well," Schrader said. "We weren't wrecking anything, and our engines were holding up. I had been talking with [team owner] Bud Moore, and I was all set to drive in Fords in 1988. I had even told some people I was going there. I was sure I was going there. Then the phone rang one night—it was Jimmy Johnson, Rick's executive, on the line—and asked me what my deal was for '88. I told them I had intended to drive for Bud. He asked if I had signed anything, and I said no, not at that point, and that I had a handshake deal with Bud."

Johnson called Schrader on Tuesday, September 1, and the two met on September 2 to tour the Hendrick Motorsports facility. On

Schrader led the final lap of the 188-lap Talladega race to take the win. It was his first career victory in the Cup Series.

Schrader post-victory with Papa Joe Hendrick and Mary Hendrick, parents of team owner Rick Hendrick

Friday evening, Schrader and Johnson met in the parking lot of a gas station close to Darlington Raceway to sign the contract.

"Until then, I was dead set on going with Bud," Schrader said. "The whole scenario sort of caught me by surprise and happened really quick. I hated to do it, but I had to go and tell Bud I wasn't coming with him after all [*laughter*]. The Wood Brothers [Glen and Leonard] and their crew jokingly said they would stand about twenty feet away that Saturday morning at Darlington when I told Bud I wasn't coming with him. Bud was great about the entire situation. He understood why I took the deal with Hendrick Motorsports."

Schrader's first-year statistics were impressive, making him the perfect choice to take over the No. 25 Hendrick Motorsports Chevrolet. Hendrick's decision proved wise. In his first outing with the team in the Daytona 500, Schrader started NASCAR's most prestigious race from the pole position and finished sixth in the two-hundred-lap event.

Schrader won his first career Cup Series race at Alabama International Motor Speedway (now known as Talladega Superspeedway) on July 31 and finished fifth in the final point standings after twenty-nine starts. The second Winston Cup Series win came the following season on October 8, 1989, at Charlotte Motor Speedway. Schrader was fifth in the final standings for a second year in a row.

"Both of those wins were really special because Papa Joe and Mary were there," Schrader said. "I like to tell people I didn't drive for Rick. I drove for Pop."

On March 18, 1991, Schrader led 58 of 328 laps at Atlanta Motor Speedway and won his third career Cup Series race for Hendrick Motorsports. His final Winston Cup Series win came at Dover International Speedway on June 2, 1991, and he closed the season ninth in the final standings, with ten top-five finishes. For the 1992 season, Schrader notched eleven top-tens, finishing seventeenth in total points. In 1993, he won six pole positions and moved up to ninth in the final points standings. The following season, Schrader finished a career-best fourth in the standings. In 1995, Schrader logged two top-five finishes and ten top-tens and in 1996, he had three top-fives and ten top-tens, his final season with Hendrick Motorsports.

Schrader elected to leave Hendrick Motorsports at the end of the season after nine years. The Cup Series victories didn't come as hoped, but their relationship was strong when they parted ways and is even stronger today.

"I quit on my own to see if I was the reason we weren't winning," Schrader said. "We just weren't getting it done, so I decided to go over to Andy Petree's team. If it was me, I need to find out. But, man, I made some long-lasting friendships there at Hendrick Motorsports. We had so much fun there. Pop was such a cool guy. He and Rick came from such humble beginnings and never changed, no matter how much success they enjoyed. I miss Pop so much."

Hendrick still remembers the times he shared with Schrader and smiles about all the good they shared as driver and team owner.

"I love Ken like a brother," Hendrick said. "Yes, it's true: He did drive for Pop. We ran really well with Kenny, but we broke a lot. That was a period when we were trying to get all the power in the world, and we just didn't make it get to the end. We were fast, led a lot of laps, and won a lot of pole positions. But Kenny made it fun for everyone. That was the most fun I had racing.

"He would always borrow stuff that I never got back [*Laughter*]. I don't know how many cars he borrowed. I had this really nice Southwest Tour car that I hadn't raced very much at all. He borrowed it, and next time I saw it was pretty ragged. I never got it back either."

Schrader at Atlanta Motor Speedway after his win on March 18, 1991. He led 59 of 328 laps, including the final 43, in the No. 25 Hendrick Motorsports Chevrolet.

8 / HITTING THE ROAD: THE CORVETTE GTP PROGRAM

The Hendrick Motorsports IMSA Corvette GTP program was announced at the Goodyear Racing Technical Center in Akron, Ohio, in 1985. On the panel, left to right: Leo Mehl, Goodyear's general manager of worldwide racing, British driver David Hobbs, and Rick Hendrick. (The other two men are unidentified.)

In 1985, the newly named Hendrick Motorsports was just beginning to enjoy success as a winning organization in NASCAR when General Motors came to Rick Hendrick with an idea.

Knowing Hendrick's love and passion for Corvettes, the manufacturer wanted to revive racing them in the International Motor Sports Association (IMSA) Grand Touring Prototype (GTP) division and needed someone to lead the program. Hendrick's strong relationship with the brand made him and his race team a perfect fit for the job.

The first order of business was to search out the best leader for the project. Ken Howes, a native of Johannesburg, South Africa, was a veteran in the world of endurance road racing. While Hendrick was building his small Cup Series team in 1984 and still hoping it would survive, Howes found himself in the States doing the same some three hundred miles away in Georgia, working on his own set of problems.

"At the time, I had come over from South Africa to manage a South African–owned sports car team that was also sponsored from South Africa," Howes said. "In 1984, we worked out of Atlanta, but it was really hard because you couldn't get the right people, the traffic—everything.

"We moved the operation, which wasn't very big back then, to Indianapolis and started working out of a small shop not far from Indianapolis Motor Speedway. Looking back, it was a good move. It was a difficult move but the right one. By doing that, you had access to the right services, the right people, because you were kind of hanging on the coattails of the IndyCar industry up there."

In 1985, politics and protests back home in South Africa ultimately led the team and sponsor to withdraw from all races. The team was good to Howes and told him to continue if he could by renting the car to other drivers, but the venture didn't last.

That May, he headed a GTP team that used a Porsche engine, giving him connections to Porsche Motorsport. That opened a door to run a Porsche at Le Mans in 1985 with driver Christian Danner. After that venture, he planned to go back to South Africa to regroup and think about his future.

Then the phone rang with an unexpected offer that changed his life.

"A gentleman from Chevrolet called," Howes said. "We had talked some throughout 1984 and 1985. He asked what I was doing and what our plans were. I told him after Le Mans, I didn't have anything and didn't know if I would be able to carry on. I told him I would have to go back to South Africa. He said before I go back, I should call this person named Rick Hendrick. There's a project going on and maybe you two can help each other [*laughter*]. I said, 'Who's that?'

"We talked on the phone, and as I recall, Rick sent one of his representatives to look around the shop [in Indianapolis]. Things progressed from there. We went to Detroit and looked at the car, and it was in a shop there. It had been there for about two years.

The team's first race outing was at Road America in Elkhart Lake, Wisconsin, for the Löwenbräu Classic on August 25, 1985. Team manager Ken Howes is at left near the front of the car, and Rick Hendrick is at the rear of the car (black shirt), alongside engine builder Randy Dorton (wearing white shirt at right). Drivers David Hobbs and Sarel van der Merwe started the car from eleventh position and finished thirty-third with engine issues.

The IMSA Corvette GTP won twice in June 1986 with Sarel van der Merwe and Doc Bundy going to victory lane at events in Road Atlanta and West Palm Beach. In both races the car started from pole position and finished first. At Atlanta a record was set for the fastest lap in the race. Here the IMSA Corvette GTP is seen at speed.

SECTION 1: 1980s

ABOVE: Rick Hendrick during a 1986 photo shoot at Charlotte Motor Speedway with the IMSA Corvette GTP, the No. 5 Levi Garrett car, and the No. 25 Folgers Coffee Chevrolet.

They [Chevrolet] wanted to bring this GTP car back into competition, but since it had been about three years since it had been designed and built, they weren't sure if it could be competitive. What they were willing to do was put up some funds to test it in the fall of 1985 under the banner of Hendrick Motorsports. I could keep the few guys that I had employed, and we did that. Reliability was going to be a problem, but GM felt they could solve that. They decided to race it."

Together, Howes and Hendrick rebuilt the stalled GTP Corvette program using Howes' Indianapolis shop as home base from 1986 through 1989, with significant success against the Porsches while racing two cars.

They were winners at Road Atlanta in 1986 and also won that year at West Palm Beach, Florida, with drivers Sarel van der Merwe and Doc Bundy. Drivers for the second car included David Hobbs, Bobby Rahal, John Andretti, Michael Andretti, and Elliott Forbes-Robinson.

Howes was quite impressed with Hendrick from the minute he met him.

"It [their first meeting] was straightforward," Howes said. "We were close in age and both from the same generation. Looking back, he was sincere about what he wanted to do. He did what he said he would do. It's not always that way in racing. What he was able to bring was some stability. He understood by that time enough about the ups and downs of racing. It was more down than up, especially what we were trying to do. Sometimes you need a shoulder to lean on, and he was always able to give great perspective on situations."

Howes remained with Hendrick Motorsports after the GTP venture and became a NASCAR crew chief for Ken Schrader and Jimmie Johnson, as well as director of competition and vice president of competition before his retirement in 2020.

Hendrick remembered the venture as a bit of an underdog situation, almost a David and Goliath sort of triumph.

"I was at the NASCAR awards banquet [in 1984] and Herb Fishel [former executive director of GM Racing] came to me and said, 'We'd like to talk to you about running our GTP Corvette,'" Hendrick said. "I didn't even know what a GTP Corvette was. So, I went to the Miami Grand Prix just to see what it was. That was a deal that was kind of steered by General Motors.

"We campaigned the Corvette for a few years," Hendrick said. "We won races and won some poles. We were running a push-rod motor against those overhead-cam cars, which is hard to do. We sat on the pole of the 24 Hours of Daytona but had to pull the car before the race because we had a cracked engine block.

"We won at West Palm Beach, Florida, and won at Road Atlanta. I enjoyed it. It was high tech on one end but a shoestring effort on the other end because we were running against the factory Porsches, and we just didn't have the motor for it back in that day.

"In one race, Michael Andretti and John Andretti both drove the car. And, Bobby Rahal drove the car. So, we had a 'who's who' of drivers of that era."

OPPOSITE TOP: The Hendrick Motorsports IMSA Corvette GTP crew jumps into action during a pit stop on July 3, 1988, at Watkins Glen International in the Camel Continental event. Drivers Sarel van der Merwe and Elliot Forbes-Robinson handled the driving duties that day. The team started the race in tenth and finished third after completing the full 90-lap distance.

OPPOSITE BOTTOM: After the checkered flag fell, the Hendrick Motorsports IMSA Corvette GTP team enjoyed its eighth and final podium finish. Race winner John Morton is in the Nissan hat alongside Elliot Forbes-Robinson, Sarel van der Merwe (with mustache), second-place Derek Bell (holding Miller can), and fellow second-place finisher Chip Robinson (in Miller suit with back to camera).

9 / LINDA HENDRICK'S STEADY PRESENCE

LEFT: Linda Hendrick at the 2023 NASCAR Awards in Nashville, Tennessee. Her quiet leadership has played a key role in Hendrick Motorsports' success.

OPPOSITE: Rick Hendrick could not attend 1997's NASCAR Cup Series Awards Banquet in New York City due to difficult leukemia treatments. Linda Hendrick (pictured here with Papa Joe Hendrick [center] and Bill France Jr. [right]) spoke on his behalf, delivering the championship team owner's speech. "When Rick asked me to give the speech, I would have done anything for him," Linda said. "When I was writing the speech, I was crying the whole time. He was so sick then. When I stood to speak, I had buried my heart because it wa broken. The pain was fresh. It was new. The truth is, I had never had a reason to do that [the speech] because NASCAR was Rick's thing, and suddenly I was there by myself. I felt so empowered to do this because it meant so much to Rick, and I wanted to give that to him as a gift. Just knowing tha it would make Rick so happy during such a tough time drove me to want to do it and put my feelings behind me."

SERVICE TO OTHERS. Those three words have shaped the life of Linda Myrick Hendrick.

She spent her formative years moving with her family to various locations while her father served in the United States Air Force during the Korean Conflict. When she reached high school, they lived in Henderson, North Carolina, a town of about fifteen thousand located some forty-five miles from the state capital of Raleigh.

After graduation, Linda completed her student training at Nash General Hospital in Rocky Mount, North Carolina. She also worked as an X-Ray technician for a dentist in Henderson and a doctor in Raleigh in 1972.

One weekend afternoon, Linda's best friend, Christy Moody, was having car trouble and needed help. Linda and some friends were at the Moody family's house on Kerr Lake near Raleigh when Christy came running down to the dock.

Linda agreed to take Christy to meet her fiancé, Bob Ward, in Raleigh. Just as they got to town, Christy spotted Rick Hendrick at the CITGO station on Brentwood Road. Rick and Bob were good buddies, and Rick would know exactly where Bob would be. Linda pulled in, and a quick introduction followed. Bob had been telling Christy that Rick and Linda should meet.

In the coming weeks, Rick let Christy know several times that he was interested in getting to know Linda. The four eventually double dated and, from that point, Linda and Rick were inseparable.

"I felt I had always known him," Linda said. "People said we needed to meet each other, but we were both working hard and weren't in the social crowd or the partying crowd. We happened to meet as fate would have it or God would have it. So, that's how we officially met at that service station that was right across the street from Westinghouse where he went to school. Gene Hinson owned it, and he allowed Rick to work on cars there.

"I never liked blind dates. I really wanted to go out with people that I knew and with people that I enjoyed their company. I was pleasantly surprised because I felt like I had known Rick my whole life. I liked his gentle spirit. He was kind. That was my first impression. I'm glad he asked me out, and I'm glad that Christy helped to get us together, and it turned out to be great. On January 27, 2024, we celebrated our fifty-first wedding anniversary."

"When we got married in 1973, it was an 'us' thing and not a 'he' thing. It was just whatever we needed to do to make it. We were a team from then on. There were no dreams of

Rick and Linda Hendrick at the premiere of the movie, *Together: The Hendrick Motorsports Story*. The 2009 documentary was narrated by Tom Cruise and aired on ABC.

a business at that point. We were making it from one day to the next. I was determined to be beside him. That's what getting married is about. That's the way I was brought up."

In October 1975, daughter Lynn was born, followed by son Ricky in April 1980. The siblings became very close as they grew older.

"Lynn is my daughter, so you expect me to be so terribly proud of her, and I am," Linda said. "Rick and I both are. She has gotten her degree in neuroscience. She is helping so many people and has founded organizations for those that are underprivileged. Lynn has done so much in her adult life. She is so competitive and yet a humble and kind person. She is loving and also adventurous and very loyal to her family and friends.

"They [Ricky and Lynn] were extremely close. Extremely close. Ricky looked up to Lynn because she was almost five years older. He thought she hung the moon. Both of my children were always very caring about others. Anyone would

tell you that about them. They have always been grateful individuals. People would come to me and tell me they were some of the most caring people they had ever met."

Fast-forward forty years, fourteen Cup Series championships, and more than three hundred wins, Hendrick Motorsports is the most successful organization in NASCAR history. Throughout that time, Linda has played a vital role in supporting everything Rick Hendrick has undertaken.

"I drove for Rick Hendrick and Hendrick Motorsports from 1994 until 2005 and had some great years there," said former Hendrick Motorsports driver Terry Labonte. "Many times, I heard Rick tell me that Linda was supportive of him with whatever he was doing, whether that was owning and operating Hendrick Motorsports or any of the many, many car dealerships that he owns. [He told me] the story of how on that first car dealership he almost got cold feet as far as buying it and she encouraged him and said, 'No, you have to go for it.' She has always been there in the same capacity [at Hendrick Motorsports] as well as someone who is really solid and someone that offers a word of encouragement to Rick. Throughout all those years of driving for him, he told me many times about how she played such an important role in all his business ventures. She was always there to provide a lot of encouragement to him."

Former Hendrick Motorsports crew chief and executive Ken Howes was with the organization for decades and saw Linda's impact on the team time and again even in something so simple as the smiles she and Rick exchanged on race-day mornings.

"Linda never sought the limelight. She was always in the background," Howes said. "By the time he started the race teams, he had become successful in the car dealerships, which made All-Star Racing possible and then Hendrick Motorsports possible. By then, he had been noticed by General Motors. All these things had a thread running through it, and throughout that time, she was in the background. During the time of the airplane accident, that was a huge test for everybody. I look back a marvel at her strength to get through it all because they had lost so much and yet they were able to get up and get out of bed in the mornings."

Ironically, the racing organization and the one hundred car dealerships under Hendrick Automotive Group were never planned in the very beginning. It all began for Rick after taking a job as a salesman at a Lincoln-Mercury dealership in Raleigh in 1973.

"Rick has always impressed me," Linda said. "If there's a door that opens, he will walk through it to see how it turns out. I feel like we've been blessed, and I hope that through the years that we've been able to bless others with the successes we've had. It has never been about the money. It's been about doing what he loved to do and just following his dream and doing in life what he loved and what his gifts were.

"It's amazing to see what Hendrick Motorsports has become. We never take it for granted. Never! It's just a plan God has got for us. Life is a team sport, and we're in this together. We all have different roles to play. We try to be the very best we can every day He gives us, every time He opens the door. This is clearly His plan, not ours. I won't ever take the credit for it. People say, 'I think a lot of people have worked hard for this,' and I absolutely agree. To add to that, if God was putting together a plan and a team, He picked the best there is out there. When Rick decides to do something, he wins at it."

The Hendrick family takes a moment for a photo while at Charlotte Motor Speedway. From left to right are son-in-law Marshall Carlson, grandson Hendrick Carlson, daughter Lynn Carlson, granddaughter Kate Carlson, Linda Hendrick and Rick Hendrick.

1990s

SECTION 2

10 / GOING HOLLYWOOD: THE MAKING OF DAYS OF THUNDER

Greg Sacks drives the No. 46 City Chevrolet car during the Autoworks 500 Cup Series event at Phoenix International Raceway on November 15, 1989. Sacks was driving the Hendrick Motorsports entry as part of the filming of *Days of Thunder*. Here he passes the No. 90 Donlavey Racing Ford driven by Stan Barrett.

Tom Cruise (left) takes a break from filming for a photo with Cup Series team owner Rick Hendrick. Many of the cars used in the movie were provided by Hendrick Motorsports.

IMSA (International Motorsports Association) GTP race cars had long interested Rick Hendrick, especially because of their unique mechanical attributes, engine displacements, and sleek bodies. Their ability to be driven on road courses was phenomenal, and those who raced them were a class of respected individuals all their own.

The SCCA (Sports Car Club of America) and IMSA GTP entries Hendrick fielded opened new friendships and opportunities he never dreamed possible. One of those weekends when the Cup Series had a break in its schedule, Hendrick was invited by road racer Jim Fitzgerald to attend an event at Road Atlanta, where he met actor Paul Newman. In 1986, Newman had made a very successful movie with fellow actor Tom Cruise called *The Color of Money*. Both Newman and Cruise enjoyed driving careers of their own, and Newman was particularly successful. Newman won four SCCA National Championships, finished second overall in the 1979 24 Hours of Le Mans, and won a Trans-Am race in Brainerd (Minnesota) in 1982. Cruise entered many SCCA events and worked on becoming a professional road racer in his own right.

Hendrick and Cruise became friends after meeting at SCCA events and got together whenever their schedules would permit. During one of those visits, Cruise said, "We need to make a movie about racing in NASCAR." Hendrick honestly thought Cruise was kidding. Cruise was dead serious and had the connections to make it happen.

At the time of the conversation, Cruise had already made a dozen movies dating back to 1981. Prior to *The Color of Money* with Newman, Cruise enjoyed great popularity with *Top Gun*, also released in 1986. He was a big star in Hollywood, and if anyone could get a film made about NASCAR, Cruise was the man.

There was much to do to pull off such a feat. There was a script to write, actors to secure, and tracks to lease for filming, as well as footage of past races to be interwoven into the story. The movie was a major undertaking, and Hendrick found himself at its center, providing cars, equipment, and expertise from drivers and team personnel to ensure the project was as accurate as possible.

Previous movies about stock car racing included *Thunder in Carolina* in 1960 starring Rory Calhoun, *Red Line 7000* starring

Cruise made an appearance at Daytona International Speedway the morning of the Daytona 500 on February 15, 2009. Rick Hendrick drove the 2009 No. 46 Chevrolet on the high side, while Cruise drove the 1990 No. 46 Chevrolet in the lower groove that appeared in the *Days of Thunder* movie.

James Caan in 1965, and *The Last American Hero* starring Jeff Bridges in 1973. None gained praise as great films. The best for accuracy fell to Bridges for his loose portrayal of Junior Johnson and his early years as a moonshiner and racer. With a movie starring Cruise, there was hope that a solid and accurate film could broadly introduce the world to NASCAR.

Once Cruise received the green light from Paramount Pictures, the project began to take shape, with Don Simpson and Jerry Bruckheimer coming on as producers. Hendrick played a vital role by providing race cars and technical assistance beginning in the spring of 1989.

Hendrick tapped Dennis Connor to oversee the cars and equipment being used for the movie project. Connor was a former crew chief in the Cup Series and would later serve as crew chief for Jack Sprague's championship seasons with Hendrick Motorsports in the Craftsman Truck Series in 1997, 1999, and 2001.

Drivers Greg Sacks and Bobby Hamilton drove the Hendrick Motorsports entries in Cup Series races for filming purposes as well as in scene-setting scenarios. Hut Stricklin worked directly with Cruise in a coaching capacity upon the actor's insistence on driving in some of the race sequences. Stricklin also drove the No. 51 Exxon Chevrolet at the spring race at Darlington, South Carolina, in 1990. Tommy Ellis drove the No. 18 Hardees Hendrick Motorsports entry and filmed footage at Phoenix Raceway for the movie in 1989, though he did not qualify for the actual race. Also, Rick Mast ran laps in the 1990 Daytona 500 for filming purposes but was not an official entry in the race.

"Tom Cruise could have made a heck of a driver," Stricklin said on the *Dale Jr. Download* podcast. "His demeanor, his focus—he wanted to do things right. I know why his movies are so successful. You see how he is in person. He is so focused and dialed in. It doesn't matter if it's his fortieth take of a movie scene, it might have been right thirty takes ago, but he's still saying, 'No, I want to make it right.'"

Days of Thunder was released on June 27, 1990, to 2,307 screens in the United States and Canada. The film grossed a total of $157,920,733 worldwide. Over the past three decades, the movie has become very popular among race fans. At the time, though, Hollywood's influence didn't sit well with many longtime NASCAR's fans for accuracy reasons, including dirty and blackened cars racing at Daytona, unrealistic crashes while passing for position, and track scenes of racing a single lap with footage from four different speedways.

The character of Cole Trickle, played by Cruise, was loosely based on Tim Richmond, while the character of Harry Hogg was based on Harry Hyde, a Robert Duvall performance many felt was a carbon copy of Hyde and worthy of praise. Many scenes in the movie were based on real-life interactions between Hyde and Richmond and Hyde and Benny Parsons, such as the Highway Patrol exotic dancer scene (that actually happened in the shop with Richmond) and the ice cream scene in the pits (that happened with Hyde and Parsons at the Darlington spring race in 1987).

Overall, Hendrick felt *Days of Thunder* was a great experience, but he doesn't look to return to making any type of Hollywood movie ever again.

"I knew Tom Cruise from when we ran some SCCA races together," Hendrick said. "I met Paul Newman through Jim Fitzgerald. I became friends with Tom and Paul and got to make a movie. It was pretty special, but I don't want to do it again [*laughter*]. I tell people I've made two movies in my life: my first and my last."

Rick Hendrick (center) on set wearing a driver's suit during filming for the movie *Days of Thunder*. Hendrick Motorsports was heavily involved, providing cars, equipment, and expertise for the film.

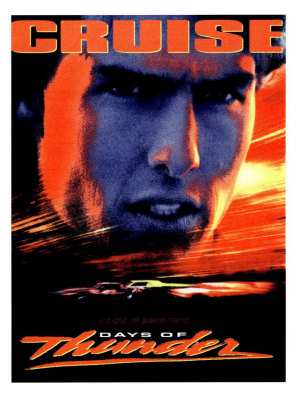

Posters promoting *Days of Thunder* appeared in theaters across the country in the summer of 1990. Tom Cruise's NASCAR-themed film grossed nearly $158 million.

11 / RICKY RUDD BRINGS SWAGGER AND STRONG RÉSUMÉ

During the 1979 Cup Series season, Ricky Rudd drove Mercurys for legendary team owner Junie Donlavey. Even though the Chesapeake, Virginia, native entered only twenty-eight of thirty-one races during the season, he finished an impressive ninth in Cup Series points.

On August 8, 1990, Rudd showed his expertise as a road racer by winning the ninety-lap Budweiser at the Glen Cup Series race for Hendrick Motorsports. Rudd led twenty laps including the final ten circuits.

When Geoff Bodine elected to leave Hendrick Motorsports at the end of the 1989 Cup Series season, the New York native had amassed a total of seven wins, forty-nine top-five finishes, eighty top-tens, and twenty-two pole positions, including eight pole positions in the 1986 season alone. Bodine had been given an offer to drive for Junior Johnson beginning in 1990, a move he felt he should make.

Hendrick wanted a motivated driver to fill his No. 5 Chevrolet who could win immediately. There was a very short list that fit the criteria, and at the top was Ricky Rudd, who had been in the Cup Series for many years and enjoyed success with several top teams.

Unknown to many, Rudd didn't initially look at NASCAR and stock car racing as a career path during his formative racing years. From an early age, Rudd had the ultimate goal of becoming a winning IndyCar driver. Older brother Al Rudd Jr. became friends with NASCAR driver and team owner Bill Champion and his son, crew chief Cliff Champion. Al Jr. and a friend volunteered to work for the Champions in the Cup Series, launching Ricky's driving career at the age of eighteen.

"I raced motocross in northern North Carolina and southern Virginia," Rudd said. "From there, it was basically on to North Carolina Motor Speedway in Rockingham, North Carolina, to race in NASCAR in 1975. Funny thing is when I was racing motorcycles and go-karts, I was so caught up trying to be successful there I didn't really know a huge amount about NASCAR. The go-kart racing kept us traveling the national circuit, but we only raced about once a month."

In four races for Champion, Rudd's best finish was tenth at Bristol Motor Speedway on March 16, 1975. Rudd logged a fourth-place finish at Talladega, Alabama, fifteen top-ten finishes in his father's Chevrolet in select Cup events from 1976 to 1978, and Rookie of the Year honors at the end of the 1977 Cup season.

By the end of the 1980 season, rides came with legendary team owner Junie Donlavey, D. K. Ulrich, and team owner Nelson Malloch. That October, the family fielded one more car in a make-or-break Cup Series effort at Charlotte Motor Speedway. Ironically, Rudd received help from crew chief Harry Hyde and Jimmy Makar, a crew chief and today an executive with Joe Gibbs Racing. Rudd qualified outside front row and finished fourth in the five-hundred-mile race.

From there, he received rides with DiGard Racing and Richard Childress, where he scored his first win at Riverside, California, on June 5, 1983. Another win came at Martinsville, Virginia, on

Rudd won the TranSouth 500 at Darlington Raceway in Darlington, South Carolina, on April 7, 1991. It was his second career victory for Hendrick Motorsports.

September 25, 1983. Wins also came with Bud Moore's team from 1984 through 1987. Rudd spent three seasons with King Racing, a Cup Series team owned by drag racing champion and IndyCar team owner Kenny Bernstein. All told, he had ten victories to his credit and proved he could win on short tracks, superspeedways, and road courses.

Hendrick knew he had the right driver in Rudd. He was good everywhere he raced and needed a consistent car under him to prove his talents. As predicted, Rudd scored a road course victory at Watkins Glen, New York, in August 1990 but was unable to log any other victories that season and was seventh in points.

After enjoying victory lane ceremonies, Rudd said, "It makes Monday mornings so much better when you've won. It makes rolling into the garage area at the next race a little more relaxed. It relieves a lot of tension and stress the guys [his pit crew] put on themselves."

In 1991, Rudd returned to victory lane at Darlington Raceway (South Carolina) on April 5 in the fifth race of the season after leading 69 of 367 laps. It was his lone victory at Darlington, a track that most drivers considered to be one of the toughest to drive.

"Anytime you can win at Darlington, it's a great accomplishment," Rudd said. "We did that when Waddell Wilson was my crew chief there at Hendrick Motorsports. That was a very special win for me. I'm happy to say we enjoyed some success while driving for Rick."

Rudd finished second in Cup Series points, a career best, 195 behind Dale Earnhardt. On September 20, 1992, Rudd enjoyed another victory at Dover, Delaware, for his lone victory of the season and logged another seventh-place finish in points. The 1992 season was Rudd's best with Hendrick Motorsports with one win, nine top-fives, eighteen top-tens, and one pole position.

On June 20, 1993, he returned to victory lane at Michigan International Speedway and finished tenth in the season's points standings. At the end of 1993, Rudd chose to leave Hendrick Motorsports to form Rudd Performance Motorsports, a company that remained on the Cup Series circuit for the next four seasons.

Rudd earned the nickname "Iron Man" after making 906 career starts in the NASCAR Cup Series for a record 788 consecutive starts from 1981 through the 2005 season. That statistic was broken by Jeff Gordon with 797 in 2015. Rudd had 117 starts for Hendrick Motorsports over four seasons.

"Driving for Rick Hendrick was a pretty exciting deal for me," Rudd said. "We nearly won the championship in 1991, and we led the points right up to the Charlotte race in the fall. If we weren't leading it, we were five or ten points apart from Earnhardt. I felt then that being with a multi-car team didn't seem like the place to be."

Hendrick feels Rudd was a great asset to Hendrick Motorsports during his tenure with the organization.

"Ricky was an intense guy and a great road racer," Hendrick says today. "He raced like he had somewhat of a chip on his shoulder. He just didn't like the multi-car teams and told us that going in, and that's really why he started his own team after he left Hendrick Motorsports. He was a great driver everywhere he raced."

Rudd won the Peak Antifreeze 500 at Dover, Delaware, on September 20, 1992, leading the final twenty-five laps to take the victory.

Rudd (left) in victory lane at Michigan International Speedway on June 20, 1993, alongside crew chief Gary DeHart. The victory marked Rudd's final win for Hendrick Motorsports.

12 CHANGING THE SPORT: JEFF GORDON AND THE RAINBOW WARRIORS

Cup Series rookie Jeff Gordon alongside the No. 24 Hendrick Motorsports Chevrolet he drove during his first start at Atlanta Motor Speedway on November 15, 1992. Gordon rolled off the grid in the twenty-first position and finished thirty-first.

Throughout NASCAR's storied seventy-six-year history, very few drivers and crew chiefs have found the chemistry needed to win multiple races and championships.

The talents of Jeff Gordon and Ray Evernham combined in 1990 when they met at Buck Baker's Driving School at North Carolina Motor Speedway. Gordon, a young sprint car superstar, and Evernham, a former modified driver from the northeast and crew member for 1992 Cup Series champion Alan Kulwicki, brought incredible talents from their own motorsports backgrounds.

Gordon qualified second and made his first start in NASCAR's Busch Grand National Series (now Xfinity Series) on October 30, 1990, at North Carolina Motor Speedway for team owner Hugh Connerty. Evernham served as crew chief for the initial venture that lasted only thirty-three laps, as Gordon was involved in a multi-car crash.

In 1991 and 1992, Gordon was employed with Bill Davis Racing to run the full schedule, winning three races during his second season with the Thomasville, North Carolina–based team. Hendrick signed Gordon to the No. 24 Cup Series ride in the fall of 1992, setting in motion one of the most successful unions in Hendrick Motorsports history.

The car needed a unique paint scheme, and to get it, Hendrick called on the late Sam Bass, an award-winning artist who had designed many race car paint schemes. A meeting was set for the fall of 1992, with an intended debut date for Gordon's Chevrolet on November 15, 1992, at Atlanta Motor Speedway.

"You know, it was funny," Bass said during an interview for Fox Sports on May 2, 2017, with host Daryl Motte. "I had two drawings already done. I was driving to work the morning before my presentation. I was thinking about the DuPont oval on the hood and how we needed to show a rainbow of colors.

"All the sudden, it just dawned on me as I was driving that if I arched the stripe above the DuPont logo, it would form a rainbow. I could not wait to get to the office to do that drawing. I got it done a couple of hours before the meeting. I knew when I got it done and had all the colors together that was going to be the one."

Thus the rainbow paint scheme was born, leading to the birth of the Rainbow Warriors. The metallic-blue Chevrolet was unveiled during the final race of the 1992 season with much hype about Gordon's entrance into the Cup Series. The weekend also culminated with the final race of Richard Petty's career after logging seven Cup Series championships and two hundred victories, as well as the season championship featuring six drivers mathematically eligible to win the title. Ultimately, Alan Kulwicki was crowned champion.

Gordon's first outing in the No. 24 Chevrolet resulted in a thirty-first-place finish after involvement in an on-track incident on lap 164 of 328. No wins materialized in 1993, but Gordon did collect seven top-five finishes, eleven top-tens, and one pole position.

Gordon's breakthrough victory came in the 1994 Coca-Cola 600 at Charlotte Motor Speedway on May 29. He started from the pole position, led a total of sixteen laps, and held off Rusty Wallace of Team Penske during the final nine circuits to secure the win.

In 1995, the team logged seven wins, seventeen top-five finishes, twenty-three top-tens, and eight pole positions that resulted in Gordon's first Cup Series championship.

In 1996, the No. 24 team amassed ten victories, twenty-one top-fives, twenty-four top-tens, and five pole positions. The season served as a foundation for the incredible success of 1997 and 1998, when Gordon and Evernham logged a combined twenty-three victories, forty-eight top-five finishes, fifty-one top-tens, and eight pole positions. Together, they were one of the most dominant driver and crew chief combinations in NASCAR history—three titles with forty-seven wins in just six and a half years. Among those wins were two of Gordon's three Daytona 500 wins and two of his five Brickyard 400 wins at Indianapolis Motor Speedway.

"When we were in it, I think it was just a lot of passionate people that had a goal to rise to the occasion and build the best race cars and the best race team we could build," Gordon said. "It was also about me being the best race driver I could be for that team as well. Ray Evernham was always looking at things as, 'How can I provide the best resources for these guys because they have a lot of talent' and that was proven."

Gordon with his sprint car during a break in the race action in late 1989. He enjoyed considerable success as an open-wheel racer before moving to NASCAR competition.

Gordon (24) passes Joe Nemechek (41) before eventually taking the checkered flag in the 1994 Coca-Cola 600 at Charlotte Motor Speedway on May 29. The win was Gordon's first of ninety-three career victories spanning twenty-five Cup Series seasons.

Gordon recounted how everyone on the crew was somewhat new to the sport and were laser focused on winning and being successful in NASCAR's top level of competition.

"I think we had a bit of a chip on our shoulders to go and prove that we had what it took . . . even though we were young and inexperienced," Gordon said. "I think everybody was marching in the same direction, had the same goals, and had a lot of ability, talent, ideas, and work ethic and had the resources to achieve those goals.

"Every time we kind of set out to achieve something, it didn't come easy; we eventually checked that box and it built confidence in everybody and we would go to the next thing on the list and check that one off, the next thing we know, three championships later, here we are. It was just a special time; things were clicking, and things were happening at a rapid rate, and we were sort of riding the wave. I don't think we knew just how special it really was until today when we look back on it."

From day one, Evernham was on a mission to succeed. There were specific keys to success that made the Rainbow Warriors so dominant in the early to mid-1990s: his own personal experience and something he saw that no one else in the Cup Series was doing. Also, Evernham looked outside the sport at how others in professional sports were building long-term success.

"It's rare that you get a group of people together that are not only talented, but they work as a true team," Evernham said. "There were a lot of overachievers on that team. They used a combination of strength and support for one another to continue to get better. When I look back at the Rainbow Warriors, I feel really fortunate to have been a part of that group.

"It's very much like being Don Shula, the coach of the National Football League's undefeated 1972 Miami Dolphins. Then there's the Pittsburgh Steelers or the Dallas Cowboys, sports organizations that have created their own dynasties. It's really about the commitment that their players made to their teams.

LEFT: Gordon poses with his first Cup Series championship trophy November 12, 1995. He won seven Cup Series races that season on his way to claiming the first of his four career titles.

ABOVE: Gordon (left) with crew chief Ray Evernham at Daytona International Speedway in 1995. Gordon and Evernham won forty-seven Cup races together from 1992 through 1999 and three Cup championships in 1995, 1997, and 1998.

"Coming from the Penske organization, I understood culture and leadership and efficiency," explained Evernham. "Being new to the game at that time, I really started to look at the rapid growth of NASCAR, and it wasn't really a very professional high-level sport at that time. We could gain an advantage by setting up the 24 team like a professional team. To do that, we needed a coach and leadership and organization to get out ahead. I looked at a lot of different sports teams. One of the biggest differences came when I read a book called *The Winner Within* by Pat Riley, a fantastic coach and organizer and manager. I learned a lot of things from reading that book and decided that we were going to build the 24 team like a professional sports franchise the best that we could. We found a lot of efficiencies by doing that."

13 HOME GAME: BRAGGING RIGHTS AT CHARLOTTE

Darrell Waltrip, driver of the No. 17 Hendrick Motorsports Chevrolet, closes in on winning the Coca-Cola 600 at Charlotte Motor Speedway on May 28, 1989. It was Waltrip's second win for Hendrick Motorsports and the first win for Chevrolet's Lumina body style.

Jimmie Johnson (left) in victory lane with Rick Hendrick (center) and crew chief Chad Knaus at Charlotte Motor Speedway on May 29, 2005.

Since the official opening of Charlotte Motor Speedway in June 1960, the 1.5-mile facility has been considered one of the premier tracks on NASCAR's Cup Series circuit.

It was built by visionary O. Bruton Smith, a business entrepreneur who worked for decades to make the track a showplace for all race fans to enjoy. His partner in the venture was Curtis Turner, a moonshiner turned racer who kept the grandstands filled through his daring ability to thread race cars at high rates of speed to victory on seventeen occasions from 1949 to 1968.

Drivers love to win on any racetrack. To do it at Charlotte offers a special charm with more prestige because it's one of the crown-jewel tracks on NASCAR's Cup Series schedule. It's the centerpiece of the sport, especially since most of the Cup Series race teams are located within a fifty-mile radius of the speedway.

That includes Hendrick Motorsports, located less than a mile from the venue. The uniquely shaped track has been home turf to the Hendrick organization since its inaugural season in 1984.

Even before All-Star Racing—the original name given to Rick Hendrick's dream race team—came to mind, Rick was associated with winning on stock car racing's hallowed ground. In 1983, Dale Earnhardt won a Budweiser Late Model Sportsman Series (now Xfinity Series) victory on May 28 at Charlotte in a Pontiac owned

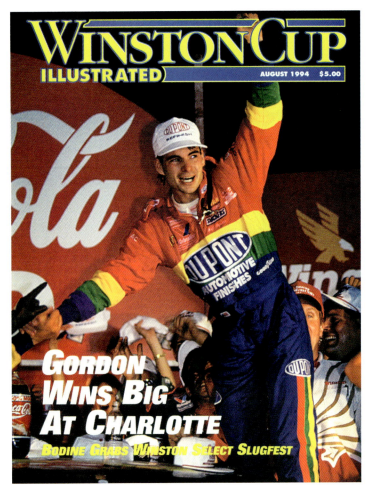

Jeff Gordon on the cover of the August 1994 *Winston Cup Illustrated* magazine. The victory lane photo was shot at Charlotte Motor Speedway after he'd won the Coca-Cola 600 in May of that year. It was the first of Gordon's ninety-three career wins in NASCAR's premier Cup Series division.

by car builder and Earnhardt's father-in-law, Robert Gee. Financial support that day came from Rick Hendrick's City Chevrolet, making it the first win of Hendrick's NASCAR career.

On May 29, 1988, Darrell Waltrip drove the Hendrick Motorsports Chevrolet to victory lane for the team's first Cup win at Charlotte Motor Speedway. The Owensboro, Kentucky, native overcame a last-lap bid from Rusty Wallace and pushed his No. 17 Chevrolet to his first win of the season and his fourth career win at Charlotte.

"We won ourselves a whale of a race," Waltrip said after the win, as quoted in the Winston Cup '88 yearbook. "But it was a tough day emotionally. I saw a lot of guys run very good and all of a sudden, I'd come around and they'd run into the wall.

"The consistent speed we'd decided on gave us no problems with our tires. It kept us out of trouble. and we knew we'd be there at the end because we knew we had a very strong car. We just had to save it to the finish."

Waltrip defended his victory in May 1989 by leading eighty-seven of the race's four hundred laps, holding off Hagan Racing's Sterling Marlin and Hendrick Motorsports teammates Ken Schrader and Geoff Bodine for the win.

"Charlotte Motor Speedway was always a great track for me," Waltrip said. "We won six races in 1989, and that was also the fifth and final Coca-Cola 600 win of my career. To win in one of Rick's Chevrolets was so special to me. Everything just seemed to come together so well that day. I consider it one of my biggest victories."

Another victory came in the 1994 Coca-Cola 600 during Jeff Gordon's second full season of competition. Gordon became the first driver since David Pearson and Wood Brothers Racing in 1976 to win the 600 from the pole position. Gordon led four times for sixteen laps, including the final nine circuits.

"Rusty [Wallace] had the race won because he was in the dominant car that day," Gordon said. "We kept ourselves in position to win. We fought hard to stay in contention, and sometimes that's all you need to do is be in position to capitalize. We had a great strategy call near the end with a two-tire pit stop, which was a fast two-tire pit stop. Rusty made a four-tire stop at the end, and that was the difference.

"We led the last ten laps or so [actually nine laps] and went on to win it. There was a lot of emotion wrapped up in that win because I felt like it was a huge accomplishment. I wanted to win so badly because we had struggled in 1993. I wanted to win in the Cup Series. I wanted to win at that level. I realized right away how competitive and difficult the Cup Series was going to be. To win the 600 at Charlotte in 1994 for my very first win . . . really meant the world to me."

Gordon's victory opened the floodgates for Hendrick Motorsports in the coming years. That memorable and emotional win began a string of fifteen additional Cup Series victories for the organization from 1997 through 2021 on the 1.5-mile oval and the 2.28-mile road course. Tim Richmond also enjoyed wins in 1985 and 1986 in Busch Grand National races at Charlotte Motor Speedway in a Pontiac Ventura.

Seven-time champion Jimmie Johnson leads the list with a record eight wins at Charlotte, his first on May 25, 2003 followed by four straight wins there in 2004–2005. It was only his second full-time season in the Cup Series and fourth of eighty-three-career victories. Johnson's final victory at the track came in the five-hundred-mile event on October 9, 2016.

"That seems like such a long time ago," Johnson said. "Charlotte Motor Speedway is one of my favorite tracks and a place where I've had so much success throughout my career. It is just one of those places where I feel comfortable and a place that fits my driving style, I guess. You put that with the great cars that I had with Hendrick Motorsports and great people working with me there, and you can understand how we were able to win at Charlotte so many times. [Crew chief] Chad [Knaus] and I had just seemed to have a great feel for our cars there. I think that's why we were so successful there."

Terry Labonte, Schrader, Casey Mears, Kasey Kahne, Chase Elliott, and Kyle Larson all have one victory each at Charlotte as of 2023. Elliott also has two victories in the ROVAL, the speedway's 2.28-mile) road course, while Larson has one.

"Charlotte Motor Speedway is special because it's right there. It's my home track since we're only a mile away from it here at Hendrick Motorsports," Hendrick said. "People don't understand that Bruton Smith and I were close friends. You wouldn't think that would be true since we were competitors in the automobile business. Bruton and his kids—Marcus and David—are real close to me and my family. I would always kid Bruton about taking his money.

"You want to win at Charlotte because all of our employees are there, the dealership people are there. Winning the 600 was and is an important race for us to win and always has been."

Chase Elliott (9) and teammate Kyle Larson (5) lead the field during the Coca-Cola 600 at Charlotte Motor Speedway on May 30, 2021. Larson won ten Cup Series races as well as the 2021 championship that season.

14 T-REX: CREATING A MONSTER

The 1997 Chevrolet Monte Carlo, built by a Hendrick Motorsports team led by crew chief Ray Evernham with engineers Rex Stump and Phil Hammer, was one of the most innovative race cars in NASCAR history.

Rex Stump, a talented engineer with Hendrick Motorsports, was instrumental in the design of the Chevrolet dubbed "T-Rex." Stump's innovations were well ahead of their time and drove NASCAR to make changes to its rule book in direct response to the car.

In August 1996, Rick Hendrick had an idea. He assembled Hendrick Motorsports team members Ken Howes, Rex Stump, and Phil Hammer and crew chief Ray Evernham and asked them to think about how to build the ultimate race car with bold ideas for a single experimental chassis. The car would be entered in The Winston (now called the NASCAR All-Star Race), a special non points event at Charlotte Motor Speedway on May 17, 1997.

In the beginning stages of the building process by the research and development department, the working blueprint name for the car was Elsie. With sponsorship from the 1997 *Jurassic Park* film and dinosaur emblem on the hood, as well as Rex Stump's involvement, the car affectionately became known as "T-Rex."

The future 1997 Chevrolet Monte Carlo was to be driven by Jeff Gordon and was built with some rather unique features, such as an aluminum drive shaft, a raised floor pan, and dropped frame rails to get the best underbody aerodynamics possible. The chassis was stiffened and featured hollow axles and lighter gears with shocks made to work much smoother and moved outside the frame rails. The overall low center of gravity and emphasis on aerodynamics were keys to the car's success, almost as if it were a slot car pegged in a groove on the 1.5-mile track.

Ironically, early testing of the car proved disappointing. Speed and handling characteristics were not as impressive as everyone had hoped. Hundreds of hours had been invested in the car, but something was still missing. With Hendrick Motorsports located less than a mile from Charlotte Motor Speedway, other Hendrick Motorsports teams took the car to the track during test sessions to see what they could discover during their time on the track. Terry Labonte drove it, as did Ken Schrader and Ricky Craven. No one was getting anything special out of the car as hoped.

Then crew chief Ray Evernham applied some basic short-track thinking to the car. One late afternoon, while the track was slick and hot, Evernham put a crazy setup under the car and asked Gordon to try it. It was so loose that some crew members felt Gordon could possibly get hurt if he crashed. But loose meant fast, and Evernham knew Gordon's talented seat-of-the-pants driving style could handle it.

Evernham cautioned Gordon to work up to speed for a lap or two and not try to be a hero. He also told his young driver he had no idea how the car would handle. A click of the stopwatch as Gordon crossed the start-finish line confirmed he was a second faster.

Gordon rolled into the garage. His wide brown eyes said everything Evernham needed to know. Calculations indicated later that they had dropped the front end, making the underbody aerodynamics they designed work perfectly.

"I put the radical setup under the car because nothing else was working," Evernham said. "We had some time that afternoon, and I always wanted to see how some of these things worked. Coming from a background of modifieds, IndyCars, and things like that, I always wondered why it wouldn't work on a stock car. That day,

The front end and body of T-Rex emphasized aerodynamics, allowing the car to handle exceptionally well through the turns of 1.5-mile Charlotte Motor Speedway. Its driver, Jeff Gordon, won 1997's The Winston race with very few challenges over the course of the special non-points event.

we were kind of screwing around. We had time. I said, 'Let's just try this and see what happens. I want to know why it doesn't work.' We found out that it would work.

"Basically, what's really cool is that ten years later, it became kind of the way people were setting cars up, and it's the way they still do. We didn't spend enough time trying to figure it out. In the end, T-Rex got outlawed by NASCAR. But that setup with real soft front springs and a more equal platform in the car is still used. We were on to something there, for sure, but we did it because I couldn't understand why it wouldn't work, and it turns out it would have with the right car."

Evernham is quick to point out there were many people involved in the T-Rex project and not just himself.

"The T-Rex car has become an urban legend, and I'm proud to have been part of it," Evernham said. "People think about me when they think about that car, but I was only a small part of it. That car was Rick Hendrick's idea. That car was Rex Stump's design. All Jeff and I did was race it. I had come up with some ideas and some things that went into it, but so did all the other crew chiefs that were working at Hendrick Motorsports at that time."

Gordon drove the famed T-Rex Chevrolet Monte Carlo to victory that night and pocketed $275,000 for Hendrick Motorsports. NASCAR deemed the car legal, as it met the rulebook, but Hendrick and Evernham were told to never bring it back to the racetrack.

Gordon thought of the car as one of the very best of his thirty-one-year-career in NASCAR.

T-Rex proved far superior to its competitors in The Winston event. Following the car's dominant win, Gordon smokes the tires for the crowd.

"We were building our own chassis at the time, and we brought Rex Stump on to sort of advance the vehicle engineering of things," Gordon said. "A few with some ideas and thoughts got together and packed it all together and put it into that car. All I can speak about is what it was like to drive it. It was pretty obvious right away that the car had something unique about it. It just seemed to do all the things that I wanted a race car to do and gave me a ton of confidence.

"Ray tells the story that right in the beginning, it didn't show promise, but I remember it being pretty spectacular. When I got into the race, it was our race to lose. The car just had a ridiculous amount of grip and speed compared to our competitors. I could put that car anywhere I wanted to.

"What was fun about that was we had T-Rex through the *Jurassic Park* promotion and Rex Stump worked so hard on the car and all that came together. Back in those days we had names for all of our cars where the chassis have numbers today."

Hendrick was extremely proud of everyone who worked on the car, and future cars, and appreciated their abilities and passion for innovation.

"NASCAR said it was okay at first, but [after the race] they said, 'Don't bring it back!'" Hendrick said. "Rex Stump and Ray Evernham took a clean sheet of paper, came up with it, and the thing was in a different league. I'd say our legacy in NASCAR will be that we made them change a lot of rules. We went from Twisted Sister [Gen4-body-style cars] to the way we corkscrewed the cars. Other teams would complain and then they [NASCAR] started lining up the bodies. Then it went from that to the chassis, and they'd say you can't do anything to this or that. So, all those changes were because of us."

15 TERRY LABONTE ICES ANOTHER CHAMPIONSHIP

Terry Labonte, in the No. 5 Hendrick Motorsports Chevrolet, takes the high line around Dale Earnhardt at Atlanta Motor Speedway during a Cup Series race in 1996. He finished fifth there in November to secure the Cup Series title that season.

Labonte at speed in 1996. The Texas native won Cup Series races that year at North Wilkesboro, North Carolina, and Charlotte, North Carolina.

On November 10, 1996, Terry Labonte (right) notched his second career Cup Series title at Atlanta Motor Speedway after finishing fifth behind his younger brother, race winner Bobby Labonte.

With ten races remaining in the 1993 Cup Series season, Terry Labonte was beginning to feel rather dejected, as his future in the sport wasn't looking very promising. The native of Corpus Christi, Texas, had been on top of his career by winning the 1984 Cup Series championship with team owner Billy Hagan and was in the last year of his contract with the fellow Texan.

Labonte left Hagan's team in 1987 to join legendary team owner Junior Johnson through the 1989 Cup Series season. He joined Richard Jackson's team in 1990, recording no wins but managing four top-five finishes and nine top-tens. The Texas native returned to Hagan in 1991, hoping to rekindle the days when wins and a championship kept them in the headlines. The magic was gone the second time around, as the best they could muster was five top-five finishes, thirty-four top-tens, and one pole position in eighty-eight starts over three seasons.

The thought crossed Labonte's mind that his career might be over.

"We were having some decent runs in Billy's cars from time to time in 1993, but it wasn't like 1984 when we won the championship," Labonte said. "The thing was I had made one trip down to Spartanburg and visited with Bud Moore because he wanted me to drive his number 15 Ford. I had been on the phone with his sponsors and had a contract and had seriously been thinking about taking that ride. It looked like that was going to happen for 1994."

Labonte realized the glory days of winning championships with Hagan were gone, and so were the people who helped make it happen. Less-than-stellar equipment made the situation worse. The cars, equipment, and money weren't there and made Labonte look like he had lost his edge, which couldn't have been further from the truth.

Little did he know something was happening behind the scenes in Concord, North Carolina, that was playing heavily in his favor. Driver Ricky Rudd had greatly enjoyed his time at Hendrick Motorsports but was never a fan of multi-car teams and wanted to form his own operation for 1994.

Rudd informed Hendrick of his intention not to return in 1994, leaving the No. 5 seat without a driver. Hendrick and Hendrick Motorsports executive Jimmy Johnson began looking at a list of potential replacements and saw Labonte—a name they hadn't thought of.

"I was surprised to find out Ricky was leaving Hendrick Motorsports, to be honest," Labonte said. "I think Rudd liked being there, but he wanted his own team, and that opened the door for me to come over and drive the 5 car. I don't know all the circumstances there, but I can't say I was unhappy that he left. Him leaving was one of the greatest things that happened in my career, if not the best."

Hendrick remembers how he chose Labonte, which turned out to be a pleasant surprise.

"It was kind of funny," Hendrick said. "Jimmy and I were looking down the list through the statistics and looked at Terry and thought Terry was older. We said, 'He's won a championship and won some races. And eventually we talked to him, and he came on board.'"

The weekend after the meeting between Hendrick and Johnson, the next race on the schedule was at North Wilkesboro, North Carolina, a track where Labonte seemed to excel. That October Sunday, he led fifty-three of the race's four hundred laps and remained in the top ten throughout the race.

RIGHT: From left, Rick Hendrick, Labonte, and Gary DeHart in victory lane at Atlanta Motor Speedway after winning the 1996 Cup Series championship.

BELOW: Labonte at Atlanta Motor Speedway on November 10, 1996. Two victories, twenty-one top-five finishes and twenty-four top-tens built the foundation for the second championship of his career (his first was in 1984 with team owner Billy Hagan).

"I watched him lead that race in a car that really wasn't strong enough to lead," Hendrick said. "I remember thinking how well he was getting through the turns while doing battle with cars that were much better than his. He showed me he still had it as a race car driver. I made a mental note to keep an eye on him the rest of the year."

Labonte found out that Hendrick was interested in talking with him, and he met with Hendrick and Johnson to tour their facility. After seeing the first-class operation and meeting those who would build and maintain his Chevrolets, it was an easy decision to make. Kellogg's requested to come on board as primary sponsor, and the deal was quickly put in place. Gary DeHart was named Labonte's crew chief, reuniting them from years past.

"It was really good," Labonte said. "I knew Gary from the 1984 championship team. He was our lead fabricator in Hagan's shop in High Point [North Carolina] when Hagan had his shop there. There wasn't a real learning curve because we knew each other. I first met Gary back in 1980."

During the 1994 season, Labonte, DeHart, and the No. 5 Hendrick Motorsports crew recorded three wins (North Wilkesboro, Richmond Raceway, and Phoenix Raceway), six top-five finishes, and fourteen top-tens, followed in 1995 by three wins and fourteen top-five finishes. In 1995, he posted a near carbon-copy season of the previous year with wins coming at Richmond, Pocono Raceway, and Bristol Motor Speedway, as well as seventeen top-tens and one pole position.

Both seasons set the stage for the incredible year Labonte enjoyed in 1996. After twelve years, he returned to center stage as Cup Series champion after victories at North Wilkesboro and the October five-hundred-mile event at Charlotte Motor Speedway. Teammate Jeff Gordon finished thirty-first in the latter race and dropped from a 111-point lead to a 1-point lead in the standings over Labonte.

Labonte finished third behind race winner Ricky Rudd and second-place Dale Jarrett the next week at North Carolina Motor Speedway at Rockingham. Gordon finished twelfth, helping Labonte gain thirty-three points. Labonte became the new point leader by thirty-two points and held it for the rest of the season.

Another third-place finish at Phoenix International Raceway in October was a highlight, especially as Labonte was driving with a hand broken in an earlier practice crash! Gordon managed a fifth-place finish but could not make up ground lost in previous races.

In the final race at Atlanta on November 20, Bobby Labonte, Terry's younger brother and driver of the No. 18 Joe Gibbs Racing Pontiac, won his only race of the season. Gordon finished third. Terry was fifth, clinching his second-career Cup Series championship. It's the only time in NASCAR history one brother has won a Cup Series race the day another brother won a championship.

Even though Gordon scored the most wins of 1996 with ten, he and crew chief Evernham lacked consistency in the final stretch of the season. Labonte remained consistent in the last four races of the season, and he won his second-career title by thirty-seven points.

Labonte enjoyed a successful career with Hendrick Motorsports. All told, from 1994 through 2005, he achieved twelve wins and one championship.

"Mr. H is the only guy I've ever driven for that I'd never heard anybody say anything bad about," Labonte said. "You know, and that tells you something right there. He is just the most pleasant person to be around. And he thinks so much of all of his employees. He's just that kind of guy."

Hendrick also returned the compliment about his former championship racer. The two are still very close friends nearly twenty-eight years after their championship in 1996.

"What a great guy and a great racer," Hendrick said. "I loved Terry's 'take no crap' attitude on the track when he was driving. I loved his 'you mess with me and I'm gonna whip your butt' Texas way of doing things. Nobody wanted to mess with him."

16 TRUCKIN': JACK SPRAGUE DELIVERS THREE TITLES

Jack Sprague driving the No. 25 Hendrick Motorsports Silverado during NASCAR's inaugural Craftsman Truck Series season in 1995. Sprague finished fifth in points that year.

During the inaugural season of NASCAR SuperTruck Series by Craftsman (now NASCAR Craftsman Truck Series) in 1995, several NASCAR Cup Series team owners also formed teams in the new division to further showcase their drivers and sponsors throughout the twenty-race schedule. The season began at Phoenix Raceway on February 5 and ended at the same track on October 28.

Hendrick elected to enter the series with various drivers during the first season. Rick himself was in the driver lineup at Topeka, Kansas, on July 29, 1995, for the twelfth race of the year, as he wheeled his only Truck Series entry for Hendrick Motorsports. Hendrick finished twenty-third in the thirty-three-truck field after suffering transmission problems on lap forty-five of sixty.

Hendrick's drivers represented the organization well in the series' first season. Scott Lagasse Sr. competed in the full twenty-race schedule, while Jack Sprague completed seven races, Roger Mears four, and Terry Labonte three. Among them, Labonte enjoyed a victory at Richmond International Raceway on September 7.

Sprague's path to Hendrick Motorsports' garage was an interesting journey.

In a September 26, 2015, article for NBC Sports, Sprague discussed his early years in the Truck Series after moving up from late model racing.

Recalling his time with Bruce Griffin Racing in early 1995, Sprague said, "I remember being totally intimidated, cause we're out there with all these trucks and a lot of them were raced by Cup owners. Terry Labonte was racing, [Ron] Hornaday was racing [Dale] Earnhardt's truck, all these guys with big ol' teams. Here we are: four guys with a truck [and] no spare nothin'. [I'd] never been there before in my life and went out there and ran sixth."

Sprague and his crew notched nine top-ten finishes over the next twelve races, something quite impressive against the well-funded teams.

Sprague had stayed in touch with Dennis Connor, an engine tuner on the No. 24 Hendrick Motorsports Cup Series Chevrolet who had also worked with crew chief Harry Hyde and driver Tim Richmond in 1986 and 1987. Sprague desperately wanted to drive full-time for Hendrick's team and made his interest known by calling Jimmy Johnson, general manager at Hendrick Motorsports.

"Two or three times a week I would call and bug the crap out of him [Johnson]," Sprague recalled.

Sprague ultimately completed thirteen Craftsman Truck Series races with Griffin in 1995. During that time, Sprague got an invite to see what Hendrick Motorsports had to offer. "I couldn't get there fast enough."

In a follow-up call, Hendrick asked Sprague, "You think you can win races in my piece-of-junk truck?" Sprague answered, confidently, "Absolutely," knowing he could get the job done in a truck he knew for certain was not junk.

On August 19, 1995, Sprague made his first start in the No. 25 Hendrick Motorsports Chevrolet Silverado at Fleming, New Jersey, and finished fourth. Sprague went on to log three top-five finishes and five top-tens in Hendrick Motorsports trucks that season with Dennis Connor serving as crew chief.

In 1996, Sprague was named to drive the No. 24 Truck Series Silverado for his first full season with Hendrick Motorsports. His talent was apparent from the very start, and he posted victories at Phoenix International Raceway, Nazareth Speedway, and the Milwaukee Mile. He logged another first at Phoenix and closed the season with a win at Las Vegas Motor Speedway. Sprague finished the season second to fellow Chevrolet driver Ron Hornaday Jr.

In 1997, Sprague returned with a vengeance hoping to claim the title. Wins at Phoenix, Nazareth, and Nashville Fairgrounds Speedway, along with sixteen top-five finishes, twenty-three top-tens, and five pole positions made for an impressive first championship

Sprague (24) leads Johnny Benson (18) and Ron Hornaday Jr. (16) at Phoenix International Raceway during the 1996 Craftsman Truck Series season. Sprague won five races that year and finished second in points.

Sprague takes a break with his No. 24 Hendrick Motorsports Chevrolet Silverado during the 1997 season. His racing career began in street stocks on short tracks near his hometown of Spring Lake, Michigan.

Sprague in victory lane after winning the Kroger 200 at Richmond International Raceway on September 6, 2001. Sprague led 196 of the race's 200 laps.

Sprague wheels the No. 24 Hendrick Motorsports Chevrolet Silverado in 1997. That season, he won at Nashville, Tennessee, and logged nine top-five finishes and fifteen top-tens.

season. A strong 1998 season saw Sprague post five wins, sixteen top-five finishes, twenty-three top-tens, and four pole positions, to finish second in points.

Sprague returned to the Truck Series championship stage in 1999, clinching the title with three wins, sixteen top-five finishes, nineteen top-tens, and one pole position. A tough 2000 was his least impressive season with Hendrick Motorsports, falling to fifth in points. A return to form in 2001 locked his final championship season with four wins, fifteen top-five finishes, seventeen top-tens, and seven pole positions. Over seven seasons with Hendrick Motorsports, Sprague finished first in points three times, second twice, and fifth twice, logging twenty-three wins for the team in the series.

Hendrick looks back on the team's time racing in NASCAR's Truck Series as a highly successful experience.

"Anytime you can win a championship, it's great," Hendrick said. "Jack was a great driver. He was aggressive, and he knew how to win. Having him and Dennis Connor together was a great combination. At about that same time, we had Ricky [Hendrick] running in the trucks, so to be able to base Ricky off of Jack's success was great. Jack was a workman, one of those good, aggressive short-track guys."

Ricky Hendrick added a victory to the Truck Series win tally at Kansas Speedway on July 7, 2001, and Chase Elliott clocked a win at Canadian Tire Motorsport Park at Bowmanville, Ontario, on September 1, 2013. All told, Hendrick Motorsports posted a total of twenty-six victories before they ceased competing in the series at the end of the 2013 season.

17 / THIS ONE'S FOR YOU: DAYTONA SWEEP STIRS EMOTIONS

Terry Labonte (left), race winner Jeff Gordon (center), and Ricky Craven (right) stand in victory lane after finishing first, second, and third in the 1997 Daytona 500 for Hendrick Motorsports. With owner Rick Hendrick at home fighting cancer, it was an emotional win for the team.

Gordon (24) crosses the finish line ahead of teammates Terry Labonte (5) and Ricky Craven (25) in the Hendrick Motorsports sweep of the 1997 Daytona 500.

In November 1996, the optimism that had served as a foundation for Hendrick Motorsports was threatened: its founder and leader, Rick Hendrick, was diagnosed with chronic myelogenous leukemia, a form of bone marrow cancer, at age forty-seven. He was told 95 percent of people his age with a similar diagnosis passed away within two years of their cancer being detected.

In a letter sent to all his employees in January 1997, Hendrick wrote, "I want to share a deeply personal matter with you because I regard all of you as family. I have been diagnosed with a rare but treatable form of leukemia. This disease was detected in its early stages. My doctors believe that the treatment has a good chance of forcing the disease into remission. There will likely be side effects for some period of time."

Hendrick began six months of treatment with alpha interferon and received a bone marrow transplant. He was prescribed a course of two injections of cancer-fighting drugs a day for nearly 1,100 days.

Each of the one hundred fifty employees at Hendrick Motorsports at that time moved into a higher gear in honor of Hendrick in an effort to make the team even more successful. As a result, Sunday, February 16, 1997, proved to be one of the most historic days in Hendrick Motorsports history as well as the history of Daytona International Speedway.

Leading up the running of the thirty-ninth annual Daytona 500, Jeff Gordon, Terry Labonte, and Ricky Craven (the newest driver to the Hendrick Motorsports fold) entered ten days of Speedweeks with high hopes of recording a victory in "The Great American Race."

The trio of drivers and their crew chiefs, Ray Evernham, Gary DeHart, and Phil Hammer, faced the normal challenges of Speedweeks, passing car inspections, finding the desired speed during practice sessions, and qualifying for the two starting spots in the front row to lead the forty-two-car field to the green flag. All the cars in the field carried decals in Hendrick's honor that urged fans to call 1-800-MARROW-2 to help in the fight against blood cancers.

Gordon and his No. 24 team finished runner-up in the second of two 125-mile qualifying events, placing him sixth on the starting grid for the 500. Labonte started eighteenth and Craven fortieth after he crashed in his qualifying race. All three drivers were slightly off on speed and hoped their performances in the race would show improvement. By the end of the last practice, Gordon and Evernham were feeling confident, as changes made to the car had made it faster.

Then a change to the race-day engine caused concern, as Gordon could feel a flutter at times when he put his foot on the floor. He was forced to go with what he had and hoped the issue would not worsen.

When the green flag fell, Gordon felt he had a strong race car—that is, until a cut tire on lap 110 in the 200-lap race sent him high in turn one. Evernham and the crew sprang into action after Gordon radioed to tell them exactly what the problem was.

As the field came off turn four, Gordon left pit road and was up to speed. He held off the Fords of Mark Martin, Bill Elliott, and Dale Jarrett that were barreling down on him. Gordon realized his Chevrolet was fast and that he had a legitimate shot at winning the race if he could keep them from putting him a lap down. Just twelve laps later, Greg Sacks spun and crashed on the backstretch, allowing Gordon to pit once again to stay in contention on the lead lap. Gordon moved from eighteenth to third with fifteen laps remaining.

A multi-car crash developed off turn two with twelve laps remaining involving leaders Jarrett, Dale Earnhardt, and Ernie Irvan. Gordon got a wheel mark from Earnhardt just before the latter flipped after contact with Jarrett, but Gordon's damage was only cosmetic.

With seven laps remaining after a caution for a multi-car crash on the backstretch, Elliott led the field across the start-finish line when the green flag waved. He continued to lead back to the start-finish line with six laps remaining and Gordon, Labonte, and Craven in second, third, and fourth behind him. Gordon dropped as low as possible to get around Elliott going into the first turn, with Labonte and Craven racing in the high groove.

A twelve-car crash occurred in turn four with only three laps remaining, ending the race under caution. With a sea of cameras flashing, Gordon, Labonte, and Craven finished first, second, and third, making Hendrick Motorsports the first organization in NASCAR history to take the first three finishing positions in the Daytona 500.

Immediately upon entering victory lane, Gordon was handed a cell phone with Rick Hendrick on the line from his Charlotte home for a heartfelt conversation. The No. 24 crew, led by Evernham, showed their signature "Refuse to Lose" T-shirts under their fire suits.

"Rick had won the Daytona 500 before [in 1986 with Geoff Bodine and 1989 with Darrell Waltrip], but the 24 team and myself had not," Gordon said. "When I think of the 24 team right from the very beginning, we were strong at Daytona and had a winning car, just not a winning driver in my rookie season. Daytona was always something that I was excited about going to and felt confident in. I was learning every time I went there, so it was amazing to finally pull off that first win.

"The disheartening part about it was Rick wasn't there to be a part of that special moment," Gordon continued. "Primarily, it was accomplishing something for him, which was the 1-2-3 finish in the biggest race that there is and just how huge that was. We knew he was smiling while at home watching. I could tell when I got on the phone with him while I was in victory lane how much that meant to him. He was pretty excited and that win lifted his spirits."

Hendrick recalled, "I was at home battling leukemia watching the race with Dr. Steve Limentani [Hendrick's oncologist]. Bill France Jr. [president and CEO of NASCAR] called me right after the race to congratulate me. That was something at that point in my life that was very, very special. Nothing could have lifted me more than to see Hendrick Motorsports finish first, second, and third that day."

The same year Gordon won the first of three career Daytona 500s, Hendrick chartered the Hendrick Marrow Program, a nonprofit fundraising organization that worked with the Be The Match Foundation to support the National Marrow Donor Program. The initiative raised funds to add volunteers to the Be the Match registry, which helped patients find a bone marrow match and aided recipients with uninsured transplant costs.

From its inception in 1997, the Hendrick Marrow Program raised millions of dollars, added more than one hundred thousand potential donors for the Be the Match registry, and eased the financial burden of nearly six thousand patients with grants from the Hendrick Family Fund for Patient Assistance.

Hendrick and his wife, Linda, were honored in 1999 with the Be The Match Foundation's Leadership for Life Award, which recognizes individuals who have made an extraordinary commitment to serve marrow transplant patients. Though The Hendrick Marrow Program no longer exists, some of its work is continued by the Hendrick Family Foundation.

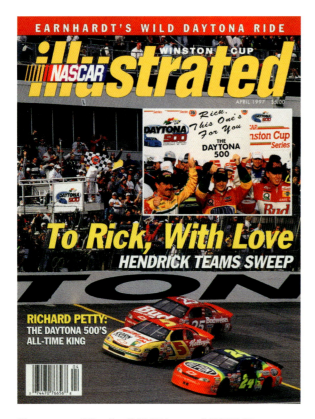

The cover of the April 1997 issue of *NASCAR Illustrated* tells the story of Hendrick Motorsports' dominance of NASCAR's most prestigious race. No other Cup Series organization in the race's sixty-six-year history has finished in the top-three positions in the 500.

Gordon (24) battles Dale Earnhardt (3) during the 1997 Daytona 500. Earnhardt and Gordon raced close enough for Earnhardt to leave a tire mark on the side of Gordon's Hendrick Motorsports Chevrolet.

Gordon celebrates after exiting his No. 24 Hendrick Motorsports Chevrolet in victory lane. Before being greeted by the crowd that had assembled there, Gordon spoke with Rick Hendrick by cell phone. Hendrick was at his home in Charlotte, North Carolina, while suffering from life-threatening chronic myelogenous leukemia.

SECTION 2: 1990s   83

18 / IT'S ALL ABOUT PEOPLE: RICK HENDRICK'S WINNING CULTURE

CULTURE.

Its definition is the set of shared attitudes, values, goals, and practices that characterizes an institution or organization.

There might be one word missing from the description that would characterize Rick Hendrick and anyone who has ever worked for him or, better yet, worked *with* him. That word is *passion*, for cars, auto racing, and people.

Passion for competition can be felt within all five hundred thousand square feet of shops, administrative space, and museums located on the campus of Hendrick Motorsports that continues to grow. Sure, there are fleets of brightly colored Chevrolets, engineers to design them, and mechanics who build them. There are lightning-fast pit crews to service them, public relations representatives who work with the drivers who drive them, and crew chiefs who call the shots from pit road. There are marketing personnel promoting the sponsors that support them. It's a fast-paced, well-oiled machine that's managed right down to thousandths of a second for thirty-eight race weekends per Cup Series season.

According to Hendrick, the secret ingredient to success at Hendrick Motorsports is the people who make it happen. That's the way it's been since the day the first race cars were loaded onto a single transporter in February 1984 headed for Daytona Beach, Florida.

One memorable family outing in the early 1980s gives a foundational look at the thinking of Rick and Linda Hendrick and what is most important in their lives. Marshall Carlson, former president of Hendrick Motorsports and current president of Hendrick Companies, remembered a Christmas Eve when his future in-laws showed their tremendous generosity.

"When Lynn [Hendrick] and I first started dating, she invited me over to their house in Charlotte," Carlson said. "It was the day before Christmas, and we were on break from high school. She said, 'My folks are going to do something, a little tradition they do every year, if you would like to come along. They do some charitable work.' I said, 'Absolutely. That would be neat.' I didn't know them that well at this point.

"Her dad had gotten a van from City Chevrolet and had it there. They loaded up as a family and we went to the women's shelter and the men's shelter. There was a family there they had heard about that was split up. The mother and daughters were on the women's side, and dad and sons were on the men's side.

"They picked them up, and we all went to lunch, and everyone had a nice holiday meal. Then we went to a big department store and did all the Christmas shopping together. The parents went and got things for the children and got things they needed and things they wanted. Then Lynn's parents put them up in a hotel for the holidays. There's no one else I know like them, socioeconomically, that's doing that the day before Christmas. It was really cool."

Jeff Andrews, president of Hendrick Motorsports, defines the culture of Hendrick Motorsports as every employee genuinely caring for each other.

"The family aspect is at the root of our culture," Andrews said. "Our culture really starts with respect for each other first and foremost. It's easy in this business to point fingers when things aren't going well. It's easy to say, 'It's not my area.' This company doesn't do that. Our culture is to treat each other with dignity and respect, and we work as a team. I will drop in a phrase by Mr. Hendrick and that is, 'No one person is better than all of us together.' We live by that. All the latest technology, all the best equipment, our incredible campus and facilities—those mean nothing if it's not for the

LEFT: Hendrick's iconic logo is recognized around the United States for its Hendrick Automotive Group car dealerships and the championship-winning Hendrick Motorsports NASCAR team. Hendrick Motorsports began with five crew members in 1984 and now employs over five hundred people. To date, it has logged fourteen Cup Series titles and more than three hundred Cup Series victories—both all-time records.

BELOW: Hendrick Motorsports' state-of-the-art racing facility features the most up-to-date equipment for building some of the best race cars in the world. More importantly, the people who build them are placed first within the plan for success.

belief and respect that we have for one another. Another is, 'They will never tear us down from the outside. We'll only tear ourselves down from the inside,' and that's another of Mr. Hendrick's sayings. Those words for me resonate every minute of every day, and that starts with respect for one another. What makes all the technology and all the great equipment work is the people."

Alan Gustafson, a crew chief for Hendrick Motorsports since 2005, has seen many changes within the company over nineteen years. He knows exactly why the organization tops all others in wins and championships with fourteen Cup Series titles and more than three hundred victories through 2023: Hendrick puts people first.

"There have been huge amounts of success over forty years, and there's lots of people who have come through here [at Hendrick Motorsports] and had a lot of success, but it's all on his [Hendrick's] coat tails," Gustafson said. "He's the one who sets the tone, and I think he's the one who does carry that example. He always puts people first, and he sets that tone. I think he is the one who deserves the credit for being the patriarch and the guy who really has set that example for a countless number of people. I don't personally feel like he gets the credit he deserves."

Dale Earnhardt Jr., a driver for Hendrick Motorsports from 2008 through 2017, saw firsthand why the organization won races and championships. All the pieces of the puzzle fell right into place after seeing the infrastructure from within.

"I knew Hendrick Motorsports was the best, but I had never seen behind the curtain as to why they were the best," Earnhardt Jr. said. "Any driver wants to drive the cars that are capable of winning. I knew they had those. I had never been behind the curtain to see the culture and how they go about putting their cars out on the racetrack. I learned that over the course of a long period of time. It wasn't obvious, and you didn't see it immediately. As you walked about the place and got to know everybody and sort of got to see

how it worked, you could start to see how successful and how sustainable it was. You felt a lot of pressure as a driver to go out there and get it done because there were really no excuses because you had preparation, people, equipment, talent inside the shop. They had everything you needed."

Hendrick has used the same business strategy since opening his first dealership nearly five decades ago. It's a simple plan that puts employees and customers first and foremost.

"We spend a lot of time talking about culture," Hendrick said. "I believe in servant leadership. I tell the people that work with me all the time that your people are your biggest asset. How do you take care of them? How do you deal with them? Do you have people that want to see you succeed? How do you develop relationships with sponsors that want to stay with you? All of that is culture and people skills. Culture here at Hendrick Motorsports is that it's a family and it's big, and how do you keep it like that?

"The answer is you surround yourself with people that believe like you do. You talk about family. Your audio has to meet your video, so to speak. If you say you're going to take care of people, then you've got to do it. If you say you're a family, then you've got to do things such as scholarships for their children, good insurance, reward them for a job well done, but mostly treat them with respect and treat them like family.

"I've done that with eleven thousand people in my dealerships and six hundred in the race shop. We started with five in each company, and it's grown over almost fifty years. It's grown fifty years in the car business and forty years in racing, and I've never changed my philosophy. People before profits because people are your biggest asset. We are in the people business. We're really not in the racing business, and we're really not in the car business. We are in the business of developing people and getting people to work together."

Jeff Andrews (left), president and general manager of Hendrick Motorsports, says the organization's culture is rooted in family.

Rick Hendrick speaks during a Hendrick Motorsports sponsor event. Fostering long-term corporate partnerships is a critical component of the team's success.

Driver Kyle Larson (left) presents a donation from the Hendrick Family Foundation to the Philadelphia-based Urban Youth Racing School.

2000s

SECTION **3**

19 RICKY HENDRICK: AN EMERGING LEADER

Ricky Hendrick (center) enjoys victory lane ceremonies with parents Linda and Rick Hendrick after his Craftsman Truck Series win at Kansas Speedway on July 7, 2001.

In the spring of 1982 during a trip to a store to buy boating equipment, two-year-old Joseph Riddick Hendrick IV, known simply as Ricky, asked his father to buy him a motorized car he could ride. After being told he was too young and that he could get it as soon as he was old enough to drive it, Ricky walked back to where it was parked.

As his father talked to the salesman, Ricky hopped aboard and drove it to the counter. Father and son left the store with young Ricky beaming and kid car securely aboard. There was no question he would follow his father into stock car racing, as Ricky's world was filled with real cars in NASCAR's Cup circuit beginning in 1984, just before his fourth birthday. Eleven years later, Ricky got his opportunity to drive a Legends Car in the Summer Shootout Series at Charlotte Motor Speedway. In 1996, he joined the Summer Shootout Series' Legend Car Semi-Pro Division, winning one race and posting four top-five results.

In 1997, Ricky moved to the NASCAR Late Model Stock Series, where he quickly adapted to the larger, full-bodied cars. In 1998, he notched three wins and three poles all at Concord Speedway. From there, he moved up to the NASCAR Craftsman Truck Series in May 2000. Racing the series full time in 2001, he claimed victory at the inaugural race at Kansas Speedway, becoming what was then the youngest driver to win a race in the truck division at age twenty-one.

Ricky showed he had talent, and a move forward to NASCAR's Busch Series (now the Xfinity Series) full time in 2002 was a natural progression. A promising season start was interrupted when he suffered a violent crash at Las Vegas Motor Speedway in just the third race of the year, and the resulting shoulder injury put him out of commission for the next six events.

He returned to the track for the race at Richmond and continued to compete through the season. His final start came on September 28, 2002, at Kansas. An accident in the Kansas event led to follow-up testing at Atlanta Motor Speedway. Ricky realized he was no longer

Ricky Hendrick after winning in Legends Summer Shoot Out competition at Charlotte Motor Speedway in 1995.

Ricky Hendrick during a late model test session in 1998. He showed natural talent as a race car driver.

100 percent and made the difficult choice to retire from driving at age twenty-two.

He pursued a management role at Hendrick Motorsports, becoming the owner of the No. 5 Busch Series team. His first decision was to hire Brian Vickers as the driver for 2003, and they won three races and the series championship that year.

Rick Hendrick remembered, "When he got hurt at Las Vegas and when he was testing at Atlanta, he called me and said, 'You know, my neck hurts. There are people better than me at driving this car. I'm not one hundred percent.' He tore up his shoulder and his neck.

"That's when Brian Vickers got in it and won the championship. He wasn't afraid to get out and say, 'I don't need to do this.' He was very mature for his age."

Vickers moved to the No. 25 Hendrick Motorsports Cup Series ride, and Ricky also became a part-owner of that team alongside his grandfather, Papa Joe Hendrick.

Tragically, Ricky passed away on October 24, 2004, as a passenger on an aircraft that crashed en route to Martinsville Speedway.

Seven-time Cup Series champion Jimmie Johnson remembered Ricky as one of his very best friends. The two met before Johnson became a driver for Hendrick Motorsports beginning in 2001 with select Cup Series races.

"I met Ricky while hanging out on Lake Norman there in North Carolina close to Charlotte," Johnson said. "We were similar in age and had similar friends. We all liked to wakeboard at the time and just being on the water in fast boats and kind of hanging out. I got to know Ricky and we formed a great friendship.

"What's really crazy for me in this whole experience was that Ricky and I were friends first. And of course, I wanted to drive for his dad first but never wanted to cross that line with him and ask him to put in a good word for me or ask him to take me around the shop or anything like that.

"So, when I met Jeff Gordon, when all of that transpired in September of 2000, and I signed my contract, it became very apparent to me the belief Ricky had in me as a driver. I couldn't believe all the work he had done behind the scenes with his father and with Jeff. And again, I never crossed that line and never asked for that help. But we had a very deep friendship and he truly believed in me. He was selling me, and the team never considered another driver for that fourth car.

"I think back to my 2000 statistics and my first year in the NASCAR Busch Series. I hit everything [logging only six top-tens in thirty-one starts and three races he did not finish]. I was crashing left and right. Ricky saw something in me and convinced his father.

Ricky Hendrick (left) in victory lane with his father, Rick Hendrick, after winning the Craftsman Truck Series race at Kansas Speedway on July 7, 2001.

That's how this whole opportunity came about."

Johnson also recalled a story about Ricky and a number that meant so much to him.

"I take great pride in my time at Hendrick Motorsports," Johnson said. "I truly know that Ricky had such a massive role in that. When I was facing my seventh championship, [I recalled that] Ricky was a big fan of the number seven and wrote it out a certain way. On social media I use that, the way he wrote seven, as a hashtag. I was really trying to honor Ricky through the chase for that seventh championship. To win it again brought another really deep bonding moment for myself and Rick and Linda. Leading into the season finale allowed us to talk about Ricky.

"I'll never forget being inside the media center after winning the seventh and we were in the hallway waiting to go into the media room for questions. All three of us were in the hallway crying and talking about Ricky and all that had transpired since he passed away in 2004."

His father often thinks of his son's qualities and what a perfect fit he was in his all-too-brief time at Hendrick Motorsports. His calm demeanor, decisiveness, and genuine care for others is still felt around the company.

"Ricky had an unbelievable ability to make friends and make people like him," Hendrick said. "People were attracted to him. He was fun loving. When you talk about people skills, he had as good as I've ever seen because he had so many friends. But he wasn't afraid to make a decision. Sometimes I procrastinate a little bit longer than I think he would have. He would have done a super job at Hendrick Motorsports. I think he would have been better than I am at it. People wanted to work with him. He had tremendous leadership skills.

"He loved to have a good time. He connected with Jimmie [Johnson] and Jeff [Gordon]. He told me Jimmie was going to be a champion; he told me Dale Earnhardt Jr. was going to drive for us one day. I said, 'That will never happen.' He and Dale were already talking about it. The plan was for him to take over and I was going to step back, but that just didn't work out. His people skills and the way he treated people, and the way people were attracted to him, were going to be an amazing fit."

Today, the Ricky Hendrick Centers for Intensive Care at Charlotte's Levine Children's Hospital offers a fully equipped pediatric intensive care unit, and his competitive spirit is embodied in Hendrick Motorsports' state-of-the-art race day command center, which is also named for him.

OPPOSITE TOP: Brian Vickers was Ricky Hendrick's choice to replace him in the NASCAR Busch Series in 2003 after Hendrick was injured in a Las Vegas Motor Speedway crash in 2002. Here Vickers leads the field in the final race at Homestead-Miami Speedway in November 2003. He went on to win the championship for team owner Ricky Hendrick and Hendrick Motorsports.

OPPOSITE BOTTOM: Driver Brian Vickers and Ricky Hendrick with the Busch Series championship trophy at Homestead-Miami Speedway on November 15, 2003.

20 / STEPPING IN: JOHN HENDRICK AT THE HELM

On March 5, 1995, Terry Labonte enjoyed his first victory of the Cup Series season at Richmond, Virginia. Labonte is joined in victory lane by team owner Rick Hendrick (far left), Labonte (center), Papa Joe Hendrick (second from right), and John Hendrick.

John Hendrick was born January 15, 1951, in Richmond, Virginia, and grew up near the small town of South Hill. He was active in baseball, basketball, and track at Park View High School and shared an interest in racing with his father and his older brother, Rick.

John graduated from high school in 1969 and from the University of Cincinnati in 1973 with a Bachelor of Science degree before moving to North Carolina. He worked in the funeral business but after a time decided upon a different career.

John began working in the automotive industry in 1979 at City Chevrolet in Charlotte before becoming general sales manager at Rick Hendrick Honda in West Columbia, South Carolina. He later founded JL Hendrick Management Corporation, which operates six car dealerships throughout the Carolinas and Florida.

On January 28, 1997, John was faced with one of the biggest challenges of his life. His older brother was diagnosed with leukemia and began a six-month course of treatment. With Rick's strength quickly draining due to the extreme medical regimen, John found himself in a new and unexpected role as the 1997 NASCAR season began—president of Hendrick Motorsports.

"It was a year I will never forget," John said in *Twenty Years of Hendrick Motorsports*. "Rick and I met two or three times about me running Hendrick Motorsports until he was strong enough to come back. I thought he was kidding.

"Rick called me the first time and said, 'I need for you to do something for me. I need you to run Hendrick Motorsports.' After two or three meetings, I said, 'Wait a minute, he's serious.'"

Out of respect for his older brother, John took on the role and did it well. Rick's health improved, and he eventually returned to the helm. In the meantime, John kept the company in championship form while his brother fought for his life.

"It was an opportunity of a lifetime for me, and it gave me the chance to pay Rick back for all the things he's done for me," John said. "It was an honor for me to help out during a tough time."

Helping others defined John Hendrick. He was an incredible person who devoted his life to giving back to those in need. John loved kids and showed that by establishing the Hendrick Foundation that supported programs and services that benefited children with illness, injury, or disability.

John also served as chairman of the board for the Nazareth Children's Home in Rockwell, North Carolina, and served on the board of directors for Elon Homes for Children in Charlotte. A weekly Bible-study program for employees started by John continues today at Hendrick Motorsports.

Jeff Andrews, president of Hendrick Motorsports, worked with John in 1997 when Rick had to step away. Andrews gained a great respect for the younger Hendrick for his leadership in a very tough situation.

"I enjoyed my relationship with John," Andrews said. "I didn't know him that well until he stepped into the day-to-day operations of our company in 1997 when Mr. Hendrick got sick. He was passionate about his faith. He brought our weekly Bible study to

John Hendrick began working in the automotive industry in 1979, eventually operating multiple car dealerships in the Southeast.

John Hendrick (34) was Rick Hendrick's younger brother. He enjoyed all forms of competition, playing basketball and other team sports throughout high school.

Driver Brian Vickers (left) looks on as crew chief Peter Sospenzo (right) and John Hendrick (center) study race data in the garage area at Charlotte Motor Speedway while preparing for the 2004 Coca-Cola 600.

our campus that we still have today on Wednesdays, which is the John Hendrick Fellowship Lunch. I valued my relationship with him. Much like Mr. Hendrick, he valued our people tremendously. His guidance and his leadership led us to our fourth championship with Jeff Gordon in 1997. I also remember John for his huge heart and generosity. I remember having conversations with him about his belief in helping children in need. There was little doubt that he was a true Hendrick, in my opinion. He just had that way about him. He had learned that from Papa Joe and his brother. In Mr. Hendrick's absence, it was very warming to have that true Hendrick presence here."

Rick felt there was no one better to call upon at a very difficult time in his life. John was a trusted confidant who Rick knew would be capable of leading Hendrick Motorsports when he was forced to step away.

John passed away on Sunday, October 24, 2004, in the airplane crash that also took the lives of his daughters, Kimberly and Jennifer, as well as Ricky Hendrick and other members of the Hendrick Motorsports family.

"John was a good leader. He held everything together," Rick said. "He was a very caring, dedicated person of deep, deep faith. He did the Bible study and worked with the children's home. His life was about giving back. I think he would have been a great preacher. Both of us saw our mom and dad sacrifice, give to us, and how they were respected in the community. He had some loyal people that worked for him in his dealership group. They still celebrate him today. That is a great measure of a man when he's not there anymore and people still talk about him and bring up things that he did and have a John Hendrick Award for Excellence that they still present at his stores."

When Rick Hendrick was battling leukemia, John stepped in to serve as president of Hendrick Motorsports.

Not one to seek the spotlight, John enjoys watching Jimmie Johnson's No. 48 Hendrick Motorsports team celebrate a win from the side of victory lane at Pocono Raceway on June 13, 2004. John later lost his life in an airplane crash while en route to Martinsville, Virginia, on October 24, 2004.

21 / LIVE FROM NEW YORK! IT'S JEFF GORDON AND SATURDAY NIGHT LIVE

It took the encouragement of friends to convince Jeff Gordon to accept an invitation from NBC executives to host the network's classic late-night franchise. Here he delivers the show-opening monologue on January 11, 2003.

It's true: Jeff Gordon excels at most things he undertakes. That included parking his Hendrick Motorsports Chevrolet between seasons 2003 and 2004 to try his hand at acting on a national stage in front of millions of people.

On January 11, 2003, he was given the opportunity to host NBC's popular late-night sketch comedy show *Saturday Night Live*, a program known for its edgy, anything-goes content. The Vallejo, California, native proved an onscreen natural.

At first, Gordon didn't feel comfortable with that type of challenge.

"At first, I said, 'No way,'" Gordon laughed. "I was flattered, but I didn't think I was capable of pulling it off. It just seemed to me like it was too big of a task. It was a six- or seven-day commitment with the schedule and everything else and I just thought, 'Man, I'll look like a fool doing this.'

"I've had a lot of amazing opportunities in my career, but that one really rises way up there. Off the racetrack, *SNL* was probably the number-one opportunity that I was able to be a part of. But it didn't come without a little bit of reluctance on my part because I didn't want to do it the first time they came to me when NBC was coming into the sport. And they had the idea."

Twice during postseason NASCAR banquets, in 2001, the year of his fourth Cup Series championship, and 2002, NBC executives slipped him envelopes with invitations to be a guest host. After the 2002 banquet, he went to dinner with friends in New York City and mentioned that for a second time he had been asked to host the show.

When the table of friends went crazy with encouragement and told him he couldn't turn it down a second time, he had to take NBC up on their offer. It was simply too big of an invitation not to do it. It was a once-in-a-lifetime opportunity.

The wheels were put into motion, and suddenly Gordon was on set running through scripts. In a whirlwind, it was showtime and he was on stage. Then it was lights, camera, action in a world as frightening as the speeds at which he drives.

No worries. Gordon nailed his timing and delivery. During his opening monologue, he interacted with Southern race fans played by Rachel Dratch and Chris Parnell, who then revealed themselves to be sophisticated New Yorkers disguised as race fans.

Other skits included wearing a fake mullet wig, handlebar mustache, and T-shirt that read, "1 Tequila, 2 Tequila, 3 Tequila, Floor." He strums an air guitar interspersed with karate chops in a laundry room as Parnell, playing Cousin Terrye Funck, tapes his so-called "The Terrye Funck Hour" talk show while sitting in blow-up chairs in front of a washer and dryer, all punctuated by Steve Miller Band music and hilarious dialogue. Gordon plays ladies' man and chain-store photographer Rickye Funck in that skit.

Gordon as Rickye Funke. He and cousin Terrye Funke (played by *SNL*'s Chris Parnell) staged a radio talk show from their basement laundry room.

In another skit, Gordon played a Southern-speaking Captain Jack "Cougar" Kelly, an air force pilot addressing a group of school children in a "bring your parent to school" scenario. Gordon keeps the children excited with his thrilling stories of saving them from harm, hands out pilot's wings, and flusters teacher Amy Poehler because he is so handsome. Seth Meyers has little to offer as a carpet salesman. He fades quickly, as the children lose interest in what he has to say.

Gordon was thankful his friends talked him into making the *SNL* appearance.

"I feel very, very fortunate that I have friends in New York that convinced me to do it," Gordon said. "They convinced me that I should do it, no matter how much of an idiot I made of myself. As it turned out, it was an amazing experience and one I will never forget. Doing it put me in the elite category of athletes, the very few that have done that. Nobody in motorsports other than myself that I'm aware of has done it. It was so special. I had a blast."

Gordon is a perfectionist at heart and wanted to give his all. He got completely into character with every skit.

"Yes, I let completely loose, especially with the Rickye Funke character," Gordon said with a laugh. "When I do things, I want to do really well. I want to put a lot of effort into what I do. I want to be proud of what I do, and I want others to be proud of what I do. I knew I was representing more than just myself in that moment. I worked hard at it."

Steve Waid, former executive editor of racing publications *NASCAR Scene* and *NASCAR Illustrated Magazine,* remembered the impact Gordon's appearance on *Saturday Night Live* had on NASCAR as a sport.

"At that time, many athletes had hosted *Saturday Night Live*; I don't believe any race car drivers had ever hosted the show before Jeff," Waid said. "People had heard of Jeff because of his achievements since coming to NASCAR during the final race of 1992. Other than the NASCAR crowds that had seen the sports pages that had followed his career, no one outside of the sport had seen him on a national basis across the board. If you had not read the sports pages, you didn't know him very well.

Gordon portrays Robert Forgey of the Lancaster Zoo during a visit to Brian Fellow's (played by Tracy Morgan) "Safari Planet." The other guest is Orpheus, the snake held by Gordon.

Gordon's *SNL* appearance opened further television and movie doors, including a cameo in 2003's *Looney Tunes: Back in Action*.

"Because of his flawless performance on *Saturday Night Live*, they took notice and suddenly knew who he was," Waid explained. "They had never seen any race car driver do that. He was an instant hit. That, in turn, put an injection into NASCAR and brought more people to the sport who wanted to see what it was all about just because of his appearance there. The fact that he hosted *SNL* was a great marketing boost for NASCAR. They had seen him in an entirely different light and, in turn, saw NASCAR in an entirely different light as well."

Over the past two decades, Gordon has also appeared on such shows as *Live with Regis & Kelly, Taxi, Spin City*, the *Late Show with David Letterman, The Tonight Show with Jay Leno, Today, Jimmy Kimmel Live!, Ellen, 60 Minutes*, the *Rachael Ray Show*, and *The Tonight Show Starring Jimmy Fallon*, among others.

22 / NO. 24 TEAM'S FOURTH CHAMPIONSHIP CEMENTS PLACE IN HISTORY

From left, team owner Rick Hendrick, driver Jeff Gordon, and crew chief Robbie Loomis celebrate after winning at Kansas Speedway on September 30, 2001. It was their sixth victory of the season, en route to winning the Cup Series championship.

When the green flag waved over the 2001 Daytona 500, there was great optimism that the season would be one of NASCAR's greatest. Some three hours later, the weight of seven-time champion Dale Earnhardt's death during the race's final lap was felt to its depths, and in some ways, it remains heavy to this day.

Every team competing within NASCAR's Cup Series division that year, including those at Hendrick Motorsports, pledged to continue on in the spirit of Earnhardt's success and determination. Each gave their all with every lap completed to honor their lost close friend and competitor.

"I had seen Dale go through some pretty horrific crashes during his career, and he walked away," Gordon said. "If he was injured, he would show up at the racetrack the next weekend. He was just one of those guys that you just thought would always be there until the day he walked away on his own terms.

"That was really tough for all of us when we lost him at Daytona that day in February of 2001. All of us had our own relationship with him. He took me under his wing and helped me a lot on and off the racetrack. I appreciated that. He didn't have to do that, but he did. He saw the bigger picture. It wasn't necessarily wanting to help Jeff Gordon. He just wanted to see what he could do to help the sport continue to grow and saw the potential that was there. No one could do it like Dale could. There was a lot of responsibility on all of us as competitors to fill those shoes the best that we could. I had a lot more to learn from him, and that certainly stands out to me.

"I did feel like it was important to step up. I think we had FOX Sports and NBC that year, and I think that was the first year of the new TV rights deal with NASCAR. There were a lot of eyeballs on the sport and they [the networks] were going to help the sport as well."

Gordon certainly did step up. He enjoyed an amazing 2001 season, one that was the culmination of a couple years of changes for the No. 24 team. Ray Evernham had been Gordon's crew chief since joining Hendrick Motorsports in 1992 for the final race of that season. Together, they amassed forty-seven victories and three Cup Series championships. Then in late 1999, Evernham had been given the opportunity of a lifetime to form his own team, Evernham Motorsports, with backing from Dodge. The automaker was returning to NASCAR after a lengthy absence; it had previously backed Richard Petty and Petty Enterprises for nine of their ten championships (Petty had won his final championship in 1979 with Chevrolet).

Gordon gave Evernham his blessing and began thinking of a new crew chief. The list of replacements was short, as there was really only one particular crew chief Gordon had in mind. His name was Robbie Loomis.

Loomis had worked with Petty for many years and proved he was not only smart but very efficient and calm, running his team with an organized game plan. After several phone calls and a few secret meetings, Loomis agreed to take the job. In their first season together, Gordon and Loomis put together a ninth-place finish in points in 2000, with three wins, eleven top-fives, and twenty-two top-tens.

Gordon (24) leads the field during a Cup Series race at Dover Downs International Speedway on June 6, 2001. He went on to win the race that day.

104 HENDRICK MOTORSPORTS 40 YEARS

From their first meeting, their bond and ability to communicate was obvious. Success came at Talladega, Sonoma, and Richmond. Their start was impressive with the hope of much more to come.

Then came 2001, when Gordon collected his fourth and final NASCAR Cup Series championship with six race victories along the way. All told, Gordon amassed eighteen top-fives finishes and twenty-four top-tens, with an average finish of eleventh over thirty-six races.

Gordon clinched the 2001 NASCAR Cup Series title at Atlanta Motor Speedway one week before the final race with his sixth-place finish, joining Richard Petty and Dale Earnhardt as winners of four or more NASCAR Cup Series Championships. As the 2001 season came to an end, Gordon's winning average was 20 percent, winning one race of every five starts. At the conclusion of 2001, he had fifty-eight victories in 293 races.

"Robbie was such a great addition to the team," Gordon said. "I hated to see Ray leave, but I understood why with such a great opportunity. Robbie fit in well with our team. Our entire team welcomed him and rallied around him. The veteran guys wanted him, and so did the new guys.

"There was something magical between 2000 and 2001. We had made some huge gains between those seasons, statistics wise. The team worked hard between 2000 and 2001 to get us back into championship form. We proved it from the win at Las Vegas at the start of the year, and I knew then we were going to have a great year.

"I think what makes you a championship team is to go through changes and still be able to adapt to them and run like a championship team and remain successful. The way we came together motivated me to work hard and help win that championship. The year started out tough losing Dale Earnhardt at Daytona, and then 9/11 happened in September, and that was the other major challenge for our sport and our nation. But we held it together as a team and as a sport and prevailed in the end."

Jeff Gordon hoists his Cup Series championship trophy at Atlanta Motor Speedway. The title was secured with one race still remaining in the season.

OPPOSITE TOP LEFT: Gordon (24) and Kevin Harvick (29) lead the field at Kansas Speedway on September 30, 2001. Gordon led fifty-three of 267 laps and collected six wins that season.

OPPOSITE TOP RIGHT: Gordon (24) leads Robby Gordon (Lowe's) and Kevin Harvick (white Chevrolet) on the road course at Watkins Glen International on August 12, 2001. Gordon went on to record the victory, his fourth and final win on the 2.4-mile track.

OPPOSITE BOTTOM: From left, team owner Rick Hendrick, team manager Brian Whitesell, crew chief Robbie Loomis, and champion Jeff Gordon alongside the Cup Series title trophy in November 2001 at Atlanta Motor Speedway.

23 DALE EARNHARDT JR.'S MOVE ROCKS NASCAR

Dale Earnhardt Jr. collected his second career Daytona 500 on February 23, 2014. The Kannapolis, North Carolina, native considers the win to be one of the greatest of his nineteen-year career.

The relationship between the Hendrick and Earnhardt families goes back decades. In fall 1983, Dale Earnhardt Sr. (right) tested a car for Rick Hendrick (left) in preparation for Hendrick Motorsports' NASCAR debut the following season.

Earnhardt Jr. in his No. 88 Hendrick Motorsports Chevrolet racing to the checkered flag at Michigan International Speedway on June 15, 2008. Earnhardt led 14 of the race's 203 laps.

Dale Earnhardt Jr. remembers countless visits to his grandmother's home on his father's side, Martha Earnhardt, at the corner of Sedan and V8 Streets in Kannapolis, North Carolina, and his grandfather Ralph's shop in the backyard. His grandfather Robert Gee, on his mother's side, was a player in Rick Hendrick's world very early in the racing game in Palmer Springs, Virginia.

"He passed away in 1994," Earnhardt Jr. said of Gee. "I remember going to his house close to Charlotte Motor Speedway, especially during Charlotte race weeks. I'm biased, but a lot of people said he was the best body man in the business. He worked on the K&K Insurance Dodge [driven by 1970 champion Bobby Isaac] and ended up going to Rick's and working for him. He had real good craftsmanship and built beautiful cars. He would polish every piece of aluminum to a mirror finish. He just took a lot of pride in it.

"He didn't have much of a filter. He told you what he thought. He didn't have time or patience for B.S. or people dragging their feet," Earnhardt Jr. recalled. "On the other side of that, he could also be the life of the party. Rick has told me about past celebrations, and when the party got going, he would get on stage and sing. When Robert got older and had health issues, Rick kept him on the payroll for morale purposes."

Throughout the late 1980s and early 1990s, Earnhardt Jr. watched his father become a seven-time Cup Series champion. A few years on some North and South Carolina short tracks paved the path toward two Busch Grand National Series (now called Xfinity Series) championships in Dale Earnhardt Inc. Chevrolets in 1998 and 1999. That led to five Cup Series starts in 1999 and his first Cup Series win at Texas Motor Speedway for DEI in 2000.

Over the next seven seasons, Earnhardt Jr. logged seventeen victories, including the 2004 Daytona 500. A conversation that began through the sale of a boat that Dale Jr. bought from Ricky Hendrick a year earlier would eventually put him at Hendrick Motorsports.

"On occasion, I would go to Ricky's house on Sundays after races," Earnhardt Jr. said. "He was incredibly, incredibly nice to me every time I saw him. We'd be out on the lake joking around. But I would talk about getting pretty frustrated with things at DEI. This had to be in 2003. I'm telling him, 'I think I'd like to go there.' Ricky said, 'We need to do that. We need to figure out how to make that happen.' When my contract is up, we really do need to sit down and really think about it. I might stay. I might not. I don't know. I want to talk about it if you all are interested in hiring me. It sounds like fun. What I'm doing right now isn't any fun. We would just sit on the boat and just daydream about it more than anything."

Then came October 24, 2004. Earnhardt Jr., along with the rest of the racing world, felt unspeakable sadness upon learning of Ricky's death in a plane accident near Martinsville, Virginia. Earnhardt Jr. remained with DEI through the 2007 season, but in spring of that year he signed his first contract with Hendrick Motorsports to drive in the 2008 season.

"I really enjoyed the communication I had with Rick from the onset when he sat down and said, 'I'm interested in this. How can we make this happen?'" Earnhardt Jr. said. "It was comfortable and

Crew chief Steve Letarte (left) alongside Earnhardt Jr. after winning the 2014 Daytona 500. The pair also won Cup Series races twice at Pocono Raceway and once at Martinsville Speedway that year.

easy. He went above and beyond to make it happen. I could tell it mattered to him. We were having a good time going about putting the deal together and meeting with sponsors and getting excited and testing at Daytona and Vegas that very first year."

Fourteen races were completed before victory came at Michigan International Speedway on June 15, 2008.

"We felt like it should have happened sooner," Earnhardt Jr. said. "When we were doing the negotiations, talking about it, and listening to the media build up to the season, Darrell Waltrip said he thought we would win five or six races, and I honestly felt like that was a legitimate possibility. We came out of the box at Daytona and won a qualifying race and the Shootout at Daytona. We were getting reasonably good finishes, but we weren't winning races. We had some close ones. We just weren't winning. That was getting more and more frustrating. Winning that race at Michigan was a big relief."

Over the next three seasons, the team went winless through 108 races, with only three second-place finishes at Talladega, Martinsville, and Kansas City. Earnhardt Jr. was deeply concerned.

"Stalled would be an understatement. My career had nearly ended," Earnhardt Jr. said. "I was out of ideas. There was not a lot of excitement about how to get better, and there didn't look like there were a lot of people around me excited to try and help me get better. I wasn't sure how to get the right people around me to help me succeed."

Talk of crew chief changes were in play, and Dale Jr. was at the center of the discussions. Jeff Gordon offered a solution that seemed to work best. He switched to Alan Gustafson, Mark Martin switched to Lance McGrew, and Earnhardt Jr. moved over to Steve Letarte.

"They called me and said, 'What do you think about this idea?'" Earnhardt Jr. said. "So, when I heard that, I said, 'You're going to put me in the shop where Jimmie Johnson and Chad Knaus have won five championships in a row? Heck yeah, I want to do that!' They were the best team. I want to be next to them. If I can stand next to them every day for the next year, I want to do it."

Letarte and Earnhardt Jr. both felt they had something to prove. Earnhardt Jr. had won no Cup Series races in 2010, but by joining Letarte there was hope they could build from the ground up and begin winning again. They met for dinner and formed a plan.

"Letarte came to my house," Earnhardt Jr. said. "He said, 'We're backed in a corner. You're going to do everything I ask you to do. We're going to give it our all. We have to make this work to continue.' I said, 'I'll deliver.' I had been racing for twentieth and finishing twentieth and twenty-fifth in points. It was pretty bad. I was afraid we had flamed out and that was going to be the end of my career."

Earnhardt Jr. opened the 2014 Cup Series season by winning his second-career Daytona 500 and logged three additional Cup Series victories, twice at Pocono and another at Martinsville.

"Winning the 500 was awesome because it was Letarte's first Daytona 500 win, and I was able to help him achieve something that meant a lot to him," Earnhardt Jr. said. "At that point, our relationship had become so close. We were like family. That win did a lot, but that whole year was a nice little spell of redemption and getting back to victory lane. We won a good chunk of races and showed we could be competitive in the right scenario with the right people."

They continued their quest for consistency and became a championship-contending team.

"Letarte kept saying, 'I want you to run in the top fifteen. So, start with that,'" Earnhardt Jr. said. "We worked hard to run in the top fifteen. Then those top-fifteens became top-tens. He would notice it, and he would say, 'Hey, starting from here, we're a top-ten team. That's our goal.' It took some time. It wasn't an easy process. Midway through the 2014 season, he said, 'Now we're a top-five team. You can do it. We're there.' That's what we were. We were top three. We could see that potential. So, we got the performance we were looking for. That was incredible to me. That was very methodical and very planned. By 2014, we were where we needed to be as a race team. That year, we were a top-five team if not a top-three team."

Earnhardt Jr. earned his final Cup Series win on November 15, 2015, at Phoenix International Raceway. His final start came on November 19, 2017, in the Ford EcoBoost 400 at Homestead-Miami Speedway. Earnhardt Jr. finished his Cup career with twenty-six wins, nine coming with Hendrick Motorsports. He remains one of the most popular drivers in NASCAR history.

He is extremely grateful for the deep friendship he and Hendrick have shared over the years.

"I like to think of Rick as one of the kindest and most caring people that I've ever met," Earnhardt Jr. said. "He has the ability to give anything to help somebody, and he does it. If somebody needs assistance financially, if he knows about it, he does something about it. I've always appreciated that about him, and I try to model my own decisions based off of that kindness and generosity. He has been such an incredible influence on so many people. The good that he does for the world influences us to be the same. That to me is my most favorite part about him, but I also love how competitive he is. It's fun to be around successful people and find out why they are successful."

Dale Earnhardt Jr. clinched his final Cup Series win on November 15, 2015, at Phoenix Raceway.

24 / SEVENTH HEAVEN: THE JIMMIE JOHNSON AND CHAD KNAUS DYNASTY

The No. 48 Hendrick Motorsports team celebrates Jimmie Johnson's first career Cup Series victory at California Speedway on April 28, 2002. Johnson and crew chief Chad Knaus are standing behind their crew in this photo.

Longtime Hendrick Motorsports crew chief and executive Ken Howes looks on during a Cup Series event. Howes was Johnson's first crew chief during the initial three races of his career in 2001.

During the summer of the 2000 Cup Series season, Ricky Hendrick made a statement to his father that seemed a bit strange and caught him off guard. "You really need to think about putting Jimmie Johnson in one of your cars. He can win championships in the Cup Series."

Rick didn't understand Ricky's line of thinking at all. Having Johnson at Hendrick Motorsports wasn't on his radar. Ricky was certain that Johnson had talent as a driver and that with the right crew chief and the strong engines Hendrick Motorsports could provide, there was great promise for the future.

But while Johnson had shown a lot of potential in the early years of his Busch Grand National Series career, he had crashed more than most and his statistics were not great.

"Jimmie didn't show that much in the [Busch] Series," Hendrick said. "Ricky had already been talking with Jeff [Gordon] about it. Jeff had a lot of confidence in Jimmie, and Ricky did as well. Chad left us to go and be a crew chief with another team, and Ken Howes wanted to bring him back. I don't take credit for that one. I approved it, but it wasn't my idea. I was the marriage counselor that had to keep it together as long as it was."

Johnson and Knaus met for the first time on pit road during the next-to-last race weekend of the season at Homestead-Miami Speedway on Saturday, November 11, 2000. Johnson was walking toward his Busch Series race car before the start of the race. Knaus was crew chief for Melling Racing with driver Stacy Compton. Jay Guy, a crew chief and friend of Knaus, mentioned to Johnson that Knaus should be his crew chief for his limited-schedule Cup effort with Hendrick Motorsports planned for 2001. It was small talk among friends, but Johnson and Knaus met again in September 2001 when Knaus was one of three crew chiefs being interviewed for the 2002 season.

Ken Howes served as Johnson's interim crew chief in 2001 for a limited schedule of three Cup Series races, while Knaus remained with Melling Racing. Howes requested that Knaus come back to Hendrick Motorsports as crew chief for Johnson when he went full-time in 2002. Knaus had previously been with the No. 24 team as a crew member and operated the chassis and fabrication shop.

The duo opened the season by winning the pole position for the Daytona 500, and their first victory came on April 28, 2002, at Fontana, California. For Johnson, it felt like the monkey was off his back.

"Winning at Fontana such was a relief, on top of such excitement and emotion," he said. "I dreamed of winning a Cup race. That was my dream. It wasn't becoming a champion or a seven-time champion. I wanted to win at the highest level, and there I was. So, all those emotions were running around my mind. I was just enjoying the moment.

"The relief for me, which might sound crazy, involved a backstory. In 2001, Jeff [Gordon] won the championship, and then they took all his cars and equipment and put number 48 on all of that, and we have this fleet of championship-winning cars, parts, and pieces. I put a lot of pressure on myself to succeed because I felt if I didn't win in my rookie season, I wouldn't have a job. And so, granted, the win came in my tenth race of my rookie season, and it was my thirteenth race in the Cup Series. My emotions were very high, but close behind in my mind was, 'I'm going to have a job. I'm going to be around for a while. This isn't going to just be a flash-in-the-pan moment.'"

Johnson and Knaus enjoyed nineteen wins over the next four seasons with three in 2002, three in 2003, eight in 2004, and five in 2005. On the championship front during those years, Johnson had come close to winning the championship with a fifth-place finish, two seconds, and another fifth in points through 2005. Too many championships had slipped away, a fact that was disturbing to Hendrick, Johnson, and Knaus.

The tension led to a special meeting that took place between the pair and their team owner.

At the end of 2005, there was serious talk of Johnson and Knaus ending their relationship as driver and crew chief. Communication was becoming strained, and another championship had been lost in the final race of the season. Opinions were mounting that a possible change may have been best for all involved.

"Mr. Hendrick sat Jimmie and me down because there was a lot of frustration," Knaus said. "We didn't win the [2005] championship, and it was due to lack of performance or lack of accomplishing the goal of winning the championship. He sat us down because we were acting like a couple of children. He walked in with a plate of chocolate chip cookies and a half gallon of milk and said, 'Well, if you guys are going to sit here and act like children, we're going to eat these cookies and then we're going to go and take a nap.'"

Johnson and Knaus rest against the No. 48 Hendrick Motorsports Chevrolet during a break in the action. The pair won seven Cup Series championships from 2006 through 2016.

Johnson enjoys the victory lane celebration after winning the Brickyard 400 at Indianapolis Motor Speedway. Note the unique trophy given to all Brickyard 400 winners dating back to 1994.

Point made.

"The three of us did a deep dive as to what was going on and where we were at," Knaus continued. "We came to the conclusion that we wanted to continue to push and continue to grow. As Mr. Hendrick does, he helped us figure out a plan to go into 2006.

"I think 2006 was a good year for us in general. We had done a lot of off-season planning with restructuring the team where the team members were holding more responsibility as a group. The car chief, engineer, mechanics, shock specialists all had skin in the game and more help in the decision-making process. We distributed the workload more to focus on everybody being an integral part of the team. That was really key, and I think pivotal to our success moving forward."

The result of all the team's work was the 2006 Cup Championship. "I look at Mr. Hendrick as an unsung hero for winning the 2006 championship," Knaus said. "I don't know if he realizes how impactful he was going into that [season]."

Five Cup championships in a row from 2006 to 2010, followed by two more in 2013 and 2016, gave Johnson the distinction of becoming only the third driver in NASCAR history to score seven titles, alongside NASCAR Hall of Famers Richard Petty and Dale Earnhardt.

"I don't know what it was, but I know what I felt, and I know what we had," Johnson said. "I know without question that's what separated us from everyone else, but I don't know the why aspect of it. We both were young in our positions and new in these roles. I think building this team from scratch created a deeper bond for Chad and myself. There were layers of accountability and ownership in the program.

"There was a lot to put my finger on, but especially in that era of NASCAR, the data in the race cars and the driver–crew chief relationship, it was my job to feel out the race car and explain what I felt. Our ability to communicate was tremendous. I would explain things to Chad and what I felt, and somehow in his mind's eye, not being in the vehicle, he could understand what it was doing and what we needed from an aero standpoint. We just had this thing going on that was incredible to experience.

"With more time that passes, and I look back on it, the less real it seems. When you're in it day after day, you never savor the moment. Before you know it, twenty years are gone and you say, 'We did all that? Really?'"

When Johnson left Hendrick Motorsports at the conclusion of the 2020 Cup Series season, he had 83 wins, 232 top-fives, 374 top-tens, 36 pole positions, and 7 Cup Series championships (2006, 2007, 2008, 2009, 2010, 2013, and 2016) with Hendrick Motorsports.

"Jimmie was capable of driving high-horsepower race cars, which were harder to drive than the Xfinity cars," Hendrick said. "Chad came up with more ideas and could dream up more stuff and had such attention to detail. He would always push the envelope to be right on the cutting edge of every rule they [NASCAR] had. Chad would try to get as much out of the car as he could. When you put those two combinations together, they were deadly. Nobody knew they would be that good. We had no way of knowing Jimmie was

TOP: November 20, 2016: Team owner Rick Hendrick stands between driver Jimmie Johnson (left) and crew chief Chad Knaus (right) with all seven of their Cup Series championship trophies in the foreground. That day Johnson had won the race at the season finale at Homestead-Miami Speedway, adding the seventh trophy and title to the collection.

RIGHT: Team owner Rick Hendrick and Cup Series champion Johnson confer on pit road at Charlotte Motor Speedway in 2016. Johnson won the five-hundred-mile race there on October 9.

going to be that good. No one knew that No. 48 crew would be as amazing as they were as long as they were.

"They were like brothers. They had their periods and their times. Chad was the one that came up with all those twisted bodies for the templates. He was always super creative and very aggressive and wanted the very best pit crews and best people, and he didn't care what it took. He was going to make it happen. It was twenty-four hours, seven days a week with him. Jimmie would eat right and be the very best athlete he could be. You just don't know if you're going to end up with it when it happens.

"That was a storybook ending."

25
THE TRIUMPH AND TRAGEDY OF MARTINSVILLE

Race winner Geoff Bodine (just under floral wreath) celebrates with his team at Martinsville Speedway on April 29, 1984. To Bodine's left is crew chief Harry Hyde. Had they not won, All-Star Racing, known today as Hendrick Motorsports, would likely have had to close its doors.

The race cars of Kyle Larson (5), Chase Elliott (9), Alex Bowman (48), and William Byron (24) lined up at Martinsville Speedway. Byron won the April 7, 2024, race followed by Larson second, Elliott third, and Bowman eighth. All four cars sported the ruby red colors indicating Hendrick Motorsports' fortieth anniversary.

Each time the Hendrick family planned a trip to Martinsville Speedway, it was tough for Rick to sleep the night before. For him, childhood visits to racetracks and dealership showrooms, where new cars were unveiled each year, were as exciting as Christmas morning.

Rick and John Hendrick first entered the gates of Martinsville in the early 1960s when they were in their teens. Colorful race cars filled its pit road and garage area.

"I grew up near the track and watched a lot of modified races there," Hendrick said. "We went to Martinsville because it wasn't far from Palmer Springs and South Hill, Virginia, where we lived. Most of the tracks I had been to were dirt. Just smelling the rubber was different.

"Years and years later, we won our first race at Martinsville in 1984, and that enabled us to go on and continue. If we hadn't won that race, we wouldn't be here today. We owe Geoff Bodine and that track so much. We've won twenty-nine races there at Martinsville Speedway."

For fans and employees of Hendrick Motorsports, as well as members of the Hendrick family, the mention of the track's name brings forth feelings that cover both ends of the emotional spectrum.

Two dates immediately come to mind: April 29, 1984, the day of Bodine's team-saving win, and October 24, 2004, the day a Hendrick Motorsports airplane was tragically lost en route to the half-mile Virginia short track.

"The spring race is not as hard; it's the fall race that's hard," Hendrick said. "I usually don't go to that race, just because it's that time of year.

"The weather is changing, and it's getting cooler. The leaves on the trees are changing, and all of that brings back memories from 2004. It's not the track's fault, but that's where it happened [at Bull Mountain]. It's almost two different worlds. The spring race at Martinsville kept [Hendrick Motorsports] alive, and the fall race is when the accident happened. All the things around fall bring it back when that race comes around."

Jimmie Johnson (48) battles Jeff Gordon (24) for position during a Cup Series race at Martinsville, Virginia, in 2009. Johnson went on to record his fourth of seven career titles that season while driving for Hendrick Motorsports.

That Sunday morning in 2004, the fog was thick. Other teams flying to the area diverted to Danville, Virginia, but the Beechcraft Super King Air 200's pilots decided to stay with the original plan and land at Blue Ridge Airport near Martinsville in Patrick County, Virginia. It proved to be a fateful decision.

Those lost that day were Rick and Linda Hendrick's only son, Ricky; Rick's brother and Hendrick Motorsports president, John Hendrick; John's twin daughters, Kimberly and Jennifer; the organization's general manager, Jeff Turner; chief engine builder Randy Dorton; DuPont executive Joe Jackson; Tony Stewart's helicopter pilot, Scott Lathram; and pilots Richard Tracy and Elizabeth Morrison.

Hendrick learned something was wrong shortly before the race. While he was driving home after visiting his mother, his mobile phone rang. It was Ken Howes, director of competition with Hendrick Motorsports, who asked him to pull over. He shared the news that the plane was missing.

Hendrick drove home to tell his wife, Linda, hoping the plane had diverted to another airport. But he knew they would have called, and he feared the worst. Family and friends began assembling at the Hendrick home. By late afternoon, the phone rang again. It was NASCAR president Mike Helton confirming the plane had been found. There were no survivors.

Back at Martinsville Speedway, officials asked the Hendrick Motorsports drivers, including race winner Jimmie Johnson, to report to the NASCAR transporter in the track's infield to share the grave news. All victory lane ceremonies were canceled. Jim Hunter, NASCAR's vice president of communications, made the public announcement that the plane was missing, and information was still being gathered.

During the next weekend at Atlanta Motor Speedway, all the Hendrick Motorsports drivers and crew chiefs gathered to express their thoughts during a press conference carried live by CNN and other major outlets. The Cup Series race was won by an emotional Johnson.

In the days after the crash, Hendrick felt it was vital that he address the organization's employees, whom he considered his extended family. With him was Linda Hendrick and their daughter, Lynn, and son-in-law, Marshall Carlson. They wouldn't let him go alone.

"I needed to go and at least let everyone see me," Hendrick said of the days after the accident. "I knew everyone was very upset. But I also knew that we needed to go on, no matter how hard it was going to be. I needed to go over there and try to pull everyone together the best that I could. I just felt like I needed to see them [the employees].

"I wasn't thinking about racing. I was thinking about family because that's what we always talk about: family. I knew it was going to be painful, but I had this overwhelming feeling that we were going to work through this, that we were going to finish the job that everyone on the plane loved and cared for. I walked in, and the first person I made eye contact with was Jeff Gordon. I went up there on the stage, and I remember just how emotional it was, how hard it was just to try to talk. But I had to thank them and tell them I was thinking about them."

The day of the accident, Ricky Hendrick had driven his black 2004 Chevrolet Z71 Chevrolet Tahoe to the airport before boarding the plane. All these years later, Hendrick sometimes still drives it to feel close to his son.

In many ways, Martinsville Speedway continues to be a joyful place for Hendrick Motorsports. As of April 2024, the team has collected twenty-nine Cup Series victories there, the most of any team at any track. Gordon and Johnson each have nine Cup Series wins there. Darrell Waltrip has four, William Byron has two, and Bodine, Dale Earnhardt Jr., Alex Bowman, Chase Elliott, and Kyle Larson have one apiece.

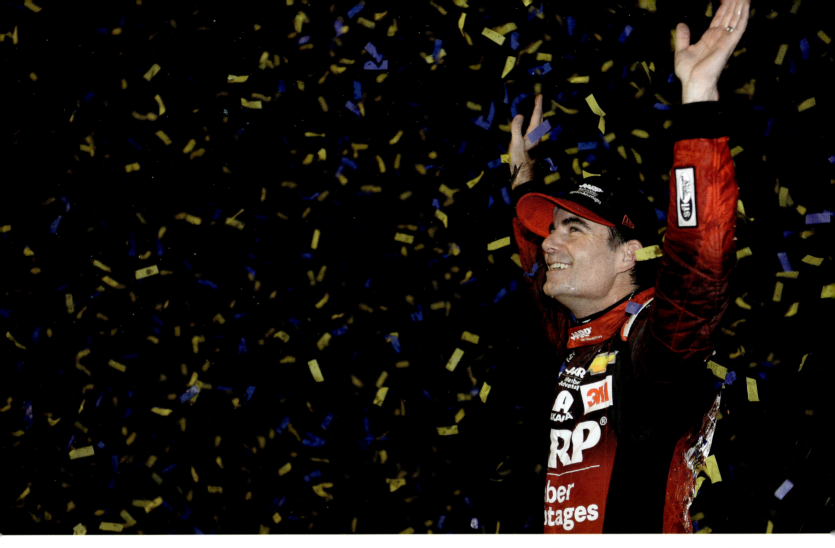

Jeff Gordon strikes a triumphant pose after winning his ninety-third and final race at Martinsville Speedway on November 1, 2015. All told, Gordon enjoyed nine career Cup Series victories on the 0.526-mile Virginia short track.

Gordon, despite nine wins at Martinsville including his ninety-third and final career Cup Series victory on November 1, 2015, still remembers feeling lost when he first came there for Busch Grand National Series competition in 1990. But something clicked when he got to Hendrick Motorsports that put him on a winning path.

"It wasn't until we did a test when I got to Hendrick Motorsports that I was able to go there [Martinsville] and make laps and try all kinds of things," Gordon said. "Ray Evernham was trying to do things to the car setup that weren't working, and nothing changed. I realized I had to change what *I* was doing. As I found something making all those laps, it started to click, and it did throughout the rest of my career. It was such a pleasure to go to Martinsville from then on.

"No matter what the rules were, the car, the tires, my age, it seemed like that was the one place I could go where I could consistently run up front and be a threat to win. When I look at the number of wins I had [there], and what that meant to Hendrick Motorsports and the end of my career, I don't think there was a better track to win my final race."

The race on April 7, 2024, was particularly sweet. Gordon and Bodine served as grand marshals, and the four Hendrick Motorsports cars each featured ruby red fortieth anniversary paint schemes. Seven buses had carried employees and family members to take in the race, and the 1,500 in attendance were not disappointed. Byron led a 1-2-3 Hendrick Motorsports sweep at the checkered flag to become the ninth driver to win at the track for owner Hendrick. He crossed the line just ahead of teammates Larson (second) and Elliott (third). It was the first 1-2-3 finish for a single organization in Martinsville Speedway history and the eleventh win there for the No. 24 car. Most importantly, the performance marked the fortieth anniversary of Hendrick Motorsports' inaugural victory in 1984.

"There are so many men and women [behind the win] and this is a tribute to all the hard work in the shop," Byron said of the win. "It's just a really good environment to work in. They have built something so special over the years, and I am thankful to be a part of it and to drive the No. 24.

"It's way bigger than me."

26 / A WINNING COMBINATION: HENDRICK MOTORSPORTS AND CHEVROLET

HENDRICK MOTORSPORTS AND CHEVROLET have become synonymous. Looking back into NASCAR's storied history, Bill Blair and Al Wagoner were the first to enter their own Chevrolets in NASCAR competition on September 25, 1949, at Martinsville, Virginia. Blair finished fifth with Wagoner following in eighth in the sixth race of NASCAR's inaugural Strictly Stock season, today known as the Cup Series.

The first driver to win in a Chevrolet in NASCAR competition was Fonty Flock on March 26, 1955, at Columbia, South Carolina, while driving for team owner Frank Christian.

On March 24, 1957, Buck Baker scored Chevrolet's first "factory-backed" (in quotes because of the Automobile Manufacturers Association self-imposed racing ban then in effect) victory at Hillsborough, North Carolina, leading fellow Chevrolet drivers Speedy Thompson and Jack Smith under the checkered flag. Baker collected ten wins, thirty top-fives, and thirty-eight top-ten finishes over forty races and stamped the brand's legitimacy in the hearts of passionate car buyers and fans.

When Rick Hendrick decided to form the original All-Star Racing team in 1984, there was no question as to the type of race car he would enter. His family drove Chevrolet passenger cars and trucks on the farm and had for generations. There was no other brand to be considered.

"I grew up loving Chevrolets, racing a Chevrolet, and wanting Chevrolets," Hendrick said.

"Once you're a Chevrolet person, you're always a Chevrolet person. I've gotten to do some of the coolest things through our partnership. In 1976, we opened our first Chevrolet dealership in Bennettsville, South Carolina. I've always been grateful for that opportunity and have been fortunate to develop incredible relationships with the people at General Motors. Over nearly fifty years together, I've become one of their biggest dealers. I take a lot of pride in my association with them. I've never raced anything but Chevrolets."

Jim Campbell, vice president of GM Performance and Motorsports, interacts with Hendrick on a weekly basis. The two have been longtime business partners and friends.

"There's something Rick has done over the years in NASCAR and that is he's been racing up front with his teams and winning championships at all different levels of the sport," Campbell said. "He's a great example of the whole point of winning, whether you're running a car business or running a race team. You want to win. Rick, in partnership with Chevrolet, showed how to win in NASCAR at the top level, what it took in terms of preparation, execution, and hiring the right team members and creating the right chemistry. Also, importantly, leveraging the people on the team and with Chevrolet and bringing everyone together with the right technology and engineering and the approach to building fast race cars."

Rick Hendrick outside his flagship City Chevrolet car dealership in Charlotte, North Carolina, in 1985.

"When I think about Rick Hendrick, I think about someone who values people at the highest and challenges them to bring their best performance to work every day. The chemistry he creates to work together inside of his race teams and the way they've worked with Chevrolet over the years is amazing. That combination is so powerful, getting the results that we can be proud of and that are worth celebrating."

Campbell deeply appreciates the relationship he has shared with the championship team owner. It's a genuineness that hasn't changed, no matter how much success has been enjoyed by Hendrick Motorsports.

Jim Campbell, US vice president, Performance Vehicles and Motorsports for General Motors, presents NASCAR Cup Series driver Jeff Gordon with the Inaugural Chevrolet Lifetime Achievement Award during the 2015 NASCAR NMPA Myers Brothers Awards Luncheon at Encore Las Vegas on December 3, 2015. Campbell is a key part of Hendrick Motorsports' relationship with Chevrolet.

Hendrick Motorsports' Chevrolet dominance in action: Jimmie Johnson (48) and Jeff Gordon (24) have eleven Cup Series championships between them.

"Rick is always kind and has such a great sense of humor and makes every conversation fun, but he also gets work done," Campbell said. "He values friendships and values hard work. Whether it's the dealerships business, the accessories business, or winning races, it's always a valuable conversation. I'm always lifted to do better in our joint projects. That's Rick. He inspires you to do better."

Throughout the forty-year history of Hendrick Motorsports, the organization has won fourteen Cup Series championships. Jimmie Johnson won titles in 2006, 2007, 2008, 2009, 2010, 2013, and 2016. Jeff Gordon collected four in 1995, 1997, 1998, and 2001. Terry Labonte, Chase Elliott, and Kyle Larson have one each in 1996, 2020, and 2021, respectively.

Brian Vickers won the 2003 NASCAR Xfinity Series championship with Ricky Hendrick as team owner. Jack Sprague won Craftsman Truck Series championships for Hendrick Motorsports in 1997, 1999, and 2001.

Overall, throughout the sport's history, Chevrolet has more than 850 Cup Series victories. Among them, more than 300 of those victories belong to Hendrick Motorsports.

At the conclusion of the 2023 Cup Series season, Hendrick Motorsports had amassed 4,705 starts, 301 victories, 1,232 top-fives finishes, 2,112 top-tens, and 246 pole positions over a forty-year period with fifty-one drivers, all coming in Chevrolets.

2010s

SECTION 4

27 TALENTED KASEY KAHNE JOINS THE TEAM

Kasey Kahne celebrates after winning the Brickyard 400 for Hendrick Motorsports on July 23, 2017. Kahne notched six Cup Series wins during his time with Rick Hendrick.

Jimmie Johnson (48) and Kahne (5) lead the field at Chicagoland Speedway on September 16, 2012. Johnson started from the pole position and finished second, while Kahne started sixth and finished third.

During his fifteen-year Cup Series career, Kasey Kahne was one of the sport's most popular drivers.

When Kahne was seventeen, he began racing open-wheel sprint cars at Deming Speedway in Deming, Washington, and also Skagit Speedway in Alger, Washington, before moving to USAC (the United States Auto Club). In 2000, open-wheel icon Steve Lewis hired Kahne to drive his Sprint Cars, just as he had done for other racing greats such as Jeff Gordon, Stevie Reeves, Tony Stewart, Kenny Irwin Jr., Jason Leffler, Dave Darland, J. J. Yeley, and Bobby East. In Kahne's first year on the circuit, he won Rookie of the Year honors and the national midget championship. He continued to run USAC, as well as the Toyota Atlantic Series and the World of Outlaws.

Kahne came East to run in the NASCAR Busch Grand National Series (now the Xfinity Series), where he scored eight victories, forty-six top-fives, eighty-seven top-tens and nine pole positions. While in the Cup Series, Kahne logged eighteen victories, ninety-three top-fives, 176 top-tens and twenty-seven pole positions.

The bigger opportunity came at the start of the 2004 season when Kahne replaced Bill Elliott in the No. 9 Dodge for Evernham Motorsports in the Cup Series. Kahne logged thirteen top-five finishes and fourteen top-tens.

In 2005, Kahne scored his first career Cup Series victory at Richmond International Raceway. In 2006, Kahne logged wins at Atlanta Motor Speedway, Texas Motor Speedway, California Speedway, and Michigan International Speedway and twice at Charlotte Motor Speedway.

Kahne went winless in 2007. In May 2008, he won his second career Coca-Cola 600, his first points-paying win of the season. Kahne also became the sixth driver to win the 600 and NASCAR's All-Star Race in the same season. He also won the Pocono 500 from the pole position in June of that year.

Kahne's new team for 2009, Richard Petty Motorsports, was the result of Petty Enterprises and Gillett Evernham Motorsports merging. Kahne won at Sonoma, California, in June for his first road course win. In September, Kahne collected his second win of the year at Atlanta. Kahne struggled to get back into contention for the championship and finished tenth in the final season standings. On September 10, 2009, it was announced that Richard Petty Motorsports would merge with Robert Yates Racing alongside drivers Elliott Sadler, A. J. Allmendinger, and Paul Menard.

Kahne signed with Hendrick Motorsports in 2010, even though his tenure with the organization would not begin until 2012. After

SECTION 4: 2010s   125

Kahne (right) with crew chief Kenny Francis at Michigan International Speedway during the 2012 Cup Series season. Kahne finished fourth in Cup Series points that year.

Kahne celebrates after winning the Coca-Cola 600 at Charlotte Motor Speedway on May 27, 2012, for Hendrick Motorsports. Kahne led 96 of the race's 400 laps.

an early release from Richard Petty Motorsports in October of 2010, he joined Red Bull Racing for the 2011 season. Kahne collected one victory for the team on November 13, 2011, at Phoenix International Raceway. It was his first victory in over two years. He finished the season fourteenth in points.

At the start of the 2012 Cup Series, Kahne partnered with crew chief Kenny Francis who had come along from Red Bull. Unfortunately, he finished no better than fourteenth in the first five races. He improved significantly by winning the Coca-Cola 600 in May at Charlotte—his 300th Cup Series career start. Kahne followed that victory by winning at Loudon, New Hampshire, in July and ended the season a career-best fourth place in the points, with two wins, four poles, twelve top-five finishes, and nineteen top-tens.

In 2013, Kahne won at Tennessee's Bristol Motor Speedway in March and collected a second victory at Pocono in Pennsylvania in August. Kahne finished fourteenth in Cup Series points that year. In 2014, a single win at Atlanta at the end of August offered hope for more wins before season's end, but it was not to be. The team managed only three top-fives and eleven top-tens amid thirty-six starts that year. No wins were logged in 2015 or 2016. Kahne's final victory for Hendrick Motorsports came on July 23, 2017, at the Indianapolis Motor Speedway in the Brantley Gilbert Big Machine Brickyard 400.

Kahne finished his Cup Series career with Levine Family Racing for 25 starts in 2018. His career totals: 529 starts, 18 victories, 93 top-five finishes, 176 top-tens, and 27 pole positions.

"I was super excited to go to Hendrick Motorsports in 2012 when I got the call to go over there with Jimmie [Johnson] and Jeff [Gordon] and Dale [Earnhardt Jr.]," Kahne said. "It was great to be part of an organization that had won so many races and so many championships while I was in the sport. Some of them came before I got into the sport. I did compete against those guys and got beat by them. I did get to beat them at times, but truth be told, I got beat by them often. It was really cool that at thirty-one years of age I was going to spend some time racing for Rick Hendrick."

Kahne felt confident with crew chief Kenny Francis by his side at Hendrick Motorsports. The two had worked together since the final race of 2005 and had built a strong relationship. Their time together at Hendrick paid off with some high-profile victories.

"Kenny was pretty quiet and reserved, but I was quiet often as well," Kahne said. "Kenny was always watching, listening, and paying attention and had such a good handle on things. We brought a lot to [Hendrick Motorsports] the first year and really got everything going over there. He was a great crew chief and a great guy to have on your side.

"We didn't win nearly enough races with Hendrick Motorsports, but we did win the 600 at Charlotte, the Brickyard 400 at Indianapolis, and won at Bristol Motor Speedway. I always felt good to be part of the team. I loved being a part of the debriefs with the other teams and drivers and how we prepared for each race.

We looked at each race throughout the race weekend, and I loved the way we went about it. To me, there was always a lot of structure built into Hendrick Motorsports. It was fun to be a part of such a big operation."

Kahne has always felt incredible respect for Hendrick, especially at times when Kahne was inspired through accomplishments and the owner's ability to pull people together to achieve the goal of winning races and championships.

"The thing about Rick is that I always felt good listening to him speak, whether it was at our Christmas parties, whether it was at a lunch after team wins, or when he spoke to drivers and crew chiefs at our team debriefs," Kahne said. "He definitely made you feel like you were part of the team and that everyone there was working together to get better. I enjoyed those times and I think you could see it in the room. We would all get quiet, and we listened and learned, and it was always really good to hear Mr. H talk."

Looking back, Kahne felt he could have achieved more for himself and for Hendrick Motorsports during his six-year tenure.

"I've never felt like I got everything out of Hendrick Motorsports that I should have for whatever reason," Kahne said. "But it was just enjoyable to work hard and try to win races and ultimately a championship. We were able to [accomplish] some of that, and I enjoyed my time there but never felt like I did what I could have or should have during my years there."

Hendrick felt Kahne was a great asset to his racing organization.

"Kasey was a heck of a talent." Hendrick said. "Just as soon as we put him in our car, he was fast. He did a great job for us."

ABOVE: Kahne (left) and Rick Hendrick at Homestead-Miami Speedway prior to the start of the final Cup Series race of the 2017 season. This race also marked Kahne's final start with Hendrick Motorsports. All told, Kahne collected six victories for the team.

TOP: Kahne won the Brickyard 400 at Indianapolis Motor Speedway on July 23, 2017. It was the eighteenth and final victory of Kahne's Cup Series career.

28 / CHASE ELLIOTT: SECOND-GENERATION CHAMPION

Chase Elliott celebrates clinching his first Cup Series championship by winning his fifth race of the season at Phoenix Raceway on November 8, 2020. Elliott outpaced the Fords of Brad Keselowski and Joey Logano.

Elliott driving his HendrickCars.com-sponsored Chevrolet during a short-track late model test in 2011.

Elliott and his crew celebrate in victory lane after winning the Craftsman Truck Series event at Canadian Tire Motorsport Park in Bowmanville, Ontario, on September 1, 2013.

From a very early age, Chase Elliott has been around racetracks with his parents, 1988 Cup Series champion Bill Elliott and Cindy Elliott, a former photo editor for two national auto racing publications in the early 1990s.

Go-karts, pro late models, and the ARCA Series all set the path for his career. No matter what he drove, Chase was winning races, and everyone was taking notice.

After hearing about the fifteen-year-old driver from another Cup Series team owner, Rick Hendrick called and asked to meet him. "James Finch said to me, 'Have you been watching that Elliott kid?' I said, 'No, not really,'" Hendrick recalled. "I found a video of Chase racing and liked what I saw. With his pedigree and looks and that kind of talent, I thought if I put him in the right spot, he's going to be really good."

Hendrick offered to support Chase's career path and help with race cars and equipment in hopes of eventually putting him in a Cup car. In February 2011, Hendrick Motorsports announced it had signed the high school freshman.

"I took a chance on him pretty early and started helping him when he was fifteen," Hendrick said. "Bill and I met, and he started laying out the program. I said 'Bill, here's the deal. I'm going to give you what you need, and you run it. You know what you're doing.'"

Chase made nine starts in the Craftsman Truck Series for Hendrick Motorsports in 2013, winning once that season at Canadian Tire Motorsport Park in Bowmanville, Ontario, on September 1.

An opportunity came to drive for JR Motorsports, where he won three Xfinity Series races and the championship in 2014. He won one race in 2015 and finished second in points that season. Chase also ran five Cup Series races in 2015 in the No. 25 Hendrick Motorsports Chevrolet, his first on March 29 at Martinsville Speedway. It was a race he had dreamed of all his life, having seen his father win Cup Series races and a championship.

"It was a huge time for me," Chase said. "That was obviously a dream coming to fruition. At that point in time, if Jeff [Gordon] had announced his retirement [January 2015], that was going to be his last year. Rick wanted me to come over and drive the 24 car (beginning) in 2016. I just didn't have a lot of big track experience at that point in time or experience in general in the heavier cars."

Chase qualified for the race but finished thirty-eighth after an on-track incident. The young rookie looked at the experience as the start of a rewarding journey.

He returned to NASCAR's Xfinity Series with JR Motorsports for six races in 2016 and won in the season-opening three-hundred-mile race at Daytona International Speedway. Chase also got his first taste of success on NASCAR's biggest stage by winning the pole position for the 2016 Daytona 500, NASCAR's most prestigious event. He remains the youngest pole winner in the race's history.

"Yeah, that weekend as a whole was a whirlwind," Chase said. "I ran the Xfinity race for JR Motorsports and ended up winning, which was really neat, there at Daytona on Saturday. We qualified the Sunday before, back then for the 500. I'm not going to lie; it was a lot for me at the time. I didn't really feel like I deserved to be starting on the pole for the Daytona 500 at that point. I stepped into a solid team and the speedway racing side of things. That was a huge strong suit for [crew chief] Alan [Gustafson] and the 24 team, and it had been for Jeff over the couple of seasons before I got there. So, I just stepped into a really good situation."

Chase spun on lap twenty and ultimately finished thirty-seventh, completing 160 of the race's 200 laps.

In 2018, Elliott switched his car number from No. 24 to No. 9, a legacy set by the Elliott family.

"It's really pretty simple," Chase said. "It was just my favorite number and the number that I've related to my family's history. It was also the number that I have run since I had started racing

Elliott made his first Cup Series start at Martinsville Speedway on March 29, 2015. He started twenty-seventh and finished thirty-eighth after suffering front-end damage.

go-karts and everything. Because of that, it's always going to be special regardless of if I was ever going to have the number. I didn't really anticipate that change happening just because it wasn't something that was a part of the history of Hendrick Motorsports.

"Really and truly, I'm not sure I would have had the nerve to even ask. Dale Jr. was kind of the one that pushed me along to make that request because I really wasn't going to do that. Who was I to say, 'Hey boss, I haven't done anything for you or for your company, but I would love to switch numbers, you know?' It just was a tough thing for me to ask. Dale just felt like if it was something meaningful to me that it made a lot of sense for me to try and get that number because it was not being used."

Added Earnhardt Jr., "I was trying to foreshadow the idea. Chase was going to be great and win a lot of races and a lot of championships. Does he want to do that driving the number 24 or does he want to do those things adding to that number 9, what his dad created? Would that matter to him? He said it would. He drove the number 9 for us at JR Motorsports, so I knew how he had already added to that [legacy] because he had already felt the impact using it was having in our sport.

"I was looking at Chase as the next big superstar. If that guy is doing all these things in the next twenty years, it would be better for NASCAR, long term, than him doing it in the number 24. Honestly, I think it [number 24] is a better fit with William Byron. He doesn't have a family legacy with the 24, so this is a great way for him to carry the number 24 on by a driver that can set his own legacy. In a way, I think it worked very well for everybody.

"I said to Chase, 'The longer you wait [and] the more you accomplish in the 24, the harder it will be to convince yourself and everyone else to change to the number 9. If you want to be in the 9, it's now or never.'"

Chase was especially proud to have brought the thirteenth Cup Series championship to Hendrick Motorsports in 2020 after logging five wins, fifteen top-five finishes, twenty-two top-tens, and one pole position in 2020. Elliott won his way into the Championship 4 with a "walkoff victory" at Martinsville to advance to the title race. From there, he rallied from having to start at the rear of the field to be crowned the champion following the first Cup Series title race held at Phoenix Raceway.

"The landscape of that season was very different from what we all went through with COVID," Chase said. "But man, everything was just clicking, and we got hot there at the right time. We were firing on all eight [cylinders], and with the way this points format is now, that's kind of what it takes, getting hot right there at the end of the season. If you can squeak your way into the round of twelve in the playoffs and get hot there for those last six or seven weeks, man, you're sitting in really good shape. Fortunately, that was the case for us. Everything just played out in our favor."

The Dawsonville, Georgia, native would go on to reach the Championship 4 in both 2021 and 2022. Elliott claimed his sixth consecutive National Motorsports Press Association Most Popular Driver Award in 2023. His father has a total of sixteen most popular awards to his credit.

ABOVE: Elliott with crew chief Alan Gustafson (far right) and his crew after winning the pole position for the 2016 Daytona 500.

RIGHT: Chase Elliott is joined by his mother Cindy and father Bill Elliott in victory lane at Phoenix Raceway on November 8, 2020. Bill Elliott enjoyed a long NASCAR career and was Cup champion in 1988. Chase won the Cup Series race that day and also secured his first career Cup Series championship.

29 AN UNCONVENTIONAL PATH BRINGS WILLIAM BYRON ON BOARD

William Byron's No. 24 Hendrick Motorsports Chevrolet is showered in confetti following his race-winning drive in the 2024 Daytona 500.

Byron in victory lane after winning the NASCAR K&N Pro Series East Granite State 70 at Loudon's New Hampshire Motor Speedway on July 17, 2015.

Byron leads the field in the JR Motorsports No. 9 Chevrolet at Daytona International Speedway in February 2017. He would go on to win the Xfinity Series championship that year.

While most seven-year-olds may have been interested in playing T-ball or video games, William Byron credited television for shaping his career path as a winning NASCAR superstar.

The native of Charlotte, North Carolina, became interested in racing in 2005 and began following Jimmie Johnson as his favorite driver. In 2006, he and his dad attended a Cup Series race at Martinsville Speedway, furthering his desire to someday slide behind the wheel of a race car himself.

"My dad would ask me which trips I would like to go on, and I picked Martinsville Speedway," Byron said. "I just fell in love with it. We would buy tickets online and we would watch races from the grandstands. We would hit maybe five or six races a year, the ones close by and a few we had to travel to. That's how I got started watching. We also attended some races down at Daytona."

He began racing online iRacing in 2011, and through 2012 had garnered 104 wins and 203 top-five finishes.

In 2012, Byron and his dad began looking for ways he could make his dream of driving come true. Byron entered legend car races at age fifteen and won thirty-three events, becoming the Legend Car Young Lions Division champion in his first year driving race cars.

In 2014, he signed with JR Motorsports (JRM) to drive in its late model program while he continued to drive in Legend Cars competition. He scored a win and twelve top-five finishes and was second in points to teammate Josh Berry at Hickory Motor Speedway (North Carolina). While driving late models for JRM, he met Rick Hendrick and told him he was going to drive for him someday.

Byron moved to NASCAR's K&N Pro Series in 2015 and clinched the series championship by finishing ninth at Dover, Delaware. He was only seventeen years old at that time, becoming one of the few drivers to win the championship in their rookie year (future Hendrick Motorsports teammate Kyle Larson had accomplished the same thing in 2012). Byron also drove in the Menards ARCA Series in 2015 for team owner Justin Marks and scored four victories.

In 2016, he drove the full Craftsman Truck Series schedule for Kyle Busch Motorsports winning seven races to log a fifth-place finish in the point standings. That strong result earned him Rookie of the Year honors. Later that same year, Hendrick Motorsports announced it had signed a multiyear driver contract with Byron running full-time in the NASCAR Xfinity Series in the No. 9 JRM Chevrolet.

In 2017, Byron won four races with JRM in the Xfinity Series at Iowa Speedway, Daytona, Indianapolis Motor Speedway, and Phoenix Raceway and won the Xfinity Series championship. His success there prompted a move to the Cup Series in 2018, where he drove the famed No. 24 Chevrolet, a car Jeff Gordon had successfully taken to victory lane ninety-three times and won four NASCAR Cup Series championships with. Byron had no wins that season but did win Rookie of the Year honors.

"Chase Elliott was in the number 24 car for a while before I got in it," Byron said. "It was a big deal for me to be in that car, and there were a lot of expectations. But for me, I was just trying to learn as a rookie driver. I didn't really think I put a ton of pressure on myself to have amazing results, but it was definitely a tough season for us. We had a lot of inconsistent runs, and we had a lot of challenges as a team. It was difficult to jump from Xfinity to Cup because that is huge. I didn't expect that, and so just trying to learn all the nuances of the Cup Series and the grind of that every week was tough.

"In every other series, I would get a week off here and there and have a chance to reset. The Cup Series is a very difficult thing to jump into as a twenty-year-old, but I learned a ton and grew a lot through that year."

In 2019, Byron started on a strong note by winning the pole position for the Daytona 500. That season he logged five top-five finishes, thirteen top-tens and made the playoffs for the first time in his Cup

Series career. The next season, he scored his first-career Cup Series win on August 29, 2020, at the Coke Zero Sugar 400 at Daytona.

"It was really cool," Byron said. "We had made the playoffs that year [2019], but we hadn't won a race. So, our goal was obviously to win a race the next year and make the playoffs, but I think it was getting to the point where we were wondering when that first win was going to come. We were just pushing hard for it, and everything kind of came together and was down to the wire there at Daytona because we were trying to make the playoffs. Winning really kind of gets the monkey off your back because you can just focus on trying to go out there and get more wins."

In 2021, Byron's first win of the season came early in the year at Homestead-Miami Speedway, where he led 102 of the 267 laps. The win kicked off a top-ten streak in the next eleven races, including top-five finishes at Martinsville, Talladega Superspeedway, Darlington Raceway, and Dover Motor Speedway. He finished the season a career-high tenth in the points standings.

Byron collected wins at Atlanta Motor Speedway and Martinsville in 2022 and garnered six wins in 2023, finishing third in Cup Series points after making the Championship 4. Byron is extremely happy to be driving for Rick Hendrick and Hendrick Motorsports and hopes to follow in Jeff Gordon's footsteps and remain in the No. 24 Chevrolet for decades to come.

"He [Hendrick] has always been there for me with any sort of personal thing that I've gone through. When my mom had some health issues—she had cancer—he was there every step of the way," Byron said. "That just means a lot because it doesn't have anything to do with competition.

"He's always there as a resource, someone to talk to, through difficult times and the good times. He texts or calls me more when I'm running poorly than when I'm running well. It has always been a great relationship between us, and I always trust that he's going to guide me in the right direction and help give me all the tools I need to succeed."

Byron was at the forefront to help launch Hendrick Motorsports' fortieth anniversary season at the 2024 season-opening Daytona 500 on February 19, 2024, held on a Monday due to a rain delay. There were four laps remaining on the final restart, and Byron was in second in the No. 24 Chevrolet. He and Ross Chastain, of Trackhouse Racing, raced in close quarters for the lead, with Byron at the point as a big crash broke loose behind him just as he crossed under the white flag marking the final lap of the race. When the yellow caution flag was displayed, the race became official, and Byron was declared the winner, with Hendrick Motorsports teammate Alex Bowman finishing second.

Byron logged the ninth victory for Hendrick Motorsports in "The Great American Race," placing Hendrick Motorsports in a tie with Petty Enterprises for the most wins in NASCAR's most prestigious event. The win snapped Hendrick Motorsports' nine-race Daytona 500 losing streak—the last Hendrick driver to win the Daytona 500 was Dale Earnhardt Jr. in 2014—and made the twenty-six-year-old from Charlotte, North Carolina, the sixth different

Byron, driving for JR Motorsports, clinched the NASCAR Xfinity Series championship in 2017 at Homestead-Miami Speedway. The Charlotte, North Carolina, native enjoyed four victories that season.

Byron captured the pole position for the 2019 Daytona 500. To Byron's right is team owner Rick Hendrick, and crew chief Chad Knaus stands behind Byron at his left.

driver to win the 500 for Rick Hendrick. Byron's excitement could be heard throughout the headsets of everyone on his crew. His tone was a bit guarded, as he was confused about what he was hearing in his helmet.

"Did we win it? Did we win it?" Byron kept asking over his radio. The emotion he heard over his radio from crew chief Rudy Fugle confirmed he had just won the biggest race of his career.

"Well, no one told me," Byron said in post-race interviews. "Rudy was crying on the radio, so I was like, 'Dude, I hope he's crying for good reason. I guess he was a ball of emotion there, and so I was like, 'Did we actually win or not?'"

Hendrick, the winningest team owner in NASCAR history, made his way to victory lane on the actual fortieth anniversary of his first Cup start, which also came at Daytona.

"The first time we came here, we didn't think we had any business even being here," Hendrick said in victory lane. "We felt way out of our league. Now here we are forty years later. You couldn't write the script any better. To win this on the fortieth, to the day, it's just awesome."

Byron was in awe after winning the 500. He saw the race at a younger age as a fan from the other side of the fence.

"I'm just a kid [who came] from racing on computers to winning the Daytona 500. I can't believe it," Byron said.

Byron in victory lane with team owner Rick Hendrick at Texas Motor Speedway on September 24, 2023. Byron's win was historic, logging the 300th Cup Series victory for Hendrick Motorsports.

30 ALAN GUSTAFSON'S WINNING WAYS

Crew chief Alan Gustafson stands atop the pit box during a Cup Series race as he surveys the situation in hopes of helping his driver, Chase Elliott, improve his track position.

A look into Alan Gustafson's eyes shows that his mental wheels never stop turning. They have been spinning since his go-kart racing days with childhood friend Casey Yunick (grandson to legendary NASCAR team owner and engine builder Smokey Yunick) in Ormond Beach, Florida.

Gustafson worked with a friend in the Sports Car Club of America series after graduating from Seabreeze High School in Daytona Beach, Florida. He attended Embry-Riddle Aeronautical University to study mechanical engineering before moving to North Carolina to work in motorsports. Gustafson worked in the Goody's Dash Series with driver Jimmy Foster as well as on Andy Houston's Late Model Stock Car and NASCAR Craftsman Truck Series teams. A move to Diamond Ridge Motorsports in the NASCAR Busch Series (now NASCAR Xfinity Series) led to his joining Hendrick Motorsports first in the chassis department, then in 2000 as a shock specialist for the No. 5 team and driver Terry Labonte.

In 2002, he became the lead engineer for the No. 5 Chevrolet. Gustafson expressed an interest to Rick Hendrick that if a crew chief position was ever open, he would like to be considered. At the start of the 2005 season, Hendrick Motorsports announced he had been named crew chief for rookie driver Kyle Busch.

"I didn't really know what I was doing," Gustafson admitted. "I was certainly in over my head. I think everybody is when they start, and you just try to figure it out. Kyle was a young rookie, and I was a young rookie, and [neither] team at the time—that was the first year the number 5 team and number 25 team moved in together—was very good. I think the year before they were both twentieth or so in the points standing. There was a lot of work to do in getting the teams up to snuff with me managing my new job and Kyle getting acclimated.

Crew chief Gustafson (far right) and driver Kyle Busch at Atlanta Motor Speedway in 2007. Busch won one race and scored eleven top-five finishes that season to finish fifth in the Cup Series.

"Kyle had tons of talent" Gustafson continued. "By the middle of the season, we were getting the team infrastructure [together], he was doing better, and the performance was better." By the end of the 2005 season, Busch and Gustafson had achieved two wins.

During 2006 and 2007, the team recorded one win in each of the seasons and placed fifth in Cup Series points in 2007. Casey Mears drove for the team in 2008 after Busch left Hendrick Motorsports. For 2009, Mark Martin took the wheel and recorded five wins and a second-place finish in points. He remained through the 2010 season.

"It was pretty surreal for me," Gustafson said. "I've been a huge fan of his [Martin]. He was my guy growing up as a kid. I never dreamed of being his crew chief with him racing at fifty-one years old. As competitive as he was, I loved working with him. He's a dear friend of mine, and I have a huge amount of respect for him. He taught me a lot. It was fun to go through that experience with him and be able to learn from his perspective."

In 2011, Hendrick assigned Gustafson to Jeff Gordon's No. 24 team. That September, Gordon drove to victory at Atlanta Motor Speedway, marking his eighty-fifth-career win and placing him third on the all-time win list. The pair logged additional victories that season at Phoenix Raceway and Pocono Raceway along with thirteen top-five finishes, eighteen top-tens, and one pole position at Talladega Superspeedway.

Rick Hendrick (center) talks with driver Mark Martin (left) and his crew chief Gustafson at Richmond International Raceway in Richmond, Virginia, in 2009. Martin logged two top-five finishes that season at the ¾-mile short track.

Gustafson and four-time Cup Series champion Jeff Gordon at Bristol Motor Speedway in 2011. Gustafson and Gordon enjoyed three victories that season.

Across five seasons, Gustafson and Gordon recorded eleven wins, fifty-one top-five finishes, and ninety-seven top-tens. In Gordon's final full-time season of 2015, they reached the Championship 4 ahead of a third-place finish in the standings.

"Jeff is just an amazing person," Gustafson said. "And he's really a great guy, an amazing competitor, and a great driver to build a team around. Everybody has different abilities and strengths. Jeff, stem to stern, is just so good and really has no weaknesses. We're obviously still coworkers, but dear friends, too. That was really a great time for me."

In 2016, Gustafson began serving as Chase Elliott's crew chief. The team switched to the No. 9 in 2018, giving the No. 24 to William Byron and, as if receiving a lucky charm, Elliott and Gustafson proceeded to win Cup Series events at Watkins Glen International, Dover International Motor Speedway, and Kansas Speedway.

"With Chase, I was much more prepared, I think, than I was with Kyle," Gustafson explained. "It's nice to be able to take the experiences I had after working with Mark and going through the things that he had. And then Jeff and the things that he does, and the experiences with him and my experience up to that time, what I think would help Chase. It was much easier. We had a much better team and a much more solid foundation. We were in a much better position to succeed. I think we were ultra-competitive."

Even though Elliott and Gustafson went winless in 2016 and 2017, a foundation for future success was being built. Elliott finished second twice in races at Michigan International Speedway in June and August 2016, along with ten top-five finishes and seventeen top-tens for the season. In 2017, he logged more second-place finishes this time at Michigan in June, Chicago and Dover in September, Charlotte in October, and Phoenix in November. Despite the improvement, the path to victory lane eluded Elliott and Gustafson.

"Regret isn't the right word, but just the fact that we didn't win [was difficult]," Gustafson said. "We ran so good for the first couple of years, [but] we didn't win any races. I think we found every way possible to lose them, and then we finally kind of got going.

"We just hit the ground running [in 2018]. We had really good performance from the get-go. It worked out seamlessly. Chase makes things really easy on the car side and on my side of the job."

Through 2019, Gustafson had worked with several great drivers but had not won a Cup Series championship. He had come to the realization that it might never happen. Then in 2020 everything changed. Now his name is in the record book alongside Elliott's as a championship-winning driver and crew chief.

"Long story short, I had just gotten to a point in my career that, for whatever reason, I just couldn't seem to get it done. And then we did," Gustafson said. "It's a huge accomplishment because there are so many people, including Mark [Martin], who have tried for so many years and worked so hard and were not able to do it [win a championship]. So, to be able to win with Chase was a huge amount of validation, and it was a fantastic experience."

Elliott is happy that he helped make Gustafson's dream of becoming a championship-winning crew chief come true.

"One of the biggest pieces of enjoyment that I got out of winning the 2020 championship was achieving something that Alan hadn't

Chase Elliott (9) leads the field at Phoenix Raceway on November 8, 2020. Elliott won the race after starting from the pole position and clinched the Cup Series championship that day.

done," Elliott said. "Obviously, I hadn't done it either, but he's been doing this a lot longer than I have, and if anyone deserves that honor and that recognition, I feel he does.

"Through the course of my career, I take a lot of joy and pride in accomplishing things that he [Gustafson] hasn't [previously] done because he has definitely put in the time, and he's put in the work," Elliott said. "He's a guy that deserves those accolades. Now he can say he's won everything there is to win. That's pretty high on my list to check more boxes for him for as long as we're working together."

Hendrick is happy about the success Gustafson has enjoyed with so many drivers across his time at Hendrick Motorsports.

"Alan is a super-smart guy," Hendrick said. "When you ask me what impresses me the most about him, it's his loyalty, outside of his wins. He made a statement one time, saying he would sweep the floors at Hendrick Motorsports rather than go somewhere else. That's just the kind of person that he is. This is his home. I respect Alan so much for all the things he's done and for his contributions to the company."

Elliott shares the winner's circle champagne with crew chief Gustafson after clinching the 2020 NASCAR Cup Series championship at Phoenix Raceway.

31 / RICK'S REFUGE: THE HENDRICK HERITAGE CENTER

Hendrick Motorsports' extensive complex includes the Hendrick Heritage Center that houses much of Rick Hendrick's personal history.

The fifty-eight-thousand-square-foot Heritage Center is Rick Hendrick's tribute to his family as well as showcase for his classic and high-performance cars. Each automobile housed there is quite impressive, but there's so much more inside the special space that it almost takes one's breath away.

American muscle and performance cars are staged in context to his family's history, led by a colorful rainbow of 1967 Corvettes. It's all Hendrick's way of honoring his family, his roots, and expressing his passion for automobiles.

As a young man, Hendrick dreamed of having his own Corvette. When one became available locally for $1,000, it took three bank notes of borrowed money to finally make the car his.

Hendrick's passion for collecting began with two Chevrolets bought in the late 1970s. They paved the way for what has become more than 300 cars—and counting. Thus far, 122 145 of those cars in Hendrick's inventory are Corvettes.

"I've been collecting cars since 1978," Hendrick said. "In 1976, I had two matching Z-28 Camaros. I kept those cars and brought them up to City Chevrolet and put them in a hallway there. I needed money for expansion of the dealership, so I sold them.

"With my love for [1967] Corvettes, I tried to get one or two every year and put them away. So before collecting cars was a big fad, I had them in warehouses and different dealerships and little museums." But the story behind the Heritage Center runs even deeper. After the airplane accident in 2004 that took the lives of ten people associated with Hendrick Motorsports, the long process of rebuilding the organization began, both figuratively and emotionally. From the tragedy came ways to honor those lost, which included creating the Heritage Center.

"After the accident happened, some [Hendrick Motorsports] team members took Ricky's old [late model] trailer and buffed it and painted it and gave me the uniforms and helmets that he had

Hendrick's first car, a 1931 Chevrolet that he bought for $250 when he was only fourteen, is one of the many vehicles on display. He and his father, Papa Joe Hendrick, rebuilt the car and now it's been restored to its present pristine condition.

given them," Hendrick recalled. "I said then I was going to build a building for them. That's why we call it the Heritage Center. We pay tribute to my granddad's general store, the fire department he helped start, my mother's bank where she worked, the tractor shop where he built my 1931 Chevrolet, and the City Chevrolet dealership. I met Linda in the service station that's represented there, where I made a living putting camshafts in engines while I was going to school. There's the drag strip [in Person County, North Carolina] where I raced also.

"All of that helped me get started while I was growing up. It's about being able to pay tribute to the family."

The pain of losing so many loved ones was transformed by finding a way to honor them and pay tribute to the past. One can see firsthand just how important those special people were in Hendrick's life while he grew up in Palmer Springs, Virginia.

Hendrick stands alongside one of the drag boats that he raced in the late 1970s before turning his attention to creating Hendrick Motorsports.

This replica of City Chevrolet, Hendrick's flagship dealership, features several special Corvettes in the showroom and parked outside.

Hendrick's collection isn't just limited to Chevrolet, as other well-known brands have also been added over the years.

"With my love for cars, I've sort of gone over into some exotics," Hendrick said with a smile. "I started keeping Porsches years ago, and I love Ferraris. I pretty much have everything I want in the old Corvettes, [though] I'm still finding them. I have the first 1955, the first 1956, the first 1957, and I have just found the first 1958 that I'm restoring."

There's the mid-engine Corvette with VIN 0001 that was purchased at a charity auction for $3 million. The proceeds from the sale went to the Detroit Children's Fund.

In 1989, the first Corvette ZR1 rolled out of the Bowling Green, Kentucky, Corvette factory, and it is now in the Heritage Center. The museum also has King Leopold III of Belgium's two Corvettes: 1967 and 1971, both in silver. Other noteworthy additions include Roy Orbison's 1967 black Corvette and former Mexican President Gustavo Díaz Ordaz's 1967 white Corvette. Also on hand are fifty-three Camaros, both young and old, including VIN 0001 of the 2010 Camaro when it was resurrected. Several other cars have VIN numbers displaying number 1, indicating they were the first off the assembly line. There's also the 1968 Owens/Corning L-88 Corvette, the winningest Corvette race car in history.

Cars? Yes, there are plenty. There are also over 200 guitars once owned by some of the greatest musicians of all time. Jimi Hendrix and Bruce Springsteen's guitars are prominently displayed alongside 165 other notable autographed guitars from stars such as Eric Clapton, George Harrison, Tom Petty, and Zac Brown. Even a Charlie Daniels fiddle is there as one of the collection's most interesting pieces. Just as is the case with all of the cars on display, every guitar tells a fascinating story.

Hendrick loves making deals, and one of them involved rocker Sammy Hagar. Hendrick sold Hagar a red 1967 Corvette, and, to sweeten the pot, Hendrick received the guitar Hagar played in his video for "I Can't Drive 55."

The Heritage Center truly is an exceptional part of the Hendrick Motorsports campus that, done right, would take many hours to explore.

"I love going in there," Hendrick said. "I walk through and see cars I've owned thirty years, forty years, fifty years, and counting the 1931 Chevrolet I bought when I was fourteen years old, sixty years. To me, it's my happy place. I can tell you something about every car there. People love to see it. It's fun. It makes me feel good because it brings back so many great memories. I love to walk in there and walk back in time."

ABOVE: Rick Hendrick stands beside one of the Cup Series cars used in the movie *Days of Thunder*. The car sits inside the showroom of the City Chevrolet replica inside the Hendrick Heritage Center.

BELOW: "Little Joe's Speed Shop" is a tribute to Hendrick's father, Papa Joe Hendrick. The beautiful and subtly modified 1932 Chevrolet roadster speaks to Hendrick's long affiliation with the brand.

SECTION 4: 2010s

32 / HENDRICK MOTORSPORTS AND THE NASCAR HALL OF FAME

Rick Hendrick delivers his acceptance speech during his induction into the NASCAR Hall of Fame. His fellow Hall of Famers in 2017 were team owner Richard Childress, driver Mark Martin, team owner Raymond Parks, and driver/broadcaster Benny Parsons.

FOR HENDRICK MOTORSPORTS and its team members, induction into the NASCAR Hall of Fame was never a matter of if, but when. Its groundbreaking team owner and roster of legendary drivers, crew chiefs, and other accomplished contributors all but ensure a steady stream of honorees.

The final decision as to who is inducted each year is made by an esteemed voting panel that includes NASCAR representatives, manufacturers, track operators, broadcasters, media members, car owners, and drivers—and even one ballot from a nationwide fan vote. The Hall of Fame, which is located in Charlotte, North Carolina, inducted its inaugural class in 2010.

Darrell Waltrip was the first Hendrick Motorsports alumnus to enter the Hall of Fame as part of the class of 2012. He was followed in 2016 by two-time Cup Series champion Terry Labonte. Through 2024, more than a dozen people with ties to the team have been enshrined.

Owner Rick Hendrick, who helped spearhead the effort to establish the Hall of Fame in Charlotte, was inducted as part of the class of 2017. Fellow inductees that year were Benny Parsons, Mark Martin, Raymond Parks, and Richard Childress. Among the group, Parsons drove for Hendrick Motorsports in 1987, and Martin recorded five wins for the organization from 2009 through 2011.

Inductees are honored for NASCAR accomplishments and contributions to the sport. Over Hendrick's long involvement in racing, he has met those standards both personally and professionally.

Under his leadership, Hendrick Motorsports grew from five employees in its inaugural 1984 season to nearly six hundred. Through the end of the 2023 season, his Cup Series teams had amassed 301 Cup Series wins with twenty different drivers—more than any other outfit in NASCAR history.

Hendrick pioneered multi-car teams in the modern era and has garnered a NASCAR-record fourteen Cup Series championships, plus three in the Craftsman Truck Series and one in the Xfinity Series.

No matter what level of success he achieves, Hendrick remains humble and appreciative of his organization's accomplishments, crediting those around him for all they've done to bring wins and championships to the team.

In his Hall of Fame acceptance speech, Hendrick reflected on the lean times he and his wife, Linda, shared before Hendrick Motorsports was even a thought.

"There has been nobody that has sacrificed what you have sacrificed for me to do what I've done," Hendrick said to his wife. "She stood in the back of the grocery store with me and we counted our money before we went to the checkout line. Our bed in our first house had three legs and a Muncie gearbox for the fourth. When we were boat racing, she was selling T-shirts from the back of the trailer so we could raise enough money to go back and do it again."

Much has happened since those days of barely getting by. Over a period of four decades, Hendrick Motorsports has become a cornerstone of NASCAR, with its teams known as the strongest in the business.

For Hendrick, there are times when he sits back and recalls when being a part of the sport was nothing more than a seemingly impossible dream.

"It's just so hard for me to believe that a kid growing up on a rural tobacco farm in Virginia that dreamed about racing, hot rods, and waiting [to meet] Linda—those were the three things—and always wanting to be involved in racing somehow," Hendrick said. "I didn't know what I wanted to do in life, but I knew what I didn't want to do and that was to be a tobacco farmer.

"I wouldn't take anything for the time I spent with my mom and dad. They taught me something that has really been the pillar of my life: you need to take care of other people if you want people to take care of you. You need to take care of your neighbors and you need to do for others and good things will happen to you. God really blessed me by giving me terrific parents. My dad taught me how to work with my hands. It was racing that got me into the automobile business. I think back to all those lessons."

Hendrick has always realized the importance of those around him for his success in life and his rise to the top in the world of auto racing. From the people sweeping the floor to those who have lifted championship trophies, each individual has played a vital role in making Hendrick Motorsports what it is today.

"As I accept this award tonight, I think about all the people [at Hendrick Motorsports]," Hendrick said that evening. "I can't name them all, but you know who you are. Every person from the very beginning to today—everyone that laid a brick is part of this. Together we achieve more. I believe that with all my heart. I love this sport. I love the fact that we are a family. Every driver and mechanic that has been a part of it, I accept this on your behalf—past and present. It's faith, family, and friends that get you through life. When it's all over, it's the people that you've touched and the lives you've changed in this world that make a difference."

Past and present Hendrick Motorsports team members inducted into the NASCAR Hall of Fame include, from left to right, four-time champion and vice chairman Jeff Gordon (2019); seven-time champion Jimmie Johnson (2024); crew chief and vice president of competition Chad Knaus (2024); Hendrick Motorsports owner Rick Hendrick (2017); two-time champion Terry Labonte (2016); driver Dale Earnhardt Jr. (2021); and crew chief Ray Evernham (2018). Other Hendrick Motorsports inductees not pictured include former drivers Darrell Waltrip (2012), Mark Martin (2017), and Benny Parsons (2017) and crew chief Waddell Wilson (2020).

Alongside Parsons, Martin, Waltrip, and Labonte, Hendrick Motorsports drivers Jeff Gordon (2019), Dale Earnhardt Jr. (2021), and Jimmie Johnson (2024) have also been enshrined. Crew chiefs honored include Ray Evernham (2018), Waddell Wilson (2020), and Chad Knaus (2024).

Johnson and Knaus tallied seven Cup Series championships in Hendrick Motorsports' Chevrolets, including an incredible five in a row, and established a dynasty that will never be forgotten.

"We clicked right away with similar interests and with everything to prove," Johnson said. "We spent a lot of time together and became great friends. We could read each other's minds. He would somehow vividly understand what I was going through behind [his] laptop. His work ethic and ability to bring the best out of me was most impressive."

Johnson's words reflect the collaboration that has defined Hendrick Motorsports for forty years and will ensure many more Hall of Fame inductees for the team.

TOP: Rick and Linda Hendrick answer questions from members of the media after his induction.

BOTTOM: Chad Knaus (left) and Jimmie Johnson (right) were inducted into the NASCAR Hall of Fame in 2024. Here they are joined by 2017 inductee, team owner Rick Hendrick.

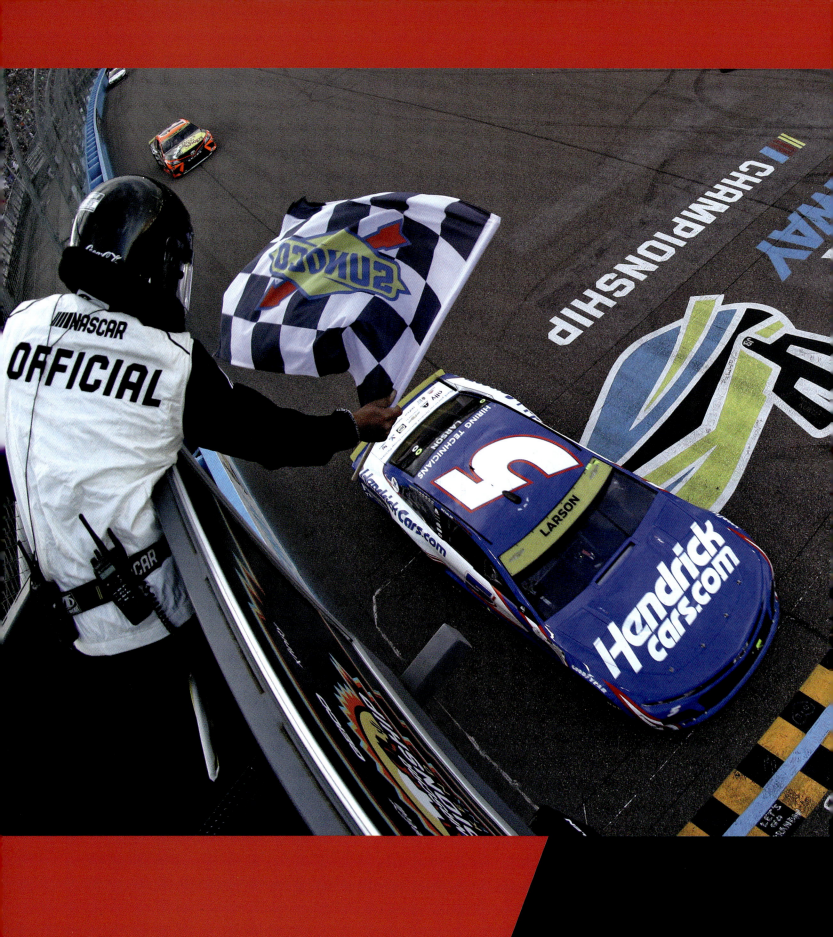

2020s

SECTION 5

33 THE ENDURING LEGACY OF RANDY DORTON

The Hendrick Motorsports engine program fostered by Randy Dorton is a keystone to the organization's ongoing success, now more than 300 Cup wins strong.

Rick Hendrick aboard one of his drag boats in the early 1980s. Dorton built engines that Hendrick used in his racing boats during that time.

With Kyle Larson's win September 3, 2023, in the 2023 NASCAR Cup Series playoff opener at Darlington Raceway, the Hendrick Motorsports engine department recorded its milestone five hundredth win in a NASCAR national series.

Through that Larson win, the tally was 356 Cup Series wins, 122 wins in the NASCAR Xfinity Series, and 22 victories in the Craftsman Truck Series division.

Geoff Bodine won the first Cup Series race at Martinsville Speedway in Virginia on April 29, 1984. Win number one hundred came at Dover, Delaware, with Jimmie Johnson on June 2, 2002. Win two hundred was Mark Martin's victory at Phoenix Raceway on April 18, 2009. Chase Elliott driving the No. 9 for JR Motorsports in the Xfinity Series earned victory three hundred at Darlington, South Carolina, on April 11, 2014. Number four hundred went to Kyle Larson in the No. 42 Chevrolet for Chip Ganassi Racing in the Xfinity Series at Daytona International Speedway on July 6, 2018, with an engine provided by Hendrick Motorsports. Larson's Darlington triumph for victory number five hundred came on September 3, 2023.

Larry Zentmeyer, a member of Hendrick Motorsports' engine department since 1988, has been with the team for all but fifteen of its points-paying Cup Series wins.

"You never think about that stuff [while working]," Zentmeyer said to sum up the milestone. "A lot of things have to go right. To think that something has gone right five hundred times, that's pretty unbelievable."

In the Cup Series, the engine shop supplies Chevrolet engines to their own Hendrick Motorsports teams as well as JTG Daugherty Racing and Spire Motorsports. For the Xfinity Series, it supports JR Motorsports, DGM Racing, and its own partial schedule. In the past, the engine department also provided engines for programs including Darrell Waltrip Racing, Chip Ganassi Racing, Stewart-Haas Racing, and Joe Gibbs Racing (when the latter two raced Chevrolets).

Hendrick Motorsports' engine shop has a storied history that began with one man back in 1984. Randy Dorton even had a role in introducing Rick Hendrick to Harry Hyde before the first Chevrolets were bought to start All-Star Racing for its inaugural season with Bodine as the team's first driver. Dorton had worked as Hyde's engine builder during other Cup Series ventures.

"I was running my own shop, Competition Engines, out of space I rented in Harry's building," Dorton said in *Twenty Years of Hendrick Motorsports*. "I had been doing some of the work on Rick's race boats and some other work for City Chevrolet when I was introduced to Rick for the first time.

"After that, Rick made a couple of random visits. Rick wanted to talk with Harry because he needed a place to store his boats and some other stuff. I was only using about thirty-five hundred feet of that ten thousand-square-foot building but Harry had other ideas for using the rest of that building other than as storage. When Rick approached Harry about using the rest of the building, Harry fed him this sad story about wanting another chance to go racing and eventually talked Rick into starting a team."

After Dorton built three initial engines for Hendrick in the fall of 1983, he never produced motors for anyone else. In May 1984, Hendrick bought Competition Engines and made it his in-house supplier. Dorton became the lead engine builder and delivered some of the best engines in the industry. He also was heavily involved in research and development with General Motors and provided other teams with leased engines.

Dorton passed away on October 24, 2004, in the Hendrick Motorsports airplane accident while traveling to Martinsville Speedway for a Cup Series race.

Jeff Andrews, president and general manager of Hendrick Motorsports, worked alongside Dorton in the engine department and knew him very well as a colleague and close friend.

"Randy was incredibly passionate about engines," Andrews said. "More importantly, or as important, was his shop and employees. He had this insatiable quest for technology. He was always hunting, always looking for the next advancement, always looking for ways to make our program better. I always considered Randy a true visionary because of his forward thinking and the way he went out and sought and brought technology into the sport.

"Dorton was known for his calm demeanor. I never saw him frustrated or nervous," Andrews said, "although I certainly knew there were times and situations that had to bother him on the inside, but he didn't show it on the outside. His office door was always open. He always made time for you and all of his employees. I was fortunate enough to spend time away from work with him as well. We had a lot of dinners together at his house. I consider him today to be one of my best friends in life. He was a true mentor to me, professionally and personally. Through him, I learned how to treat people and the importance of relationships and building a team, how important everyone was to the success of a program from top to bottom."

Andrews feels having over five hundred engine wins for Hendrick Motorsports in the record books is quite an accomplishment.

"For me, it's a testament to commitment," Andrews said. "Mr. Hendrick and Randy formed a partnership in 1984. It started with win number one, and almost forty years later [at Darlington Raceway] win number five hundred; that is just incredible to me. It's almost an unimaginable accomplishment if you think about the time frame and what it took to do that. It's humbling to know that Randy's program continues today and continues to have so much success. I think it's truly a way to pay tribute to Randy and

Dorton (left) with Jeff Gordon in victory lane at Darlington Raceway on August 31, 1997. By winning the race, Gordon also won a $1 million bonus from R. J. Reynolds Tobacco Co., then the Cup Series sponsor.

Mr. Hendrick for their commitment and their passion. And along the way, the importance of our people. We've certainly had our bumps in the road with the engine program, but at the end of the day, we believed in each other and believe in the motto, 'We win together and lose together as a team.'"

Hendrick thinks of Dorton often and what was planned for him had he been able to continue with Hendrick Motorsports.

"Randy Dorton was more than our engine guy," Hendrick said. "When I started, I had Harry Hyde, but I also had Randy. Randy had a racing background with [drag racing legends] Sox and Martin with his little engine shop. He was getting ready to close it down. I got him to continue, and we worked together. Randy was more like a general manager for the racing operation, really. I leaned on Randy a lot. He was way, way more than just the engine guy. Randy helped run the place and helped build the place.

"I look at Jeff Gordon, Jimmie Johnson, Chad Knaus, and Ray Evernham and all of their contributions too, but if it wasn't for Randy Dorton, I don't believe Hendrick Motorsports would be here today."

Jeff Andrews, president and general manager of Hendrick Motorsports, was Dorton's close friend and once worked with him in Hendrick's engine department.

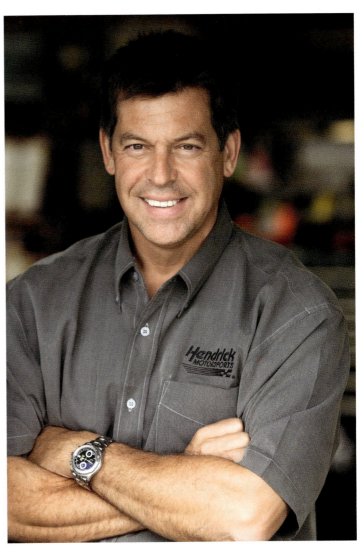

The late Randy Dorton, shown in this 2004 photo, was one of the first employees of Hendrick Motorsports and was considered a vital part of the organization. In 2024, he was nominated for the NASCAR Hall of Fame for the first time.

34 / 1-2-3-4: ALEX BOWMAN LEADS HISTORIC DOVER FINISH

Alex Bowman streaks to the finish line ahead of teammates Kyle Larson, Chase Elliott, and William Byron in Hendrick Motorsports' 1-2-3-4 sweep of Dover in 2021.

One could say Alex Bowman began his racing career by hanging out with his father, Sean. The two began watching NASCAR Cup Series races when Bowman was just seven, and he became interested in the career path of four-time Cup Series champion Jeff Gordon.

"My dad knew that Jeff started racing quarter midgets at a very young age," Bowman said. "There was a local track starting up, and one day my dad showed up with a quarter midget. That's how it started and took off from there. That was in 1999 or 2000."

Bowman traveled a long road before finding his place at Hendrick Motorsports. He started his racing career on short tracks in Arizona and California, wheeling quarter midgets in USAC (United States Auto Club) events. Six years later at age thirteen, he had a personal win tally that included nine national championships and 165 feature victories. His record certainly garnered the attention of many in the open-wheel racing world.

In 2008, Bowman collected eleven victories and won the USAC National Focus Midget championship. He won the California Dirt Focus Midget championship and was USAC National Midget Rookie of the Year in 2009. In 2011, Bowman entered the ARCA Menards Series competition, winning twice for Venturini Motorsports. A move to full-time with Cunningham Motorsports as a development driver for Penske Racing produced four additional victories.

ABOVE: Bowman is interviewed at New Hampshire Motor Speedway on July 16, 2016, before his first Cup Series start with Hendrick Motorsports.

BELOW: Bowman, triumphant, after winning the Xfinity Series race at Charlotte Motor Speedway on October 7, 2017.

Bowman's tenure in NASCAR's Xfinity Series included a full-time season in 2013 (when it was the Nationwide Series) for Robby Benton. Through the years, his time in that series included drives for Hendrick Motorsports, JR Motorsports, and Tony Townley, to name a few.

In 2014, he made his Cup Series debut with a full season driving for BK Racing. The following season he moved to Tommy Baldwin Racing. After being released from Baldwin's team, Bowman searched for any way possible to stay in NASCAR.

"When you're driving for really small teams, you have your little victories," Bowman said. "I learned a lot, and I got to make a lot of mistakes with nobody watching. I think it definitely prepared me for being able to get into Hendrick Motorsports."

Bowman's racing career took some very interesting turns beginning in 2016. While driving in the Xfinity Series for JR Motorsports, Bowman received a call from Kenny Francis of Hendrick Motorsports inviting him to work with the organization's simulator program. During that time, Greg Ives, crew chief for Dale Earnhardt Jr., reached out with an unexpected opportunity.

"Greg called me and said, 'Hey, we've always had a backup driver for Dale [Earnhardt Jr.],'" Bowman recalled. 'It's about being ready to go at any time. We don't really have that right now. We wanted to see if you were interested.' And I was like, 'Of course.'"

Bowman's mental wheels were turning as fast as the wheels on the cars he drove. Something was up, and he realized he was being pressed into action.

"They weren't looking for a far-off backup situation. There was a problem," Bowman explained. "Two days later, a Thursday afternoon [July 14, 2016], I got a call and they were like, 'Hey, there's a plane waiting. We need for you need to be at the airport in thirty minutes.'"

There was a Cup Series race scheduled for Loudon, New Hampshire, on July 17. Ives knew Bowman was the right driver to fill Earnhardt Jr.'s open seat.

"I knew Alex from being at JR Motorsports when he was there and seeing him come to Hendrick Motorsports," Ives said. "Dale got hurt, and that was a hard process for me, going through a couple of races trying to figure it all out. Dale called me and said, 'I don't think I'm good to go this weekend [New Hampshire]. I asked if he had called Mr. H, and he said I was the first person he called. We didn't have a backup driver in place, and that's how Alex came into the conversation.

"I knew Dale had put a lot of thought into it, not just when he got hurt but prior to all of this. It was about his belief in Alex, and his vision for Alex and what his capabilities were. So, I called Alex and told him to come to the shop, and that I needed him to be a backup driver for Dale. I wanted Dale to have that conversation with Mr. Hendrick, but I also wanted to have Alex ready to go in case that was going to be the plan."

Bowman exited the simulator, making up a reason he needed to leave. A day later, he found himself strapping into the No. 88 Hendrick Motorsports Chevrolet as a relief driver to Earnhardt Jr.

Earnhardt Jr. had been involved in an accident in the June 12 race at Michigan International Speedway. Initially, Earnhardt Jr. thought that symptoms following the incident were from a sinus infection, but with his history of concussions, doctors determined he had actually sustained a head injury.

Driving for the absent Earnhardt Jr. at New Hampshire Motor Speedway, Bowman was running in the top ten before an accident doomed him to twenty-sixth place. Gordon drove the next four races in place of Earnhardt, with a best finish of eleventh at Bristol Motor Speedway. However, Gordon was not available to drive at Michigan, putting Bowman front and center as a potential replacement, once again, for that August 28 race.

"In early 2016, I was selling my own seats to pay rent, and by the end of 2016, I bought a house. It was a very life-changing year for me," Bowman said. " It was also pretty intimidating, honestly. You know, taking over the 88 ride from Dale. It's hype and expectations to live up to. Obviously, Dale was super popular, so to get to drive that car was really special."

Following Earnhardt Jr.'s final full-time season in 2017, Bowman took the reins of the No. 88 for the next three seasons. He then shifted to the No. 48 in 2021 after Jimmie Johnson's final full-time season with Hendrick Motorsports.

Bowman's seven career Cup Series victories are impressive, dating back to June 30, 2019, at Chicagoland Speedway. Other wins have come at Auto Club Speedway in 2020; Richmond Raceway, Dover Motor Speedway, Pocono Raceway, and Martinsville Speedway in 2021; and Las Vegas Motor Speedway in 2022.

The most rewarding of them came at Dover on May 16, 2021, when he led teammates Kyle Larson, Chase Elliott, and William Byron to a 1-2-3-4 finish for Hendrick Motorsports. It was the first time the organization had ever swept the top-four positions in a single event.

"There were a lot of reasons that was a special win," Bowman said. "Dover has become my best racetrack and one of my favorite tracks. We should have won there a couple times before and after that, so honestly, it's so cool to be on the front side of that. Obviously, it was a historic day for Hendrick Motorsports. That gives me a little bit more bragging rights over my teammates, and that's never a bad thing. So yeah, it was a great day for us.

"To get to work with Ally Financial and everybody that's involved on the program has been super cool. We've won races together right off the bat. It's been a lot of fun."

Bowman has an incredible amount of respect for his team owner and deeply appreciates the opportunity to drive for Hendrick Motorsports.

"Mr. H is just incredible with everything that he's doing," Bowman said. "He could be doing whatever the heck he wants. He chooses to continue to run these companies and to continue to be such a huge part of my life and everybody's life at Hendrick Motorsports. We all want to win for him. Hendrick Motorsports is a special place, and he's a special guy. He worked super hard. When he talks, everybody listens, and he cares about everybody. Not just those that work for him but also those that surround him in his life."

Bowman stands and salutes the fans after winning at Chicagoland Speedway on June 30, 2019. Bowman led 49 of the race's 267 laps.

Bowman led the field in the closing laps of the Cup Series event at Dover Motor Speedway on May 21, 2021, to take the checkered for his fourth of seven career victories (through 2023).

On May 21, 2021, Alex Bowman led all four Hendrick Motorsports Chevrolets to a first-, second-, third-, and fourth-place sweep finish. Hendrick Motorsports team members pose for a commemorative photo with team owner Rick Hendrick as well as the drivers and crew chiefs.

35 — 269: A NEW WINS RECORD

Kyle Larson, driver of the No. 5 Hendrick Motorsports Chevrolet, holds the checkered flag after winning the Coca-Cola 600 at Charlotte Motor Speedway on May 30, 2021. It was Hendrick Motorsports' 269th victory, surpassing Petty Enterprises' long-standing wins record.

Jimmie Johnson logged Hendrick Motorsports' two hundredth victory on May 12, 2012, at Darlington Raceway in Darlington, South Carolina.

To the delight of a sold-out crowd at Martinsville Speedway on April 18, 1999, John Andretti drove the famed No. 43 to win number 268 for Petty Enterprises in its 1,703rd race. For over sixty years, Petty Enterprises held the record for the most NASCAR Cup Series wins by an organization, beginning on May 29, 1960, when Lee Petty earned the team's fifty-third victory at Orange Speedway. Sixty-one years and one day to the date, Hendrick Motorsports won its 269th race and took over the all-time wins record.

Several legendary drivers had added their names to what was long believed to be an untouchable number in the win column for the iconic Petty operation based in Level Cross, North Carolina. Seven-time Cup Series champion Richard Petty's 196 victories had added to Lee Petty's 54, which were further augmented by Jim Paschal's 9 wins, Pete Hamilton's 3, 2 each for Bobby Hamilton and Buddy Baker, and 1 each for Marvin Panch and John Andretti.

On May 30, 2021, the record fell when Kyle Larson won the Coca-Cola 600 at Charlotte Motor Speedway, giving Hendrick Motorsports its record 269th victory, the most in NASCAR Cup Series history.

Larson's win was the eighth of his Cup Series career and the second of his 2021 championship season. He topped teammate Chase Elliott by 10.051 seconds at the finish after leading 327 of 400 laps. Larson's only real challenges during the race came from Elliott, who led twenty-two laps, and another teammate, William Byron, who led nineteen.

"It feels great to be that guy who helped Mr. H break that record finally," Larson said.

Elliott had tied the record a week earlier with a victory on May 23 at the Circuit of The Americas road course in Austin, Texas.

Anyone who followed NASCAR, even remotely, knew of Petty Enterprises. Hendrick, who got Richard Petty's autograph as a young fan at Martinsville Speedway, certainly did.

"It feels good. I can't believe we got 269." Hendrick said. "The first one [win] was with the number 5 [Geoffrey Bodine in 1984], and this

John Andretti, driver of the No. 43 Petty Enterprises Pontiac, scored the 268th and final Cup Series victory for Petty Enterprises on April 18, 1999, at Martinsville Speedway.

one was the number 5 [with Larson]. I just remember how close it was not to finish out the first year."

In 2024, Hendrick Motorsports fields Chevrolets for Kyle Larson, Chase Elliott, Alex Bowman, and William Byron. Hendrick feels he has the very best drivers competing in the Cup Series and wants all of them to succeed in every race they enter.

"It's like having a bunch of kids," Hendrick said. "You love them all the same. It's just each one of them has different strengths and characteristics, but at the end of the day, they work well together.

"I didn't care who broke the record. I just wanted to win it. Any one of them—I pull for them all the same. It's tough when they're battling each other for the lead, but the objective in this race was to win it. Whoever could win it, that was great.

"The fact that 5 was my first number, and we decided to go back to it that year, it's pretty neat that that was the car [that won]."

There was a time when Hendrick wondered if his organization would reach such a lofty milestone. On May 12, 2012, Jimmie Johnson collected the two hundredth victory for Hendrick Motorsports at Darlington Raceway. Nine years passed before the additional sixty-nine victories were recorded.

"We were at 200 wins, just thinking how you're going to win 269 and beat the [Petty's] number," Hendrick said. "I never thought we'd get there, and then all of a sudden, the momentum started, and we had a good run.

"I want to say this about Richard: he's a class act. He has done more for the sport than anybody I know of. He's still the same Richard to all the fans. I have tremendous respect for the Petty family and what they've accomplished. Someone will probably break my record, and records are made to be broken."

Hendrick goes back to that first flagship win as the foundation of all good things for Hendrick Motorsports, as well as blessings and good fortune.

"If we hadn't won that race in Martinsville, we wouldn't be here today," Hendrick said. "God has blessed our company, and we've had a lot of great luck, and I don't take that for granted. We've had a lot of good breaks along the way and just good people."

To reach the milestone a stone's throw from the Hendrick Motorsports campus made the achievement even more special.

"I really wanted to break the record at home. I really wanted to do it in Charlotte," Hendrick said. "When the race started and it looked like we were going to be really strong, and all of them running in the top five, I thought we've really got a shot.

"I remember that I started about a mile from [the track] in a little tin building and never thought I'd win a NASCAR race. I didn't think I belonged when I got to Daytona the first time, when I looked at the Wood Brothers and Junior Johnson and Richard Petty, and I'm like, 'I don't know what I'm doing here.' I think about all those things, and I think about breaking this record because, again, it's huge for our company to win 269 races."

Three-time NASCAR champion Darrell Waltrip won nine of those races during his tenure with Hendrick Motorsports from 1987 through 1990, including the 1989 Daytona 500. He retired from driving in 2000 but has remained great friends with Hendrick.

"Rick has been, by far and away, my biggest mentor and one of my best friends," Waltrip said. "He's a visionary. His vision of what he thought the company could be, what he thought the company could do, the multi-car teams—he's done it all, and he's done it well."

Chase Elliott, driver of the No. 9 Hendrick Motorsports Chevrolet, tied Hendrick Motorsports with Petty Enterprises with 268 Cup Series victories with his win at the Circuit of The Americas road course in Austin, Texas, on May 23, 2021.

Drivers and crew members from all Hendrick Motorsports teams gather after Larson won the 269th Cup Series race for the organization. Larson led 328 of 400 laps in the event at Charlotte Motor Speedway.

SECTION 5: 2020s

36 / WASTING NO TIME: KYLE LARSON DOMINATES 2021 SEASON

Kyle Larson (left) and crew chief Cliff Daniels celebrate after winning the 2021 Cup Series championship. Larson and Daniels amassed ten victories during their remarkable 2021 season.

Larson crosses under the checkered flag at Kansas Speedway on October 24, 2021, his ninth of ten wins that season. Larson has recorded seventeen wins (through 2023) with Hendrick Motorsports, more wins in the flagship No. 5 Hendrick Motorsports Chevrolet than any other driver in the organization's forty-year history.

Going into the final race of the 2021 NASCAR Cup Series season at Phoenix Raceway, the overall feeling for the team, fans, and media was that the championship was Kyle Larson's to lose.

Larson and crew chief Cliff Daniels had dominated the season with nine wins, nineteen top-five finishes, and twenty-five top-tens going into the championship-deciding final event. The No. 5 Hendrick Motorsports team was confident they could win the Cup Series championship against fellow contenders Martin Truex Jr., Denny Hamlin, and teammate Chase Elliott. They had prepared carefully going into the final race of the season at Phoenix and hoped they would perform flawlessly during the 312-lap race.

Plus, Larson had something no other team had going into the race: momentum. The Elk Grove, California, driver had a feeling that things would go his way from start to finish. Daniels had spent days going over Larson's car, tuning his strategy and practicing pit stops with their crew. Nothing had been left to chance.

The momentum was built throughout the season with wins at Las Vegas Motor Speedway in March; a three-victory streak at Charlotte Motor Speedway, Sonoma Raceway, and Nashville Superspeedway in May and June; Watkins Glen International in August; Bristol Motor Speedway in September; and another three wins in a row at the Charlotte Motor Speedway ROVAL, Texas Motor Speedway, and Kansas Speedway in October. It was a dream season. Still, one more race was left to run, and anything could happen.

Once the green flag fell to start the 312-lap race, it was business as usual, but there were certainly nerves to be calmed throughout the race, as many things could go wrong in the blink of an eye that could toss that perfect season out the window.

Ahead of the final restart on lap 289, a flawless pit stop during the caution flag set Larson up for the title. Winning the pole position had granted Larson the first pit stall and a perfect advantage to gain the lead over Truex Jr., Hamlin, and Elliott after entering pit road in fourth. The entire season came down to one stop, and the HendrickCars.com crew got their driver out first. Larson went on to win his tenth points-paying race of 2021 and ice the title for fourteenth Cup Series championship for Hendrick Motorsports.

"There were so many points in the race where I did not think we were going to win," Larson said during his championship celebration. "Without my pit crew on that last stop, we would not be standing right here. They're the true winners of this race. They're the

Larson makes a pit stop and the Hendrick Motorsports No. 5 team, led by crew chief Daniels, leaps into action. Throughout the thirty-six-race season, the five-man over-the-wall crew helped Larson gain track position with extremely fast stops for tires and fuel on pit road.

Larson takes the checkered flag in the final race of the 2021 season at Phoenix Raceway. The victory also secured the Cup Series championship for Larson and the No. 5 Hendrick Motorsports team.

true champions. I'm just blessed to be a part of this group."

Truex Jr. could see Larson's rear bumper in the closing laps but simply couldn't catch him, with the Joe Gibbs Racing driver coming up short of his second career championship. Hamlin finished third, with 2020 Cup Series champion Chase Elliott finishing fifth.

"I knew the only way we were going to pull it off is if our pit crew got us off as a leader, and damn, they did," Larson said. "That was just crazy. I tried to do as good of a job as I could down pit road without speeding, getting my sign as good as I could, and those guys nailed the pit stop and got us out the leader.

"I still had to fight through," he added. "Martin was really fast behind me. Our car was just gripped up enough for that length of a run that we could hold them off."

Larson enjoyed the best season of his career and became just one of eleven drivers in the modern era to win ten or more races in a single season.

"I think just thinking about the journey and how tough of a road it's been to get to this point for so long, but especially the last year and a half," Larson said. " I haven't felt an atmosphere like this maybe ever. With the pressure of this race and everything that was on the line, to win this championship—every one of these fans made me feel it. I was trying to tell myself to just chill out, stop tearing up. I make fun of my dad all the time for crying, and I'm worse than he is."

Daniels felt that the relationship and chemistry outside the race car was a huge plus during the season. After Larson's win at Charlotte in May, he was asked what was important to him.

"I think, really, just to continue to deepen our connection, our friendship, our working relationship," he explained. "I think the sky really is the limit for him. We know how talented he is in any car that he gets in. There are some things that he tries to avoid thinking when there's a lot of second-place finishes that line up. He tries not to be too hard on himself, and I've been able to kind of tap into some of that with him and help him with that. So, yeah, it's been a great journey so far. Still a lot of learning and growing to do, and I'm certainly excited about it, and I think there's a lot of potential for both of us."

Daniels also offered another observation about what makes Larson a great driver in all forms of racing, no matter what type of car he drives.

"Obviously one of the biggest things that I've learned, and this is going to sound really obvious to say, he spends so much time reading a dirt track for all of these races that he goes to," Daniels said. "He watches every series that ends up on [a particular] track, and he really studies what's going on with the racetrack.

"So, for us, the more I can give him information on what I anticipate for our pavement surfaces going into a weekend, whether it's PJ1, clouds versus sun, temp changes, things like that, that's something that's just very natural for him, and again, that's what he spends a lot of his time doing to make him good on the dirt tracks. So again, it may sound obvious to say, but that's probably the biggest thing."

In 2022 and 2023, Larson added seven additional Cup Series wins for a career total of twenty-three going into the 2024 season.

Larson stands with the NASCAR Cup Series championship trophy after winning his first career title in 2021. The Elk Grove, California, native completed his eleventh year in NASCAR's premier series in 2023.

Team owner Rick Hendrick (left) with Larson after winning the 2021 Cup Series championship. Securing Hendrick Motorsports' fourteenth Cup title was a fitting way to cap off a spectacular ten-victory season.

37 / JEFF GORDON: TAKIN' CARE OF BUSINESS

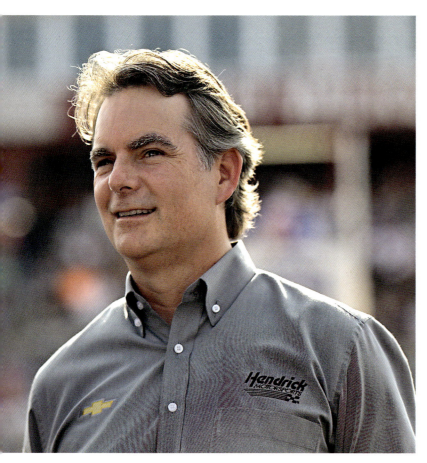

NASCAR Cup champion Jeff Gordon now serves as vice chairman of Hendrick Motorsports. The Vallejo, California, native won ninety-three races and four championships as a driver from 1992 through 2016.

From his first NASCAR Cup Series start on November 15, 1992, at Atlanta Motor Speedway until his last race on October 30, 2016, at Virginia's Martinsville Speedway, Jeff Gordon collected four championships and ninety-three wins while driving for Hendrick Motorsports. Over twenty-five years of racing, his name was on the roofline of multicolored Chevrolets built and serviced by some of the greatest crew chiefs, crew members, and engineers in the sport. After his racing retirement, Gordon went on to a successful career as a NASCAR race analyst for FOX Sports through 2021.

On January 1, 2022, Gordon took on his biggest role outside a Cup car cockpit: Hendrick Motorsports vice chairman. He is the second-ranking member of the organization to chairman and owner Rick Hendrick.

It's a role that Gordon cherishes. Hendrick Motorsports has been a huge part of his life since he joined the team in 1992. By that point, he had chosen stock cars over his childhood dream of becoming an IndyCar driver with hopes of winning the Indianapolis 500.

Gordon became an equity owner of Hendrick Motorsports in 1999, and he continues to be the only partner in the organization. He was first listed as the co-owner of the No. 48 Chevrolet when seven-time champion Jimmie Johnson began his tenure with the organization in 2001.

Hendrick, who splits his time between Hendrick Automotive Group and Hendrick Motorsports, says moving Gordon into a management role was a natural progression following his storied driving career and a successful broadcasting stint with FOX Sports.

"Jeff has been super special to me and my family," Hendrick said. "I like to look at him like a little brother rather than a son because that makes me feel too old. We've had a special relationship for a long time. I care about him a lot and love him. He has done a lot for the company. He helped build the company. He stuck with me when Ray [Evernham] left Hendrick Motorsports. Jeff could have gone with Ray, but he didn't. He's always done what he's had to do for the sake of the company. He deserves it [the vice chairmanship] and I need him."

Hendrick has come a long way and enjoys unparalleled success in NASCAR's Cup Series with 301-career victories and fourteen championships through 2023. He sees Gordon as a key component of carrying the organization forward.

"I remember when I was the youngest team owner on pit road by far and now I'm one of the oldest," Hendrick said. "Forty years is a long time. I want to carry on the heritage of our organization. My grandson loves it. Jeff Gordon loves it. His name and what his contribution has been to the company makes him perfect for that role.

"Just like the automobile side, I want to see it go on when I'm not around. Jeff will make that happen for Hendrick Motorsports."

Jeff Andrews, president and general manager of Hendrick Motorsports, has worked with Gordon for many years. He has also served as director of engine operations and vice president of competition during his time at Hendrick Motorsports.

"Obviously, Jeff's accomplishments on track speak for themselves," Andrews said. "What he is doing for our company behind the scenes is incredible. He has a true passion for winning and, of course, he knows what it takes to do that on the track. Watching him behind the scenes with our business and marketing groups, I'm personally learning from him and growing with Jeff in that area. Obviously, he bleeds Hendrick Motorsports and his dedication to the company is very strong.

"Once again, Mr. Hendrick has the best-laid plans and has always found a way to get the right people in the right positions and I don't think that's ever been truer with Jeff."

It's no secret that Ricky Hendrick was the heir apparent once his father stepped away. Fate had other plans, leaving a void that was almost impossible to fill. Gordon's ability to master everything he

Gordon became co-owner of the No. 48 Hendrick Motorsports Chevrolet when the team was formed at the start of the 2001 Cup Series season. Jimmie Johnson was the car's driver until he retired from full-time NASCAR competition at the end of 2020.

has ever been a part of made him an obvious choice to help lead Hendrick Motorsports into the future.

"I've always been impressed with his business instincts," Hendrick said of Gordon. "On some level, he's been involved in every major decision we've made over the last two decades, and his influence has continued to grow since he stopped driving. He understands our culture, our values, and the importance we place on our people and our partnerships.

"I love racing and competing, and Jeff is the only person I know who hates to lose as much as I do. I feel great physically and have no plans to go anywhere anytime soon, which is exactly why it's the right time. In the years to come, I couldn't be more energized about working arm-in-arm with him and cementing the future of Hendrick Motorsports together."

Gordon felt stepping into the role of vice chairman was the next challenge in his life. The on-track accomplishments of the Vallejo, California, native are well documented. His move into team management was the next big personal and professional step in his life.

"One of the reasons why I stepped away from television [as a broadcast analyst with Fox Sports] to do this role was that I've had so many amazing opportunities in my life through Rick," Gordon said. "I'm so appreciative of that. It also comes with the confidence that he has in me. Sometimes that's more than I have in myself. Because of that, I take a lot of pride in the role, and I take it very seriously.

"There is so much that goes on behind the scenes. Not a lot of people realize that, and I don't know that I even realized that until I got into this role.

"I stepped away from television because I just felt like I needed and wanted to be completely fulfilled in my life and my career. To do that, I wanted to have a new challenge on a pretty regular basis. I think that's what racing, as a driver, does to you. You're constantly being challenged and you're pushing yourself. You've got this goal that you're trying to achieve and that is to win races and win championships. Working in television was fun and I enjoyed it. I worked with great people. I didn't think that it would challenge me at that level. This role does."

Gordon is now in a daily position that keeps him busy with enormous tasks. Each day moves him into a place one could call uncharted territory. At least for now.

"Being vice chairman of Hendrick Motorsports is incredibly challenging because the dynamic is changing," Gordon said. "There are areas within the company that need to be managed that go way beyond the competition. Especially because it's just a unique and interesting time in the sport right now. That's true when you're talking about media right, the team charter agreement, governance and the rules, the business challenges, and how we are connecting with our fans. I am enjoying my role, there's no doubt about that. I try not to get too overwhelmed with all that's on my plate."

Gordon talks with team owner Rick Hendrick at Darlington Raceway in 2021. Gordon collected seven career Cup Series victories at the track.

Hendrick Motorsports president and general manager Jeff Andrews (left), Gordon (second from left), crew chief Greg Ives (second from right), and Alex Bowman before the start of a Cup Series race at Dover Motor Speedway in 2022.

Linda Hendrick (left), Rick Hendrick (second from left), William Byron (center), crew chief Rudy Fugle, and Jeff Gordon stand behind the Firebird 1, one of several prototypes designed by Harley J. Earl and the General Motors design team in the early 1950s. Earl's popular creation was on display at the Chevrolet Experience Center adjacent to victory lane at the Daytona International Speedway where Byron won his first career Daytona 500 on February 19, 2024.

38 NASCAR TO LE MANS: GARAGE 56 GOES GLOBAL

During a test at Virginia International Raceway in Alton, Virginia, in November 2022, driver Mike Rockenfeller worked with a variety of front splitters, rear diffusers, and drive planes as part of preparation for the Le Mans 2023 race.

On February 17, 2023, NASCAR unveiled the Next Gen Chevrolet Camaro ZL1 and livery to be entered into that year's one hundredth running of the 24 Hours of Le Mans. The Garage 56 project, approved for entry by Automobile Club de l'Ouest, was a partnership between NASCAR, Hendrick Motorsports, Chevrolet, and Goodyear. Together, they represented the team, automaker, and tire manufacturer with the most victories across NASCAR's seventy-five-year history.

Established in 1923, the 24 Hours of Le Mans is a twenty-four-hour endurance race held at the 8.467-mile (13.63-kilometer) Circuit de la Sarthe in Le Mans, France. One of the most grueling motoring events in existence, it is universally considered to be a crown jewel of global auto racing, representing a true test of man and machine.

In 2012, the event introduced Garage 56, a special category for a single noncompeting entry each year. The new classification provided an avenue for Jim France to return NASCAR to Le Mans, where a stock car had not appeared since 1976 when his father, NASCAR founder Bill France Sr., brought a Dodge Charger and a Ford Torino to the iconic race. Although the cars were fan favorites dubbed "Les Deux Monstres" ("The Two Monsters"), neither made it to the finish.

The NASCAR chairman approached Rick Hendrick, owner of fourteen-time Cup Series champions Hendrick Motorsports, who agreed to help him realize Bill Sr.'s vision by fielding the Garage 56 entry for the centenary race. Surviving the full twenty-four hours was the objective.

"The Garage 56 program was probably one of the toughest undertakings that I've ever saddled up for," Hendrick said.

Lead personnel for the effort included Hendrick Motorsports vice president of competition Chad Knaus, Garage 56 crew chief Greg Ives, and team manager Ben Wright; Mark Stielow, GM's director of motorsport competition engineering; Jim Danahy, GM's then vice president of global safety, systems, and integration; and Russ O'Blenes, director of GM's performance and racing propulsion team.

Dallara's chief designer Luca Pignacca and chief engineer Alex Timmermans brought their considerable experience in both IndyCar and NASCAR to the project. Goodyear's Stu Grant, general manager for global race tires, and Greg Stucker, director of race tire sales, created custom road racing and rain tires.

"For Hendrick Motorsports to be approached by Mr. France to take on this program, build the car, take it to Europe, race it for twenty-four hours, and to have it done in about fourteen months was a daunting task," Knaus said. "It was a real eye-opener for us as to how much confidence NASCAR and our partners Goodyear, Chevrolet, and IMSA had to even go over there and do that."

Drivers tapped to wheel the Camaro racer at the Circuit de la Sarthe were Jenson Button, Jimmie Johnson, and Mike Rockenfeller. Each of the three possessed a unique racing background: Button was the 2009 Formula 1 World Champion, Johnson tallied a record-tying seven NASCAR Cup Series championships with Hendrick Motorsports, and Rockenfeller had won at Le Mans twice. Sports car ace Jordan Taylor served as coach and backup driver.

"We couldn't have asked for a better lineup," Wright said. "Every driver was a champion, and they brought a winning attitude and drive that took us to a different level. Their combination of experience and professionalism was a major part of the equation for success. Each of them committed fully to the project and the development of the race car. Failure was not an option."

The timeline began almost a year prior to the car unveiling when the intention to enter the 2023 24 Hours of Le Mans was announced at a press conference on March 17, 2022, at Florida's Sebring International Raceway prior to the 12 Hours of Sebring endurance event.

Another important step came three months later, on June 11 and 12, when Knaus attended the 24 Hours of Le Mans on a whirlwind scouting trip with other delegates from Hendrick Motorsports.

The Garage 56 Chevrolet Camaro was unveiled at Daytona International Speedway on February 17, 2023. There were many Hendrick Motorsports and Chevrolet personnel involved in the project. From left is Hendrick Motorsports chairman Rick Hendrick, vice chairman Jeff Gordon, president and general manager Jeff Andrews, Garage 56 team manager Ben Wright, crew chief Greg Ives, and vice president of competition Chad Knaus.

During a test session at Florida's Sebring International Raceway in February 2023, the team made a twenty-four-hour test run and selected tires. They also practiced pit stops. While competing at Le Mans, the team won the pit crew competition, proving fastest among all teams in their class.

In August 2022, construction of the first race car began on the Hendrick Motorsports campus in Concord, North Carolina. On August 29 and 30, a prefatory "mule" car built by Jim France's Action Express sports car team was brought out for testing at Road Atlanta with German road-racing ace Rockenfeller as the driver. The mule would validate initial design concepts for the Garage 56 race cars.

Ives explained the thinking behind the early designs.

"The Gen 7 car is basically how it started," said Ives, the 2014 NASCAR Xfinity Series champion crew chief and a ten-time Cup Series race winner. "So, the questions began from there. How can we make it lighter? How can we make it more aerodynamic with more downforce? How can we have more horsepower and durability and better fuel mileage? How can we incorporate [tire] compounds for wet or dry racing? Do we use alternate [tread] widths on the front and rear of the car?

"We took every aspect and asked ourselves how we could improve it with the help of this group."

Changes to the Cup Series Camaro ZL1 were necessary to endure the punishing course, including the use of carbon brakes, improved aerodynamic performance, increased power, a larger fuel cell, and custom Goodyear Eagle tires.

Eventually, Hendrick Motorsports would build two Garage 56 cars. The first, G56-001, was completed in November 2022 to serve as the main test vehicle and backup race car for Le Mans. The primary Garage 56 entry, G56-002, was finished in March 2023.

Track testing began in the fall of 2022. Rockenfeller drove the backup car for its first laps on November 14 and 15 at the seventeen-turn Virginia International Raceway. A week later, custom wet weather tires were evaluated in Texas at the Goodyear Proving Ground using the mule.

Two more tests occurred before the new year. On December 7, Johnson drove the backup car at Carolina Motorsports Park's road course in Kershaw, South Carolina. On December 19 and 20, Johnson and Rockenfeller traded driving duties during two more days at Sebring that included the first six-hour endurance test.

In a January 28 press conference during IMSA's 2023 Rolex 24 at Daytona event, Johnson, Rockenfeller, and Button were officially named as the three drivers who would race in France. The following week, the trio logged 1,620 miles in two days on the Daytona road course. The test in the backup car included pit stop practice, initial assessment of the headlights and taillights, and a twelve-hour endurance trial.

During the exhaustive preparation, the stunning metallic blue Garage 56 paint scheme was unveiled February 17 in victory lane prior to the Daytona 500. The team then returned to Sebring on February 20 for the last major endurance test: a full twenty-four-hour run. The team logged 2,367 miles in the backup car as it worked through tire selections, brake modifications, pit stops, and driver changes.

The NASCAR Next Gen proposal for the Garage 56 entry was accepted by Le Mans race organizers on February 27 with Hendrick Motorsports' iconic No. 24 fittingly confirmed as its number. A week later, the primary Garage 56 race car was added to the fold for a two-day test at the Circuit of The Americas road course in Austin, Texas. The primary car also received a preliminary technical inspection by race organizers.

In mid-April, the full Garage 56 team returned to Sebring for the final time to shake down both cars before Le Mans. A group photo of the crew and the project's partners on pit lane capped the last test before the Garage 56 entry traveled to Le Mans. The final combined distance logged in testing totaled 6,894 miles. Afterward,

The Hendrick Motorsports Camaro finished thirty-ninth out of sixty-two cars entered. The No. 24 Chevrolet completed 285 laps and 2,413 miles in the 100th-anniversary race competing in the twenty-one-car GTE Am class. Former F1 driver Jenson Button, NASCAR champion Jimmie Johnson, and German endurance racer Mike Rockenfeller handled driving duties.

Jim France, NASCAR's chairman and chief executive officer, and Rick Hendrick celebrate the successful Garage 56 venture at Le Mans.

The Hendrick Motorsports team that worked on the Garage 56 project with the two Chevrolet Camaro ZL1 cars they built for the 100th running of the 24 Hours of Le Mans. Shown in front are crew chief Greg Ives, Hendrick Motorsports vice president of competition Chad Knaus, and Ben Wright, team manager for Garage 56.

forty-two-thousand pounds of cars and equipment were carefully loaded into crates and shipped to England by sea and air. From there, the cargo was transported by ground to Le Mans, where it arrived two weeks before the race.

When the Hendrick Motorsports team finally arrived at the Circuit de la Sarthe, it quickly created a buzz. During practice, the car's speed surprised observers when it was competitive with the GTE class, running as fast or faster. Then, on the Tuesday of race week, the Garage 56 pit crew won its class in the annual Pit Stop Challenge, besting the entire GTE field while performing a NASCAR-style stop with a manual jack in just 10.364 seconds. The team placed fifth in the overall competition, just 0.3 seconds behind the top crew.

"This is a special moment to be able to represent Hendrick Motorsports, represent our families, America, and NASCAR as a whole," said jackman Donovan Williams, a former tight end at the University of Connecticut.

When race day arrived, the goal was to simply finish—no easy feat in the world's most famous endurance event—but the team ended up accomplishing far more. Prior to a driveline issue that cost an hour of track time, Garage 56 stunned the event's 325,000 spectators by leading every car in the GTE class. All told, it ran 285 laps and approximately 2,413 miles—or roughly four 600-mile races at Charlotte Motor Speedway.

Appropriately it was Johnson, the stock-car champion, who drove the No. 24 Chevrolet Camaro ZL1 across the finish line to put an exclamation point on the project. Garage 56 was officially scored thirty-ninth out of the sixty-two teams entered in the event, but the impact of the effort was undeniable. It was a victory for NASCAR on the world stage.

"That car was an extremely well-performing vehicle," Knaus said. "The team operated at a very high level. To go over there and do that for the very first time was nothing short of monumental.

"It turned out to be a spectacle if you stand back and look at it. I didn't really get to see [all the attention] until after the race, but the notes, messages, the social media, the magazine articles, were really amazing about how well the car was received and how people respected it."

Hendrick praised Knaus for leading Garage 56, which stands out as a truly unique achievement in the forty-year history of Hendrick Motorsports.

"I give Chad all the credit," Hendrick said. "He did his homework. The crowd loved the car. There were thousands of articles written with mentions of the car around the world, as well as being on the cover of *Car and Driver* magazine. The fans were chanting, 'USA, USA!' The car was getting as much or more of an ovation than the Ferrari that won the entire race. Our pit crew won the Pit Crew Challenge. It was a special experience."

Although it was an undertaking with considerable challenges from beginning to end, Hendrick felt Garage 56 was more than worth the sizable effort.

"You're going to take a clean sheet of paper, and you're going to go and run twenty-four hours with a car that's only designed to run six hundred miles," said Hendrick, putting the task into perspective. "When you start out [in testing], you're five seconds slower than the class you're supposed to be equal to. Then you go over there [to Le Mans] and hope these people aren't going to boo you off the track. You work your tail off and get over there and not only do you keep up, but you're the fastest.

"It was something on the bucket list that I'm really proud of. Looking back, I'm glad we did it. It was a super hit."

39 THE DOUBLE: LARSON CHASES CROWN JEWELS

Kyle Larson's race cars for his double duty on May 29, 2024, one race at Indianapolis Motor Speedway and the other at Charlotte Motor Speedway. At left is the No. 17 IndyCar entered by Arrow McLaren and owned by Rick Hendrick for the Indianapolis 500. On the right is the No. 5 Hendrick Motorsports Chevrolet to be fielded for the Coca-Cola 600.

The No. 17 HendrickCars.com Arrow McLaren Chevrolet that Larson will race marks his first entry in the Indianapolis 500. Its 2.2 liter V-6 engine produces 550 to 700 horsepower propelling the car to speeds of up to 240 mph.

The No. 5 HendrickCars.com Chevrolet echoes the Arrow McLaren color scheme. By contrast, the Camaro's V-8 produces 750 horsepower with a top speed of 200 mph.

Open-wheel racing has been a huge part of Kyle Larson's driving career since an early age, first in micro midgets and sprint cars.

His dream of entering the Indianapolis 500 will come to fruition in 2024 with the partnership between Hendrick Motorsports and Arrow McLaren of IndyCar racing fame. The two powerhouse teams will join forces with cars, equipment, and engineering expertise to put together 1,100 miles of racing on May 26, 2024, that involves competition in open-wheel's greatest spectacle at the Indianapolis 500, followed by the NASCAR Cup Series Coca-Cola 600 at Charlotte Motor Speedway.

Arrow McLaren approached Jeff Gordon with the idea. Gordon and Zak Brown, chief executive officer of McClaren Racing, then put in place a plan to become the next group of team owners and driver to attempt to win at Indianapolis as well as at NASCAR's longest Cup Series race. Hendrick and Gavin Ward, team principal at Arrow McLaren-IndyCar, and Kyle Larson, driver of the No. 5 Hendrick Motorsports Chevrolet, began the process of bringing the plan together.

Drivers who have attempted the two-race "double" include John Andretti in 1994, Tony Stewart in 1999 and 2001, and Kurt Busch in 2014. Robby Gordon also participated in both races in 1997, 2000, and 2002 through 2004. No driver to attempt it has won either race.

Larson visited Indy in May 2023, and at the time said, "Just getting eyes on stuff a year in advance will hopefully make things a little less overwhelming for [2024]. I thought it was really important to come to a practice day and also get to come to the race for a little while, just to get reminded of how crazy this place becomes with all the people and the ceremonies and all that. I think getting eyes on it all was good, and it will hopefully knock some of the edge off next year."

Larson spent time in the simulator in October 2023 at the GM Technical Center on the Hendrick Motorsports campus, working to get accustomed to the lighter, much different race car. An announcement that Larson would race in the 2024 Indianapolis 500 was made in late December 2023. Larson drove 172 laps at Phoenix Raceway in February 2024 during a lengthy test to become more familiar with the No. 17 entry he will drive at Indianapolis followed by a successful open test at Indianapolis in April 2024.

Hendrick's excitement about being involved with an IndyCar team is palpable.

"I think [about] Daytona and the Indy 500, and I got to do the 24 Hours of Le Mans, so I'm kind of getting my bucketful here," Hendrick said. "This is such an unbelievable place here [Indianapolis], and Charlotte, doing the 600, and this race. It's going to be unbelievable.

"We all talked about it. Kyle wanted to do it. We're just very fortunate that Arrow McLaren was able to put it together for us. I can't wait to have that car in the [Heritage Center] museum."

While it's not the first time Hendrick Motorsports has discussed pursuing an IndyCar opportunity, with Larson it seemed to be a case of the right driver at the right time.

"Jeff Gordon and I talked about it, but he wasn't really keen. Jeff was so focused on driving the Cup car," Ward said. "But this is the first time that we really got serious with it . . . this is the first real effort where we said, 'Hey, let's go do it.'

"As Kyle said, no matter what the results are, he'll be a better race car driver," Ward continued. "I love that because that's kind of how I see it for the team. No matter how we do, we'll put everything into making it a success, we'll come out as better race teams. That's the mentality that I love and preach, so it's nice to hear that."

Larson (center) with Jay Frye (left), IndyCar president of competition and operations; Roger Penske, owner of Penske Entertainment Corporation, the NTT INDYCAR SERIES, IMS Productions, and Indianapolis Motor Speedway (second from left); Rick Hendrick (second from right); and Steve Phelps, president of NASCAR.

Gordon felt some extra excitement, having strongly considered IndyCar early in his career before turning his attention to NASCAR in 1990. As vice chairman of Hendrick Motorsports, and a deeply experienced racer, Gordon's encouragement of Larson and those involved with the project was most welcome.

"This is definitely going to be living out a dream of mine through this experience," Gordon said. "I'm equally excited to be a part of it in the capacity that I am, [and to] see it and hear about it through Kyle's eyes and experience."

Larson's coach for the venture is 2013 Indy 500 winner Tony Kanaan.

"Honestly, I was very happy to [learn that]—I didn't realize that Tony was sticking around to be a specialty adviser for Arrow McLaren," Larson said. "We have past experience working together, being teammates at the Rolex 24 with Chip [Ganassi]. Tony and I are the same size. We use the same [seat] insert. He's got way bigger muscles than me, but besides that, we've got, I think, a lot in common.

"He's a past champion of the event and won a number of IndyCar races. He's just so experienced. I'm going to be leaning on him the most for sure. He's so easy to talk to and work with that he's going to help me and get me steered in the right direction very quickly."

Team members of Arrow McLaren and Hendrick Motorsports join Kyle Larson (center in black shirt), Cup Series team owner Rick Hendrick (white shirt), and Hendrick Motorsports president and general manager Jeff Andrews (in black vest).

40 / 300 AND COUNTING

William Byron, in the No. 24 Hendrick Motorsports Chevrolet, took his sixth checkered flag of the 2023 Cup Series season and

Byron celebrates his win at Texas Motor Speedway in a cloud of tire smoke on the front stretch at the 1.5-mile track.

DURING THE CLOSING LAPS of the playoff race at Texas Motor Speedway on September 24, 2023, William Byron concentrated on his line on the 1.5-mile track. He gained the lead over Bubba Wallace with six laps remaining, and hanging on would mean his sixth victory of the season and milestone win 300 for Hendrick Motorsports.

That day in Texas, Byron restarted from fourth position after the eleventh caution of the day. Byron took the green flag, went low to the inside, and worked his way to the lead, where he stayed for the rest of the race. The victory meant he made it into the Round of 8 of the 2023 NASCAR Cup Series playoffs, where he ultimately finished third in points.

"It's really special," Byron said of being the driver to deliver the three hundredth Cup Series win for Hendrick Motorsports. "Growing up a Hendrick Motorsports fan, I watched win number two hundred on TV when Jimmie [Johnson] won that race [May 12, 2012, at Darlington, South Carolina]. I always felt like the gold standard was Hendrick Motorsports. So, if I could ever drive for them, once I started having success in my own career, that was the goal."

Win number three hundred was certainly on the horizon for the season, with race writers generating stories speculating as to when the milestone victory might occur.

"I knew we had talked about one of us, whether it be myself, Alex Bowman, Chase Elliott, or Kyle Larson, collecting the three hundredth victory sometime during the season when it started in February," Byron said. "I knew that weekend we were at win two hundred ninety-nine and that one of us could get it. It didn't cross my mind until I was headed to victory lane and Rudy [Fugle, crew chief] said something over the radio. Getting number three hundred for Hendrick Motorsports was extremely special to me."

Looking back, Byron had a phenomenal 2023. Only two positions separated him from winning his first-career Cup Series championship in the final race of the season at Phoenix Raceway on November 5, 2023.

"We put ourselves in position to win a lot of races," Byron said. "That was fun to see [along with] the evolution of our team, and then getting win three hundred at Texas was a huge deal because we had been inching up on it. Kyle Larson had a really good day that day, and I thought he was going to win the race. When he had problems, it kind of opened the door for us, and we were in position to capitalize."

Hendrick Motorsports broke the all-time wins mark of 269 victories by surpassing Petty Enterprises with Larson's dominating victory in the 2021 Coca-Cola 600. The team stands

Byron's Hendrick Motorsports crew reacts after their driver crosses under the checkered flag to collect his sixth Cup Series win of 2023 and the three hundredth victory for Hendrick Motorsports.

Byron in victory lane at Texas Motor Speedway. Note the large hat that he dons after every win.

alone as the only premier series organization to cross three hundred wins.

"Winning three hundred Cup Series races is just such a milestone," Hendrick said. "When you put that distance on Petty's record by a pretty good margin and at the rate we are going, we are just adding to it. Young drivers and young crew chiefs. Jeff Gordon is here helping. I don't know where we are going to go, and I am not going to set a goal because the goal for me is just winning.

"If we can win races every year and compete for championships, the numbers will come. Two hundred sixty-nine was in my brain for a long time, and I didn't think we could ever get there. I just owe it all to the people here and the drivers along the way. It is unbelievable to be at three hundred."

The milestone was reached three weeks after the Hendrick Motorsports engine shop recorded its five-hundredth national series win with Larson's victory at Darlington Raceway in the Southern 500 on September 3, 2023.

Gordon, who started his Cup Series career with Hendrick Motorsports on November 15, 1992, has tallied the most visits to victory lane for Hendrick Motorsports with ninety-three wins.

"I love what Rick always says. When he was a kid growing up, when he came into NASCAR, it's Petty Enterprises and the number of championships and the number of wins," Gordon said. "That was the benchmark. Something that I don't think anybody thought would be touched. I think

that's the way Rick looked at it from a car owner's standpoint. Yet, we were able to get to two hundred sixty-nine [wins] in 2021 and lead in that category. That says a lot about this organization, the professionalism, the performance level, and the culture of what Rick has created and been able to maintain for almost forty years now in the sport.

"That win number is a reflection on a lot of people's hard work, creativity, and great talent that we have here behind the wheel as well as working on the cars. I think it's super cool. It is a big number. Three hundred blows your mind. To think that just two years ago we were at two hundred sixty-nine, and now here we are."

Jimmie Johnson won eighty-three times for the organization. He spent twenty years with Hendrick Motorsports and is responsible for half of the squad's fourteen Cup Series championships.

"As everyone knows that has worked at Hendrick [Motorsports], it is such a family-oriented organization," Johnson said. "We all take so much pride in the long history Hendrick Motorsports has had, the winning ways, and the culture. It is just such a special feeling, and I am very thankful to be a part of it. It is just crazy to think three hundred [wins]. It is wild to think of not only the race wins but the many, many championships."

For Johnson, the success of Hendrick Motorsports comes back to Hendrick and his leadership.

(Left to right) Kyle Larson, William Byron, Rick Hendrick, Chase Elliott, and Alex Bowman pose for a photo after the three-hundredth victory for Hendrick Motorsports was reached at Texas Motor Speedway on September 23, 2023.

"The greatest success of Hendrick Motorsports is Rick's love and passion for it," Johnson said. "He is the face. That's probably one of the most important aspects I think to rally a group of people around you. He just has an ability to do that like no one else."

As the team owner describes it, the race team's success over the years is entirely about the people.

"I think any business that you're in, it's about people," Hendrick said. "We take care of our people, and we treat everybody like a family. I grew up on a farm, and that's one thing my dad taught me is you have to depend on your neighbors. I've had that philosophy all of my adult working life."

Aside from Gordon's ninety-three wins and Johnson's eighty-three wins, and through the end of the 2023 season, Elliott has eighteen, Larson seventeen, Terry Labonte twelve, Byron eleven, Dale Earnhardt Jr. nine, Tim Richmond nine, Darrell Waltrip nine, Bowman seven, Geoff Bodine seven, Kasey Kahne six, Mark Martin five, Ken Schrader four, Ricky Rudd four, Kyle Busch four, Jerry Nadeau one, Casey Mears one, Joe Nemechek one, and Brian Vickers one.

"I'd like to think our legacy will be that we will be in a position to win so many that nobody will ever break it," Hendrick continued. "People say records are made to be broken, but we took a long time to break Petty's record, so I hope it will be a long time to break ours, if they can do it.

"It feels good to get to three hundred. I'm proud of all the drivers that have driven at the company since we started because every one of them have participated in those three hundred wins, so it was really good to see William get it."

AFTERWORD
THE NEXT FORTY

On behalf of everyone at Hendrick Motorsports, I hope you enjoyed this book as much as we enjoyed working on it. Like most good things in business and in life, it was a team effort. For putting so much passion into the project, we extend a very special thanks to writer Ben White, photographer Nigel Kinrade, and publisher Motorbooks.

As Hendrick Motorsports approached its fortieth anniversary, we spent a lot of time planning. We held our first meeting in the spring of 2023 and talked about all the exciting things we wanted to do. Racing is a tough business, and I've seen a lot of teams come and go throughout my career. Forty years felt like an achievement worth celebrating.

I vividly remember the morning of the 1984 Daytona 500, our NASCAR debut. The well-laid plans for All-Star Racing had fallen apart, and I was racing out of my pocket. Standing on pit road were legends like Junior Johnson, the Wood Brothers, the Pettys, Richard Childress, and Bud Moore. I had a strong feeling that I didn't belong.

There are times I still pinch myself. I say I'm the luckiest guy in the world because I get to make a living doing the two things I love most in life, outside of my family: racing and the car business. But in 1984, I was thirty-four years old, Hendrick Automotive Group was barely established, and everything felt on the edge. With no sponsor, no investors, five crew members, and an unknown driver, I was worried it could all collapse.

On that February morning, if someone had told me we'd be right back there exactly forty years later, to the day, celebrating our *ninth* Daytona 500 win, I would've called them crazy. We were just trying to get to the next race and the next and the next. None of us knew if we could pull it off, but we had talented people who believed. It's amazing how far that will take you.

Each January, we bring everyone at Hendrick Motorsports together—now around 600 teammates—for a kickoff lunch. It feels like a pep rally. There's always energy and excitement as we approach a new season. This year, we celebrated our history but also focused on the future—our goals, how we would achieve them, and the investments we were making to ensure more wins and championships. Our anniversary got me thinking as much about the next four decades as the last.

Linda and I talk about the future a lot. Not just the next twelve months—decades down the line and how we can position the company for more growth and success. I have no plans to slow down or retire, but I believe in the concept of servant leadership. If we weren't thinking about what's ahead, we wouldn't be serving the people who worked so hard to make our organization what it is.

So, at the end of this year's lunch, we handed out footballs as a symbol of our family's long-term promise to Hendrick Motorsports and our commitment to the next forty years. Taking one signified each person's pledge to "carry the ball" and help keep the company moving forward. Everyone did.

A few weeks later, we won our record-tying ninth Daytona 500. It was quite a moment—our past, present, and future all coming together at once. Looking around victory lane, I found myself surrounded by talented, passionate people who dreamed of winning. Just like in 1984.

Legacy is usually associated with the past. For me, though, it's about building something that will thrive far into the future. Successful teams are about people, not one person. Our teammates are the true legacy—the ones who honor what we've built by taking it to even greater heights.

One word at a time, our people have written the story of Hendrick Motorsports' first forty years. Without them, there would be nothing to tell. Through wins and losses, we've done it together.

And we're just getting started.

Rick Hendrick

APPENDIX

HENDRICK MOTORSPORTS CUP RACE-WINNING DRIVERS 1984–2023

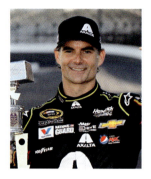

DRIVER:
JEFF GORDON

CUP WINS:
93

CUP CHAMPIONSHIPS:
1995, 1997, 1998, 2001

CREW CHIEF(S):
Alan Gustafson,
Brian Whitesell,
Ray Evernham,
Robbie Loomis,
Steve Letarte

DRIVER:
JIMMIE JOHNSON

CUP WINS:
83

CUP CHAMPIONSHIPS:
2006–2010, 2013, 2016

CREW CHIEF(S):
Chad Knaus,
Darian Grubb

DRIVER:
CHASE ELLIOTT

CUP WINS:
18

CUP CHAMPIONSHIPS:
2020

CREW CHIEF(S):
Alan Gustafson

DRIVER:
KYLE LARSON

CUP WINS:
18

CUP CHAMPIONSHIPS:
2021

CREW CHIEF(S):
Cliff Daniels,
Kevin Meendering

DRIVER:
TERRY LABONTE

CUP WINS:
12

CUP CHAMPIONSHIPS:
1996

CREW CHIEF(S):
Andy Graves,
Randy Dorton,
Gary DeHart,
Jim Long

DRIVER:
WILLIAM BYRON

CUP WINS:
11

CREW CHIEF(S):
Chad Knaus,
Rudy Fugle

DRIVER:
DALE EARNHARDT JR.

CUP WINS:
9

CREW CHIEF(S):
Greg Ives,
Steve Letarte,
Tony Eury Jr.

DRIVER:
TIM RICHMOND

CUP WINS:
9

CREW CHIEF(S):
Dennis Connor,
Harry Hyde

DRIVER:
DARRELL WALTRIP

CUP WINS:
9

CREW CHIEF(S):
Jeff Hammond

DRIVER:
GEOFF BODINE

CUP WINS:
7

CREW CHIEF(S):
Gary Nelson,
Harry Hyde,
Waddell Wilson

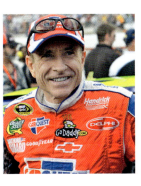

DRIVER:
ALEX BOWMAN

CUP WINS:
7

CREW CHIEF(S):
Greg Ives

DRIVER:
KASEY KAHNE

CUP WINS:
7

CREW CHIEF(S):
Keith Rodden,
Kenny Francis

DRIVER:
MARK MARTIN

CUP WINS:
6

CREW CHIEF(S):
Alan Gustafson

DRIVER:
KEN SCHRADER

CUP WINS:
5

CREW CHIEF(S):
Dennis Connor,
Richard Broome

DRIVER:
KYLE BUSCH

CUP WINS:
4

CREW CHIEF(S):
Alan Gustafson

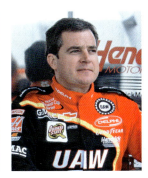

DRIVER:
RICKY RUDD

CUP WINS:
4

CREW CHIEF(S):
Gary DeHart,
Waddell Wilson

DRIVER:
CASY MEARS

CUP WINS:
1

CREW CHIEF(S):
Darian Grubb

DRIVER:
JERRY NADEAU

CUP WINS:
1

CREW CHIEF(S):
Tony Furr

DRIVER:
JOE NEMECHEK

CUP WINS:
1

CREW CHIEF(S):
Peter Sospenzo

DRIVER:
BRIAN VICKERS

CUP WINS:
1

CREW CHIEF(S):
Lance McGrew

APPENDIX

HENDRICK MOTORSPORTS CUP RACE-WINNING NUMBERS 1984–2023

103 CUP WINS
Jeff Gordon (93)
William Byron (10)

88 CUP WINS
Jimmie Johnson (83)
Alex Bowman (5)

55 CUP WINS
Kyle Larson (17)
Terry Labonte (12)
Geoff Bodine (7)
Kasey Kahne (6)
Mark Martin (5)
Ricky Rudd (4)
Kyle Busch (4)

18 CUP WINS
Chase Elliott

17 CUP WINS
Tim Richmond (9)
Ken Schrader (4)
Jerry Nadeau (1)
Joe Nemechek (1)
Brian Vickers (1)
Casey Mears (1)

11 CUP WINS
Dale Earnhardt Jr. (9)
Alex Bowman (2)

9 CUP WINS
Darrell Waltrip

APPENDIX

HENDRICK MOTORSPORTS CUP SERIES WINS 1984–2023

DATE	TRACK	CAR #	WINNING DRIVER	WINNING CREW CHIEF
4/29/1984	Martinsville Speedway	5	Geoff Bodine	Harry Hyde
7/14/1984	Fairgrounds Speedway Nashville	5	Geoff Bodine	Harry Hyde
11/18/1984	Riverside International Raceway	5	Geoff Bodine	Harry Hyde
2/16/1986	Daytona International Speedway	5	Geoff Bodine	Gary Nelson
5/18/1986	Dover Motor Speedway	5	Geoff Bodine	Gary Nelson
6/8/1986	Pocono Raceway	25	Tim Richmond	Harry Hyde
7/4/1986	Daytona International Speedway	25	Tim Richmond	Harry Hyde
7/20/1986	Pocono Raceway	25	Tim Richmond	Harry Hyde
8/10/1986	Watkins Glen International	25	Tim Richmond	Harry Hyde
8/31/1986	Darlington Raceway	25	Tim Richmond	Harry Hyde
9/7/1986	Richmond Raceway	25	Tim Richmond	Harry Hyde
11/16/1986	Riverside International Raceway	25	Tim Richmond	Harry Hyde
6/14/1987	Pocono Raceway	25	Tim Richmond	Harry Hyde
6/21/1987	Riverside International Raceway	25	Tim Richmond	Dennis Connor
9/27/1987	Martinsville Speedway	17	Darrell Waltrip	Jeff Hammond
5/29/1988	Charlotte Motor Speedway	17	Darrell Waltrip	Jeff Hammond
6/19/1988	Pocono Raceway	5	Geoff Bodine	Waddell Wilson
7/31/1988	Talladega Superspeedway	25	Ken Schrader	Dennis Connor
9/25/1988	Martinsville Speedway	17	Darrell Waltrip	Jeff Hammond
2/19/1989	Daytona International Speedway	17	Darrell Waltrip	Jeff Hammond
3/19/1989	Atlanta Motor Speedway	17	Darrell Waltrip	Jeff Hammond
4/23/1989	Martinsville Speedway	17	Darrell Waltrip	Jeff Hammond
5/28/1989	Charlotte Motor Speedway	17	Darrell Waltrip	Jeff Hammond
8/26/1989	Bristol Motor Speedway	17	Darrell Waltrip	Jeff Hammond
9/24/1989	Martinsville Speedway	17	Darrell Waltrip	Jeff Hammond
10/8/1989	Charlotte Motor Speedway	25	Ken Schrader	Richard Broome
10/15/1989	North Wilkesboro Speedway	5	Geoff Bodine	Waddell Wilson
8/12/1990	Watkins Glen International	5	Ricky Rudd	Waddell Wilson
3/18/1991	Atlanta Motor Speedway	25	Ken Schrader	Richard Broome
4/7/1991	Darlington Raceway	5	Ricky Rudd	Waddell Wilson
6/2/1991	Dover Motor Speedway	25	Ken Schrader	Richard Broome
9/20/1992	Dover Motor Speedway	5	Ricky Rudd	Gary DeHart
6/20/1993	Michigan International Speedway	5	Ricky Rudd	Gary DeHart
4/17/1994	North Wilkesboro Speedway	5	Terry Labonte	Gary DeHart
5/29/1994	Charlotte Motor Speedway	24	Jeff Gordon	Ray Evernham
8/6/1994	Indianapolis Motor Speedway	24	Jeff Gordon	Ray Evernham
9/10/1994	Richmond Raceway	5	Terry Labonte	Gary DeHart
10/30/1994	Phoenix Raceway	5	Terry Labonte	Gary DeHart
2/26/1995	Rockingham Speedway	24	Jeff Gordon	Ray Evernham
3/5/1995	Richmond Raceway	5	Terry Labonte	Gary DeHart
3/12/1995	Atlanta Motor Speedway	24	Jeff Gordon	Ray Evernham
4/2/1995	Bristol Motor Speedway	24	Jeff Gordon	Ray Evernham
6/11/1995	Pocono Raceway	5	Terry Labonte	Gary DeHart

Date	Track	Car	Driver	Crew Chief
7/1/1995	Daytona International Speedway	24	Jeff Gordon	Ray Evernham
7/9/1995	New Hampshire Motor Speedway	24	Jeff Gordon	Ray Evernham
8/26/1995	Bristol Motor Speedway	5	Terry Labonte	Gary DeHart
9/3/1995	Darlington Raceway	24	Jeff Gordon	Ray Evernham
9/17/1995	Dover Motor Speedway	24	Jeff Gordon	Ray Evernham
3/3/1996	Richmond Raceway	24	Jeff Gordon	Ray Evernham
3/24/1996	Darlington Raceway	24	Jeff Gordon	Ray Evernham
3/31/1996	Bristol Motor Speedway	24	Jeff Gordon	Ray Evernham
4/14/1996	North Wilkesboro Speedway	5	Terry Labonte	Gary DeHart
6/2/1996	Dover Motor Speedway	24	Jeff Gordon	Ray Evernham
6/16/1996	Pocono Raceway	24	Jeff Gordon	Ray Evernham
7/28/1996	Talladega Superspeedway	24	Jeff Gordon	Ray Evernham
9/1/1996	Darlington Raceway	24	Jeff Gordon	Ray Evernham
9/15/1996	Dover Motor Speedway	24	Jeff Gordon	Ray Evernham
9/22/1996	Martinsville Speedway	24	Jeff Gordon	Ray Evernham
9/29/1996	North Wilkesboro Speedway	24	Jeff Gordon	Ray Evernham
10/6/1996	Charlotte Motor Speedway	5	Terry Labonte	Gary DeHart
2/16/1997	Daytona International Speedway	24	Jeff Gordon	Ray Evernham
2/23/1997	Rockingham Speedway	24	Jeff Gordon	Ray Evernham
4/13/1997	Bristol Motor Speedway	24	Jeff Gordon	Ray Evernham
4/20/1997	Martinsville Speedway	24	Jeff Gordon	Ray Evernham
5/25/1997	Charlotte Motor Speedway	24	Jeff Gordon	Ray Evernham
6/8/1997	Pocono Raceway	24	Jeff Gordon	Ray Evernham
6/22/1997	California Speedway	24	Jeff Gordon	Ray Evernham
8/10/1997	Watkins Glen International	24	Jeff Gordon	Ray Evernham
8/31/1997	Darlington Raceway	24	Jeff Gordon	Ray Evernham
9/14/1997	New Hampshire Motor Speedway	24	Jeff Gordon	Ray Evernham
10/12/1997	Talladega Superspeedway	5	Terry Labonte	Randy Dorton
2/22/1998	Rockingham Speedway	24	Jeff Gordon	Ray Evernham
3/29/1998	Bristol Motor Speedway	24	Jeff Gordon	Ray Evernham
5/24/1998	Charlotte Motor Speedway	24	Jeff Gordon	Ray Evernham
6/6/1998	Richmond Raceway	5	Terry Labonte	Andy Graves
6/28/1998	Sonoma Raceway	24	Jeff Gordon	Ray Evernham
7/26/1998	Pocono Raceway	24	Jeff Gordon	Ray Evernham
8/1/1998	Indianapolis Motor Speedway	24	Jeff Gordon	Ray Evernham
8/9/1998	Watkins Glen International	24	Jeff Gordon	Ray Evernham
8/16/1998	Michigan International Speedway	24	Jeff Gordon	Ray Evernham
8/30/1998	New Hampshire Motor Speedway	24	Jeff Gordon	Ray Evernham
9/6/1998	Darlington Raceway	24	Jeff Gordon	Ray Evernham
10/17/1998	Daytona International Speedway	24	Jeff Gordon	Ray Evernham
11/1/1998	Rockingham Speedway	24	Jeff Gordon	Ray Evernham
11/8/1998	Atlanta Motor Speedway	24	Jeff Gordon	Ray Evernham
2/14/1999	Daytona International Speedway	24	Jeff Gordon	Ray Evernham
3/14/1999	Atlanta Motor Speedway	24	Jeff Gordon	Ray Evernham
3/28/1999	Texas Motor Speedway	5	Terry Labonte	Andy Graves
5/2/1999	California Speedway	24	Jeff Gordon	Ray Evernham
6/27/1999	Sonoma Raceway	24	Jeff Gordon	Ray Evernham
8/15/1999	Watkins Glen International	24	Jeff Gordon	Ray Evernham
10/3/1999	Martinsville Speedway	24	Jeff Gordon	Brian Whitesell
10/11/1999	Charlotte Motor Speedway	24	Jeff Gordon	Brian Whitesell
4/16/2000	Talladega Superspeedway	24	Jeff Gordon	Robbie Loomis
6/25/2000	Sonoma Raceway	24	Jeff Gordon	Robbie Loomis

(Hendrick Motorsports Cup Series Wins, continued)

Date	Track	#	Driver	Crew Chief
9/9/2000	Richmond Raceway	24	Jeff Gordon	Robbie Loomis
11/20/2000	Atlanta Motor Speedway	25	Jerry Nadeau	Tony Furr
3/4/2001	Las Vegas Motor Speedway	24	Jeff Gordon	Robbie Loomis
6/3/2001	Dover Motor Speedway	24	Jeff Gordon	Robbie Loomis
6/10/2001	Michigan International Speedway	24	Jeff Gordon	Robbie Loomis
8/5/2001	Indianapolis Motor Speedway	24	Jeff Gordon	Robbie Loomis
8/12/2001	Watkins Glen International	24	Jeff Gordon	Robbie Loomis
9/30/2001	Kansas Speedway	24	Jeff Gordon	Robbie Loomis
4/28/2002	California Speedway	48	Jimmie Johnson	Chad Knaus
6/2/2002	Dover Motor Speedway	48	Jimmie Johnson	Chad Knaus
8/24/2002	Bristol Motor Speedway	24	Jeff Gordon	Robbie Loomis
9/1/2002	Darlington Raceway	24	Jeff Gordon	Robbie Loomis
9/22/2002	Dover Motor Speedway	48	Jimmie Johnson	Chad Knaus
9/29/2002	Kansas Speedway	24	Jeff Gordon	Robbie Loomis
4/13/2003	Martinsville Speedway	24	Jeff Gordon	Robbie Loomis
5/3/2003	Richmond Raceway	25	Joe Nemechek	Peter Sospenzo
5/25/2003	Charlotte Motor Speedway	48	Jimmie Johnson	Chad Knaus
7/20/2003	New Hampshire Motor Speedway	48	Jimmie Johnson	Chad Knaus
8/31/2003	Darlington Raceway	5	Terry Labonte	Jim Long
9/14/2003	New Hampshire Motor Speedway	48	Jimmie Johnson	Chad Knaus
10/19/2003	Martinsville Speedway	24	Jeff Gordon	Robbie Loomis
10/27/2003	Atlanta Motor Speedway	24	Jeff Gordon	Robbie Loomis
3/21/2004	Darlington Raceway	48	Jimmie Johnson	Chad Knaus
4/25/2004	Talladega Superspeedway	24	Jeff Gordon	Robbie Loomis
5/2/2004	California Speedway	24	Jeff Gordon	Robbie Loomis
5/30/2004	Charlotte Motor Speedway	48	Jimmie Johnson	Chad Knaus
6/13/2004	Pocono Raceway	48	Jimmie Johnson	Chad Knaus
6/27/2004	Sonoma Raceway	24	Jeff Gordon	Robbie Loomis
7/3/2004	Daytona International Speedway	24	Jeff Gordon	Robbie Loomis
8/1/2004	Pocono Raceway	48	Jimmie Johnson	Chad Knaus
8/8/2004	Indianapolis Motor Speedway	24	Jeff Gordon	Robbie Loomis
10/16/2004	Charlotte Motor Speedway	48	Jimmie Johnson	Chad Knaus
10/24/2004	Martinsville Speedway	48	Jimmie Johnson	Chad Knaus
10/31/2004	Atlanta Motor Speedway	48	Jimmie Johnson	Chad Knaus
11/14/2004	Darlington Raceway	48	Jimmie Johnson	Chad Knaus
2/20/2005	Daytona International Speedway	24	Jeff Gordon	Robbie Loomis
3/13/2005	Las Vegas Motor Speedway	48	Jimmie Johnson	Chad Knaus
4/10/2005	Martinsville Speedway	24	Jeff Gordon	Robbie Loomis
5/1/2005	Talladega Superspeedway	24	Jeff Gordon	Robbie Loomis
5/29/2005	Charlotte Motor Speedway	48	Jimmie Johnson	Chad Knaus
9/4/2005	California Speedway	5	Kyle Busch	Alan Gustafson
9/25/2005	Dover Motor Speedway	48	Jimmie Johnson	Chad Knaus
10/15/2005	Charlotte Motor Speedway	48	Jimmie Johnson	Chad Knaus
10/23/2005	Martinsville Speedway	24	Jeff Gordon	Steve Letarte
11/13/2005	Phoenix Raceway	5	Kyle Busch	Alan Gustafson
2/19/2006	Daytona International Speedway	48	Jimmie Johnson	Darian Grubb
3/12/2006	Las Vegas Motor Speedway	48	Jimmie Johnson	Darian Grubb
5/1/2006	Talladega Superspeedway	48	Jimmie Johnson	Chad Knaus
6/25/2006	Sonoma Raceway	24	Jeff Gordon	Steve Letarte
7/9/2006	Chicagoland Speedway	24	Jeff Gordon	Steve Letarte
7/16/2006	New Hampshire Motor Speedway	5	Kyle Busch	Alan Gustafson
8/6/2006	Indianapolis Motor Speedway	48	Jimmie Johnson	Chad Knaus

Date	Track	#	Driver	Crew Chief
10/8/2006	Talladega Superspeedway	25	Brian Vickers	Lance McGrew
10/22/2006	Martinsville Speedway	48	Jimmie Johnson	Chad Knaus
3/11/2007	Las Vegas Motor Speedway	48	Jimmie Johnson	Chad Knaus
3/18/2007	Atlanta Motor Speedway	48	Jimmie Johnson	Chad Knaus
3/25/2007	Bristol Motor Speedway	5	Kyle Busch	Alan Gustafson
4/1/2007	Martinsville Speedway	48	Jimmie Johnson	Chad Knaus
4/21/2007	Phoenix Raceway	24	Jeff Gordon	Steve Letarte
4/29/2007	Talladega Superspeedway	24	Jeff Gordon	Steve Letarte
5/6/2007	Richmond Raceway	48	Jimmie Johnson	Chad Knaus
5/13/2007	Darlington Raceway	24	Jeff Gordon	Steve Letarte
5/27/2007	Charlotte Motor Speedway	25	Casey Mears	Darian Grubb
6/10/2007	Pocono Raceway	24	Jeff Gordon	Steve Letarte
9/2/2007	California Speedway	48	Jimmie Johnson	Chad Knaus
9/8/2007	Richmond Raceway	48	Jimmie Johnson	Chad Knaus
10/7/2007	Talladega Superspeedway	24	Jeff Gordon	Steve Letarte
10/13/2007	Charlotte Motor Speedway	24	Jeff Gordon	Steve Letarte
10/21/2007	Martinsville Speedway	48	Jimmie Johnson	Chad Knaus
10/28/2007	Atlanta Motor Speedway	48	Jimmie Johnson	Chad Knaus
11/4/2007	Texas Motor Speedway	48	Jimmie Johnson	Chad Knaus
11/11/2007	Phoenix Raceway	48	Jimmie Johnson	Chad Knaus
4/12/2008	Phoenix Raceway	48	Jimmie Johnson	Chad Knaus
6/15/2008	Michigan International Speedway	88	Dale Earnhardt Jr.	Tony Eury Jr.
7/27/2008	Indianapolis Motor Speedway	48	Jimmie Johnson	Chad Knaus
8/31/2008	California Speedway	48	Jimmie Johnson	Chad Knaus
9/7/2008	Richmond Raceway	48	Jimmie Johnson	Chad Knaus
9/28/2008	Kansas Speedway	48	Jimmie Johnson	Chad Knaus
10/19/2008	Martinsville Speedway	48	Jimmie Johnson	Chad Knaus
11/9/2008	Phoenix Raceway	48	Jimmie Johnson	Chad Knaus
3/29/2009	Martinsville Speedway	48	Jimmie Johnson	Chad Knaus
4/5/2009	Texas Motor Speedway	24	Jeff Gordon	Steve Letarte
4/18/2009	Phoenix Raceway	5	Mark Martin	Alan Gustafson
5/9/2009	Darlington Raceway	5	Mark Martin	Alan Gustafson
5/31/2009	Dover Motor Speedway	48	Jimmie Johnson	Chad Knaus
6/14/2009	Michigan International Speedway	5	Mark Martin	Alan Gustafson
7/11/2009	Chicagoland Speedway	5	Mark Martin	Alan Gustafson
7/26/2009	Indianapolis Motor Speedway	48	Jimmie Johnson	Chad Knaus
9/20/2009	New Hampshire Motor Speedway	5	Mark Martin	Alan Gustafson
9/27/2009	Dover Motor Speedway	48	Jimmie Johnson	Chad Knaus
10/11/2009	California Speedway	48	Jimmie Johnson	Chad Knaus
10/17/2009	Charlotte Motor Speedway	48	Jimmie Johnson	Chad Knaus
11/15/2009	Phoenix Raceway	48	Jimmie Johnson	Chad Knaus
2/21/2010	California Speedway	48	Jimmie Johnson	Chad Knaus
2/28/2010	Las Vegas Motor Speedway	48	Jimmie Johnson	Chad Knaus
3/21/2010	Bristol Motor Speedway	48	Jimmie Johnson	Chad Knaus
6/20/2010	Sonoma Raceway	48	Jimmie Johnson	Chad Knaus
6/27/2010	New Hampshire Motor Speedway	48	Jimmie Johnson	Chad Knaus
9/26/2010	Dover Motor Speedway	48	Jimmie Johnson	Chad Knaus
2/27/2011	Phoenix Raceway	24	Jeff Gordon	Alan Gustafson
4/17/2011	Talladega Superspeedway	48	Jimmie Johnson	Chad Knaus
6/12/2011	Pocono Raceway	24	Jeff Gordon	Alan Gustafson
9/6/2011	Atlanta Motor Speedway	24	Jeff Gordon	Alan Gustafson
10/9/2011	Kansas Speedway	48	Jimmie Johnson	Chad Knaus

(Hendrick Motorsports Cup Series Wins, continued)

Date	Track	#	Driver	Crew Chief
5/12/2012	Darlington Raceway	48	Jimmie Johnson	Chad Knaus
5/27/2012	Charlotte Motor Speedway	5	Kasey Kahne	Kenny Francis
6/3/2012	Dover Motor Speedway	48	Jimmie Johnson	Chad Knaus
6/17/2012	Michigan International Speedway	88	Dale Earnhardt Jr.	Steve Letarte
7/15/2012	New Hampshire Motor Speedway	5	Kasey Kahne	Kenny Francis
7/29/2012	Indianapolis Motor Speedway	48	Jimmie Johnson	Chad Knaus
8/5/2012	Pocono Raceway	24	Jeff Gordon	Alan Gustafson
10/28/2012	Martinsville Speedway	48	Jimmie Johnson	Chad Knaus
11/4/2012	Texas Motor Speedway	48	Jimmie Johnson	Chad Knaus
11/18/2012	Homestead-Miami Speedway	24	Jeff Gordon	Alan Gustafson
2/24/2013	Daytona International Speedway	48	Jimmie Johnson	Chad Knaus
3/17/2013	Bristol Motor Speedway	5	Kasey Kahne	Kenny Francis
4/7/2013	Martinsville Speedway	48	Jimmie Johnson	Chad Knaus
6/9/2013	Pocono Raceway	48	Jimmie Johnson	Chad Knaus
7/6/2013	Daytona International Speedway	48	Jimmie Johnson	Chad Knaus
8/4/2013	Pocono Raceway	5	Kasey Kahne	Kenny Francis
9/29/2013	Dover Motor Speedway	48	Jimmie Johnson	Chad Knaus
10/27/2013	Martinsville Speedway	24	Jeff Gordon	Alan Gustafson
11/3/2013	Texas Motor Speedway	48	Jimmie Johnson	Chad Knaus
2/23/2014	Daytona International Speedway	88	Dale Earnhardt Jr.	Steve Letarte
5/10/2014	Kansas Speedway	24	Jeff Gordon	Alan Gustafson
5/25/2014	Charlotte Motor Speedway	48	Jimmie Johnson	Chad Knaus
6/1/2014	Dover Motor Speedway	48	Jimmie Johnson	Chad Knaus
6/8/2014	Pocono Raceway	88	Dale Earnhardt Jr.	Steve Letarte
6/15/2014	Michigan International Speedway	48	Jimmie Johnson	Chad Knaus
7/27/2014	Indianapolis Motor Speedway	24	Jeff Gordon	Alan Gustafson
8/3/2014	Pocono Raceway	88	Dale Earnhardt Jr.	Steve Letarte
8/17/2014	Michigan International Speedway	24	Jeff Gordon	Alan Gustafson
8/31/2014	Atlanta Motor Speedway	5	Kasey Kahne	Kenny Francis
9/28/2014	Dover Motor Speedway	24	Jeff Gordon	Alan Gustafson
10/26/2014	Martinsville Speedway	88	Dale Earnhardt Jr.	Steve Letarte
11/2/2014	Texas Motor Speedway	48	Jimmie Johnson	Chad Knaus
3/1/2015	Atlanta Motor Speedway	48	Jimmie Johnson	Chad Knaus
4/11/2015	Texas Motor Speedway	48	Jimmie Johnson	Chad Knaus
5/3/2015	Talladega Superspeedway	88	Dale Earnhardt Jr.	Greg Ives
5/9/2015	Kansas Speedway	48	Jimmie Johnson	Chad Knaus
5/31/2015	Dover Motor Speedway	48	Jimmie Johnson	Chad Knaus
7/5/2015	Daytona International Speedway	88	Dale Earnhardt Jr.	Greg Ives
11/1/2015	Martinsville Speedway	24	Jeff Gordon	Alan Gustafson
11/8/2015	Texas Motor Speedway	48	Jimmie Johnson	Chad Knaus
11/15/2015	Phoenix Raceway	88	Dale Earnhardt Jr.	Greg Ives
2/28/2016	Atlanta Motor Speedway	48	Jimmie Johnson	Chad Knaus
3/20/2016	California Speedway	48	Jimmie Johnson	Chad Knaus
10/9/2016	Charlotte Motor Speedway	48	Jimmie Johnson	Chad Knaus
10/30/2016	Martinsville Speedway	48	Jimmie Johnson	Chad Knaus
11/20/2016	Homestead-Miami Speedway	48	Jimmie Johnson	Chad Knaus
4/9/2017	Texas Motor Speedway	48	Jimmie Johnson	Chad Knaus
4/24/2017	Bristol Motor Speedway	48	Jimmie Johnson	Chad Knaus
6/4/2017	Dover Motor Speedway	48	Jimmie Johnson	Chad Knaus
7/23/2017	Indianapolis Motor Speedway	5	Kasey Kahne	Keith Rodden
8/5/2018	Watkins Glen International	9	Chase Elliott	Alan Gustafson

Date	Track	#	Driver	Crew Chief
10/7/2018	Dover Motor Speedway	9	Chase Elliott	Alan Gustafson
10/21/2018	Kansas Speedway	9	Chase Elliott	Alan Gustafson
4/28/2019	Talladega Superspeedway	9	Chase Elliott	Alan Gustafson
6/30/2019	Chicagoland Speedway	88	Alex Bowman	Greg Ives
8/4/2019	Watkins Glen International	9	Chase Elliott	Alan Gustafson
9/29/2019	Charlotte Motor Speedway ROVAL	9	Chase Elliott	Alan Gustafson
3/1/2020	California Speedway	88	Alex Bowman	Greg Ives
5/28/2020	Charlotte Motor Speedway	9	Chase Elliott	Alan Gustafson
8/16/2020	Daytona International Speedway Road Course	9	Chase Elliott	Alan Gustafson
8/29/2020	Daytona International Speedway	24	William Byron	Chad Knaus
10/11/2020	Charlotte Motor Speedway ROVAL	9	Chase Elliott	Alan Gustafson
11/1/2020	Martinsville Speedway	9	Chase Elliott	Alan Gustafson
11/8/2020	Phoenix Raceway	9	Chase Elliott	Alan Gustafson
2/28/2021	Homestead-Miami Speedway	24	William Byron	Rudy Fugle
3/7/2021	Las Vegas Motor Speedway	5	Kyle Larson	Cliff Daniels
4/18/2021	Richmond Raceway	48	Alex Bowman	Greg Ives
5/16/2021	Dover Motor Speedway	48	Alex Bowman	Greg Ives
5/23/2021	Circuit of The Americas	9	Chase Elliott	Alan Gustafson
5/30/2021	Charlotte Motor Speedway	5	Kyle Larson	Cliff Daniels
6/6/2021	Sonoma Raceway	5	Kyle Larson	Cliff Daniels
6/20/2021	Nashville Superspeedway	5	Kyle Larson	Cliff Daniels
6/26/2021	Pocono Raceway	48	Alex Bowman	Greg Ives
7/4/2021	Road America	9	Chase Elliott	Alan Gustafson
8/8/2021	Watkins Glen International	5	Kyle Larson	Cliff Daniels
9/18/2021	Bristol Motor Speedway	5	Kyle Larson	Cliff Daniels
10/10/2021	Charlotte Motor Speedway ROVAL	5	Kyle Larson	Cliff Daniels
10/17/2021	Texas Motor Speedway	5	Kyle Larson	Cliff Daniels
10/24/2021	Kansas Speedway	5	Kyle Larson	Cliff Daniels
10/31/2021	Martinsville Speedway	48	Alex Bowman	Greg Ives
11/7/2021	Phoenix Raceway	5	Kyle Larson	Cliff Daniels
2/27/2022	California Speedway	5	Kyle Larson	Cliff Daniels
3/6/2022	Las Vegas Motor Speedway	48	Alex Bowman	Greg Ives
3/20/2022	Atlanta Motor Speedway	24	William Byron	Rudy Fugle
4/9/2022	Martinsville Speedway	24	William Byron	Rudy Fugle
5/1/2022	Dover Motor Speedway	9	Chase Elliott	Alan Gustafson
6/26/2022	Nashville Superspeedway	9	Chase Elliott	Alan Gustafson
7/10/2022	Atlanta Motor Speedway	9	Chase Elliott	Alan Gustafson
7/24/2022	Pocono Raceway	9	Chase Elliott	Alan Gustafson
8/21/2022	Watkins Glen International	5	Kyle Larson	Cliff Daniels
10/2/2022	Talladega Superspeedway	9	Chase Elliott	Alan Gustafson
10/23/2022	Homestead-Miami Speedway	5	Kyle Larson	Cliff Daniels
3/5/2023	Las Vegas Motor Speedway	24	William Byron	Rudy Fugle
3/12/2023	Phoenix Raceway	24	William Byron	Rudy Fugle
4/2/2023	Richmond Raceway	5	Kyle Larson	Kevin Meendering
4/16/2023	Martinsville Speedway	5	Kyle Larson	Cliff Daniels
5/14/2023	Darlington Raceway	24	William Byron	Rudy Fugle
7/9/2023	Atlanta Motor Speedway	24	William Byron	Rudy Fugle
8/20/2023	Watkins Glen International	24	William Byron	Rudy Fugle
9/3/2023	Darlington Raceway	5	Kyle Larson	Cliff Daniels
9/24/2023	Texas Motor Speedway	24	William Byron	Rudy Fugle
10/15/2023	Las Vegas Motor Speedway	5	Kyle Larson	Cliff Daniels

ABOUT THE AUTHOR
BEN WHITE

Ben White attended his first NASCAR Cup Series race in 1972 at Darlington, South Carolina, at age eleven. The Clinton, North Carolina, native drove his own race cars on a few local short tracks in the late 1970s before joining Richard Childress Racing as a crew member in 1980.

White turned his attention to writing about NASCAR in 1983 for the *Lexington Dispatch* (North Carolina) newspaper, and he continues to write for that publication today, as well as North Carolina newspapers in Fayetteville, Kinston, Burlington, and Asheboro.

From 1989 until 2010, he served as staff writer, managing editor, and senior editor of *NASCAR Illustrated Magazine* and managing editor of the "American Racing Classics" book series from 1991 to 1993.

White has authored numerous NASCAR books, including Motorbooks' *NASCAR Then and Now*, *NASCAR Racers*, *NASCAR Legends*, and *Twenty Years of Hendrick Motorsports*. Ben resides in Salisbury, North Carolina.

ACKNOWLEDGMENTS

In 2004, I had the privilege and honor of writing Hendrick Motorsports' twentieth anniversary book. Now in 2024, I am again honored by Rick and Linda Hendrick's confidence in entrusting me to chronicle the organization's first forty years. Their remarkable journey continues, as so much more has happened over the past two decades within this incredible race team, and more importantly, within this incredible racing family, including past and present employees and drivers.

Thank you also to Jesse Essex, vice president of communications for Hendrick Motorsports. You've been there every step of the way, and you are greatly appreciated and a close friend.

Many thanks to Zack Miller, Group Publisher, for Quarto Publishing's Motorbooks imprint. This book would not have been possible without your advice and unceasing work helping to build every page.

Thank you to Caitlin Fultz for your wonderful editing expertise throughout the process, as well as the work of Brooke Pelletier, the project manager for this book. Thank you also to everyone at Quarto for the beautiful design and layout.

Thank you also to Jon Edwards, Ashly Ennis, Megan Johnson, and Autumn Darracq for helping to obtain interviews with Alex Bowman, William Byron, Chase Elliott, and Kyle Larson, as well as other team personnel. Thanks to Geoff Bodine, Marshall Carlson, Dale Earnhardt Jr., Ray Evernham, Jeff Gordon, Ken Howes, Kasey Kahne, Chad Knaus, Jimmie Johnson, Terry Labonte, Ricky Rudd, Ken Schrader, and Darrell Waltrip for thoughts from their past years with Hendrick Motorsports. Also, thank you to Sam Ulrich and R. J. Kraft for help with accuracy of team facts as we put this book together.

I would like to thank my wife of thirty-five years, Eva White, for once again allowing many hours day and night to write every word of the forty chapters and photo captions that make up this fabulous story. You are wonderful and patient. I love you so much.

Finally, I dedicate this book to my grandchildren, Rex White and Theodora "Teddy" White. Please know that throughout your lives, my wish for you is that you dream your biggest dreams. Absolutely nothing is impossible.

—Ben White

PHOTO CREDITS

A = All; L = Left; R = Right; T = Top; B = Bottom

Alamy: 55; **Moviestore Collection Ltd/Alamy Stock Photo:** 101; **Andy Lyons/Getty Images:** 80; **Chris Graythen/Getty Images:** 147B; **David Becker/Getty Images:** 120; **David Jenson/Getty Images:** 146; **Dozier Mobley/Getty Images:** 150; **Fairfax Media Archives/Getty Images:** 61; **Focus on Sport/Getty Images:** 63R; **Icon Sports Wire/Getty Images:** 20; **Jared C. Tilton/Getty Images:** 7; **NBC/Getty Images:** 98, 99, 101; **Racing One/Getty Images:** 15T, 18, 19, 23R, 24, 29, 30, 31, 34, 39, 56, 62, 64, 81; **Robert Alexander/Getty Images:** 17, 26, 35; **Sean Gardner/Getty Images:** 148; **Sporting News Archive/Getty Images:** 66, 82, 112L; **Todd Warshaw/Getty Images:** 133L; **Adrian Lauerman/Hendrick Motorsports:** 170, 171T; **Andrea Miner/Hendrick Motorsports:** 173; **Hendrick Motorsports:** 6, 8, 9, 11, 12, 14, 15B, 16, 21A, 22, 23A, 25, 27, 28, 30L, 32, 33, 36, 37, 38, 40A, 41, 41, 43A, 44, 45A, 46, 47, 48, 49, 52, 53, 54, 55, 57, 58, 59A, 85B, 90, 91A, 92, 94, 95A, 97A, 107, 114, 118, 119, 140, 185 (Richmond, Waltrip), 187; **Isaiah Robinson/Hendrick Motorsports:** 171B, 172A; **Justin Nicely/Hendrick Motorsports:** 115; **Lauren Edgil/Hendrick Motorsports:** 6; **Nancy Shirley:** 194; **Ben Earp/Nigel Kinrade Photography:** 165B; **Brian Czobat/Nigel Kinrade Photography:** 112R, 183, 184 (Martin, Mears); **David Rosenblum/Nigel Kinrade Photography:** 17, 179, 180R; **Dozier Mobley/Nigel Kinrade Photography:** 63L; **Gavin Baker/Nigel Kinrade Photography:** 122, 157TL, 169, 185 (Byron); **Harold Hinson/Nigel Kinrade Photography:** 139B, 185 (Elliott); **John K. Harrelson/Nigel Kinrade Photography:** 96, 117, 130, 131T, 132, 136, 144, 147T, 157TR, 161B, 163, 164B, 168L; **Leslie Ann Miller/Nigel Kinrade Photography:** 180L; 185 (Earnhardt); **Matthew T. Thacker/Nigel Kinrade Photography:** 67, 85T, 87TR, 106, 113, 124, 128, 141A, 142, 143A, 155A, 157B, 158, 160, 165T, 181, 184 (Larson, Johnson, Gordon); **Nigel Kinrade Photography:** 50, 60, 65, 68, 69, 70, 72, 73A, 74A, 75, 76, 77, 78, 79, 83A, 87TL, 88, 93A, 102, 103, 104A, 105, 107, 108, 109, 110, 111, 113, 121, 126A, 127T, 129L, 134, 137, 138A, 139A, 153A, 154, 159, 161T, 162, 164T, 166, 167, 174, 175A, 176, 177, 184 (Busch, Kahne, Labonte, Nadeau, Nemechek, Rudd, Schrader, Vickers); **Russell LaBounty/Nigel Kinrade Photography:** 125, 127B, 129R, 133R; **Rusty Jarrett/Nigel Kinrade Photography:** 87B, 135A, 168R, 185 (Bowman); **Stephen Arce/Nigel Kinrade Photography:** 131B; **Tyler Barrick/Nigel Kinrade Photography:** 116; **Ray Evernham:** 71.

INDEX

24 Hours of Le Mans, 43, 53, 171–173

A

Action Express Racing, 171

Alabama International Motor Speedway, 41

Allison, Bobby, 21, 23, 27

Allison, Davey, 34

Allison, Donnie, 27

Allmendinger, A. J., 125

All-Star Racing, 15, 19, 20, 119

Ally Financial, 157

Andretti, John, 26, 44, 159, 175

Andretti, Mario, 27

Andretti, Michael, 44

Andrews, Jeff, 84, 86, 95, 152–153

ARCA Menards Series, 155

Arrow McLaren, 175, 176

Atlanta Motor Speedway, 20, 23, 41, 61, 90, 105, 116, 125, 134, 137, 166

Auto Club Speedway (Fontana, California), 111, 157

B

Baker, Buck, 26, 119

Baker, Buddy, 20, 23, 26, 159

Bass, Sam, 61

Beadle, Raymond, 30

Benton, Robby, 155

Bernstein, Kenny, 58

Berry, Josh, 133

Be The Match Foundation, 82

Bill Davis Racing, 61

Bingle, Pete, 36

BK Racing, 155

Blair, Bill, 119

Bodine, Geoff, 57, 66, 82, 115, 116, 117, 151, 180

Bodine, Geoffrey, 19, 20, 21, 25, 27, 28

Bonnett, Neil, 15, 19, 23

Bowman, Alex, 116, 134, 155–157, 159, 179, 180

Brainerd International Raceway, 53

Brickyard 400, 61, 126

Bridges, Jeff, 54

Bristol Motor Speedway, 20, 57, 75, 126, 156, 163

Broome, Richard, 16

Brown, Zac, 142

Bruce Griffin Racing, 76

Bruckheimer, Jerry, 54

Buck Baker's Driving School, 61

Budweiser Late Model Sportsman Series, 15, 65

Bundy, Doc, 44

Busch Clash, 23

Busch Grand National Series, 61, 66, 90, 107, 111, 117, 125, 136

Busch, Kurt, 175

Busch, Kyle, 136–137, 180

Button, Jenson, 171–172

Byron, William, 25, 116, 130, 133–135, 138, 157, 159, 179, 180

C

Caan, James, 54

Calhoun, Rory, 53

California Dirt Focus Midget championship, 155

California Speedway, 125

Campbell, Jim, 119–120

Canadian Tire Motorsport Park, 79, 129

Car and Driver magazine, 173

Carlson, Marshall, 84, 116

Carolina Motorsports Park, 171

Champion, Bill, 57

Champion, Cliff, 57

Champion Spark Plug 400, 31

Charlotte Convention Center, 145

Charlotte Motor Speedway, 15, 41, 57, 61, 65–67, 69, 75, 107, 125, 126, 159, 163, 164, 175

Chastain, Ross, 134

Chevrolet Motor Company, 42, 43–44, 49, 152

Chicagoland Speedway, 157

Childress, Richard, 20, 31, 57, 145

Chip Ganassi Racing, 151

Christian, Frank, 119

Circuit de la Sarthe, 171

Circuit of The Americas, 172

City Chevrolet dealership, 15, 19, 66, 84, 95, 140, 141, 151

Clapton, Eric, 142

Coca-Cola 600, 61, 66, 67, 125, 126, 159, 175, 179

Coke Zero Sugar 400, 134

Competition Engines, 151, 152

Compton, Stacy, 111

Connerty, Hugh, 61

Connor, Dennis, 54, 77

Cook, Jerry, 19

Craftsman Truck Series, 54, 76, 77, 79, 90, 120, 129, 133, 136, 151

CRAFTSMAN Truck Series, 145

Craven, Ricky, 69, 81

Cruise, Tom, 53, 54, 55

Cunningham Motorsports, 155

D

Dale Earnhardt Inc., 107

Dale Jr. Download podcast, 54

Danahy, Jim, 171

Daniels, Charlie, 142

Daniels, Cliff, 163

Danner, Christian, 43

Darland, Dave, 125

Darlington Raceway, 20, 29, 31, 39, 40, 54, 55, 58, 134, 151, 159, 179, 180

Darrell Waltrip Racing, 151

Days of Thunder (movie), 54–55

Daytona 500, 19, 23, 25, 28, 31, 36, 40, 54, 61, 81–82, 103, 107, 109, 111, 129, 133, 134–135

Daytona International Speedway, 23, 34, 81, 108, 129, 133, 134, 151, 171

DeHart, Gary, 34, 36, 75, 81

Deming Speedway, 125

Detroit Children's Fund, 142

DGM Racing, 151

Diamond Ridge Motorsports, 136

Díaz Ordaz, Gustavo, 142

Dickerson, Eddie, 34, 36

DiGard Racing, 57

Donlavey, Junie, 39, 57

Dorton, Randy, 116, 151–153

Dover International Motor Speedway, 41, 58, 134, 138, 157

Dratch, Rachel, 99

E

Earnhardt, Dale, 15, 20, 25, 31, 58, 65, 76, 82, 103, 105, 112

Earnhardt, Dale, Jr., 25, 86, 92, 107–109, 116, 126, 130, 156, 157, 180

East, Bobby, 125

Edwards, Frank, 14

Elliott, Bill, 31, 82, 125–126, 129

Elliott, Chase, 67, 79, 116, 120, 129–130, 133, 138, 145, 151, 157, 159, 163, 164, 179, 180

Elliott, Cindy, 129

Ellis, Tommy, 54

Elon Homes for Children (Charlotte), 95

Elsie (car), 69

Evans, Richie, 19

Evernham Motorsports, 125

Evernham, Ray, 61, 62–63, 69–70, 71, 75, 81, 82, 103, 117, 153, 166–167

F

Finch, James, 129

Fishel, Herb, 44

Fitzgerald, Jim, 53, 55

Flemington Speedway, 77

Flock, Fonty, 119

Flock, Tim, 26

Folgers Coffee, 28, 31

Forbes-Robinson, Elliott, 44

Foster, Jimmy, 136

FOX Sports, 61, 166, 168

Foyt, A. J., 27

France, Bill, Jr., 82

France, Bill, Sr., 26

Francis, Kenny, 126, 156

Fugle, Rudy, 135, 179

G

Gambler Chassis Company, 15

Ganassi, Chip, 176

Garage 56, 171–173

Gardner, Frank, 27

Gee, Robert, 15, 66, 107

General Motors. *See* Chevrolet Motor Company

Gibbs, Joe, 75

Gillett Evernham Motorsports, 125

GM Technical Center, 175

Gordon, Jeff, 25, 58, 61–62, 66, 69, 70–71, 75, 81–82, 91, 92, 96, 99–101, 103–105, 108, 111, 116, 117, 120, 125, 126, 129, 133, 134, 137–138, 145, 153, 155, 166–168, 175, 179, 180

Gordon, Robby, 175

Grand National Series, 23, 26

Grand Touring Prototype (GTP) division, 42–44, 53

Grant, Stu, 171

Gurney, Dan, 27

Gustafson, Alan, 86, 108, 129, 136–139

Guy, Jay, 111

H

Hagan Racing, 66

Hagar, Sammy, 143

Hall of Fame, 14, 112, 145–147

Hamilton, Bobby, 26, 54, 159

Hamilton, Pete, 26, 159

Hamlin, Denny, 163

Hammer, Phil, 69, 81

Hammond, Jeff, 36

Harrison, George, 142

Helton, Mike, 116

Hendrick Automotive Group, 49, 166

Hendrick Companies, 84

Hendrick, Jennifer, 96, 116

Hendrick, John, 8, 95–96, 116

Hendrick, Kimberly, 96, 116

Hendrick, Linda Myrick, 21, 47–49, 82, 84, 92, 116, 145

Hendrick, Lynn, 48, 84, 116

Hendrick Marrow Program, 82

Hendrick, Mary, 21

Hendrick Motorsports, 35, 36, 40, 58, 126, 159, 166, 167, 168, 180

Hendrick, Papa Joe, 91, 96

Hendrick, Ray, 15, 19, 23

Hendrick, Rick
cancer diagnosis of, 81, 82, 95
childhood of, 8
Hall of Fame induction, 145–147
marriage of, 47–48

Hendrick, Ricky (Joseph Riddick IV), 48, 79, 90–92, 96, 107–108, 111, 116, 120

Hendrix, Jimi, 142

Heritage Center, 140–143, 176

Hickory Motor Speedway, 133

Hinson, Gene, 47

Hobbs, David, 44

Hogg, Harry, 55

Holman, John, 27

Homestead-Miami Speedway, 109, 111, 134

Hornaday, Ron, Jr., 76, 77

Houston, Andy, 136

Howes, Ken, 42–43, 44, 49, 69, 111, 116

Hunter, Jim, 116

Hutcherson, Dick, 27

Hyde, Harry, 15–16, 19, 20, 21, 23, 27, 28, 29, 31, 34, 41, 55, 57, 77, 151, 153

I

IMSA (International Motorsports Association), 53

Indianapolis 500, 30, 166, 175

Indianapolis Motor Speedway, 42, 61, 126, 133, 179

IndyCar series, 30

International Motor Sports Association (IMSA), 42

Iowa Speedway, 133

Irvan, Ernie, 82

Irwin, Kenny, Jr., 125

Isaac, Bobby, 15, 16, 19, 20, 23, 29, 107

Ives, Greg, 156, 171

J

Jackson, Joe, 116

Jackson, Richard, 73

Jarrett, Dale, 75, 82

JL Hendrick Management Corporation, 95

Joe Gibbs Racing, 57, 75, 151, 164

John Hendrick Award for Excellence, 96

John Hendrick Fellowship Lunch, 96

Johnson, Jimmie, 25, 39, 40, 44, 67, 73, 77, 91–92, 108, 111–113, 116, 120, 126, 133, 145, 151, 153, 157, 166, 171–172, 179, 180

Johnson, Junior, 34, 35, 54, 57, 73, 160

Johns, Sammy, 27

Jones, Parnelli, 27

JR Motorsports (JRM), 129, 133, 151, 155, 156

JTG Daugherty Racing, 151

Junior Johnson and Associates, 34, 35

Jurassic Park (movie), 69

K

Kahne, Kasey, 67, 125–127, 180

Kanaan, Tony, 176

Kansas Speedway, 79, 90, 108, 138, 163

Kiekhafer, Carl, 26

King Racing, 58

Knaus, Chad, 67, 108, 111–112, 112–113, 153, 171, 172, 173

K&N Pro Series, 133

Krauskopf, Nord, 20

Kulwicki, Alan, 61

Kyle Busch Motorsports, 133

L

Labonte, Bobby, 75

Labonte, Terry, 48, 67, 69, 73, 76, 81, 120, 136, 145, 180

Lagasse, Scott, Sr., 76

Langley, Elmo, 39

Larson, Kyle, 67, 116, 120, 133, 145, 151, 157, 159, 163, 163–164, 175–176, 179, 180

The Last American Hero (movie), 54

Las Vegas Motor Speedway, 77, 90, 108, 157, 163

Late Model Stock Car Series, 90, 136
Lathram, Scott, 116
Leffler, Jason, 125
Legend Car Young Lions Division, 133
Le Mans, 43, 53, 171–173
Leopold III, king of Belgium, 142
Letarte, Steve, 108–109
Levi Garrett, 28
Levine Children's Hospital (Charlotte), 92
Levine Family Racing, 126
Lewis, Steve, 125
Limentani, Steve, 82
Loomis, Robbie, 103–105
Lorenzen, Fred, 27

M
Makar, Jimmy, 57
Malloch, Nelson, 57
Marcis, Dave, 20
Marks, Justin, 133
Marlin, Sterling, 66
Martin, Mark, 82, 108, 137, 138, 145, 151, 180
Martinsville Speedway, 14, 20–21, 57–58, 91, 108, 109, 115–117, 129, 130, 133, 134, 151, 152, 157, 159, 160, 166
Mast, Rick, 54
McGrew, Lance, 108
Mears, Casey, 67, 137, 180
Mears, Roger, 76
Melling Racing, 111
Menard, Paul, 125
Menards ARCA Series, 133
Merwe, Sarel van der, 44
Meyers, Seth, 100
Miami Grand Prix, 44
Michigan International Speedway, 31, 58, 108, 125, 138, 156

Miller High Life 500, 31
Mills, Wesley, 36
Milwaukee Mile, 77
Mitchell, Clayton, 14
Moody, Christy, 47
Moody, Ralph, 27
Moore, Bud, 16, 20, 39, 40, 58, 73
Morrison, Elizabeth, 116
Motor Racing Network, 14
Motte, Daryl, 61
Muhleman, Max, 15

N
Nadeau, Jerry, 180
NASCAR All-Star Race, 69
NASCAR Hall of Fame, 14, 112, 145–147
Nashville Fairgrounds Speedway, 77
Nashville Superspeedway, 21, 39, 163
National Focus Midget championship, 155
National Marrow Donor Program, 82
Nationwide Series, 155
Nazareth Children's Home (Rockwell, North Carolina), 95
Nazareth Speedway, 77
Nelson, Gary, 25, 28
Nemechek, Joe, 180
New Hampshire Motor Speedway, 156
Newman, Paul, 53, 55
North Carolina Motor Speedway, 61
North Wilkesboro Speedway, 20, 28, 29, 30, 39, 75

O
O'Blenes, Russ, 171
Occoneechee Speedway, 14
Orange Speedway, 159
Orbison, Roy, 142

P
Palm Beach Speedway, 44
Panch, Marvin, 26, 159
Parks, Raymond, 145
Parnell, Chris, 99
Parrott, Buddy, 23
Parsons, Benny, 31, 55, 145
Paschal, Jim, 26, 159
Pearson, David, 26, 28, 66
Penske Racing, 61, 63, 155
Petree, Andy, 41
Petty Enterprises, 26, 134, 159
Petty, Lee, 26, 159
Petty, Richard, 15, 19, 20, 26, 28, 61, 103, 105, 112, 159–160
Petty, Tom, 142
Phoenix International Raceway, 54, 75, 76, 77, 109, 126, 130, 133, 137, 151, 163, 175, 179
Pignacca, Luca, 171
Pocono 500, 125
Pocono Raceway, 29, 30, 31, 75, 109, 126, 137, 157
Poehler, Amy, 100
Porsche Motorsport, 43

R
Racing, Melling, 111
Rahal, Bobby, 44
Rainbow Warriors, 61
Ranier, Harry, 20, 34
Ranier-Lundy Racing, 34
Red Line 7000 (movie), 53–54
Reeves, Stevie, 125
Richard Childress Racing, 31
Richard Petty Motorsports, 125, 126
Richmond International Raceway, 20, 29, 75, 76, 105, 125, 157

Richmond, Tim, 19, 28, 29, 30–31, 55, 66, 77, 180
Rick Hendrick Honda (West Columbia, South Carolina), 95
Ricky Hendrick Centers for Intensive Care, 92
Riverside International Raceway, 21, 29, 30, 31, 57
Road Atlanta, 44, 53, 171
Roberts, Fireball, 27
Robert Yates Racing, 125
Rockenfeller, Mike, 171–172
Rockingham Speedway, 20
Rogers, Kenny, 15, 16, 20
Rolex 24, 176
ROVAL. *See* Charlotte Motor Speedway
Rudd, Al, Jr., 57
Rudd Performance Motorsports, 58
Rudd, Ricky, 57–58, 73, 75, 180
Rutherford, Johnny, 30

S

Sacks, Greg, 54, 82
Sadler, Elliott, 125
Salt Flats (Utah), 16
Saturday Night Live television show, 98–101
SCCA (Sports Car Club of America), 53, 55
Schrader, Ken, 39–41, 41, 44, 66, 67, 69, 180
Sebring International Raceway, 171, 172
Simpson, Don, 54
Skagit Speedway, 125
Smith, Jack, 119
Smith, O. Bruton, 65
Sonoma Raceway, 105, 125, 163
Southern 500, 31
Speedweeks, 19, 20, 34
Spire Motorsports, 151
Sprague, Jack, 54, 76–77, 79, 120
Springsteen, Bruce, 142

Spurlock, C. K., 15, 16, 20
Stacy, J. D., 20, 30
Stefanik, Mike, 19
Stewart, Cliff, 19, 23
Stewart-Haas Racing, 151
Stewart, Tony, 116, 125, 175
Stielow, Mark, 171
STP motor oil, 16
Stricklin, Hut, 54
Stucker, Greg, 171
Stump, Rex, 69, 71
SuperTruck Series, 76

T

Talladega Superspeedway, 41, 105, 108, 134, 137
Tant, Jack, 15
Taylor, Jordan, 171
Team Penske, 61, 63, 155
Texas Motor Speedway, 125, 163, 179
Thompson, Speedy, 119
Thunder in Carolina (movie), 53
Timmermans, Alex, 171
Tommy Baldwin Racing, 155
Townley, Tony, 155
Trackhouse Racing, 134
Tracy, Richard, 116
"T-Rex" car, 69–71, 70
Truex, Martin, Jr., 163, 164
Turner, Curtis, 65
Turner, Jeff, 116

U

Ulrich, D. K., 30, 57
United States Auto Club (USAC) Sprint Car competition, 39
Universal Racing Network, 14

V

Venturini Motorsports, 155
Vickers, Brian, 91, 120, 180
Virginia International Raceway, 171

W

Wagoner, Al, 119
Waid, Steve, 100-101
Wallace, Bubba, 179
Wallace, Rusty, 61, 66
Waltrip, Darrell, 25, 34, 35, 36, 66, 82, 108, 116, 160, 180
Ward, Bob, 47
Ward, Gavin, 175
Watkins Glen International, 29, 58, 138, 163
White, Rex, 14
Wide World of Sports, 14
Wilson, Waddell, 34, 36, 58
The Winner Within (Pat Riley), 63
Winston Cup Series, 31, 41, 69
Wood Brothers Racing, 66
Wood, Glen, 20, 40, 160
Wood, Leonard, 20, 40, 160
Wright, Jimmy, 15

X

Xfinity Series, 15, 61, 65, 90, 91, 107, 129, 133, 136, 145, 151, 155, 156

Y

Yarborough, Cale, 20
Yeley, J. J., 125
Yunick, Casey, 136
Yunick, Smokey, 136

Z

Zentmeyer, Larry, 151